Ambient Lifestyle

Ambient Lifestyle

From Concept to Experience

Emile Aarts – Elmo Diederiks

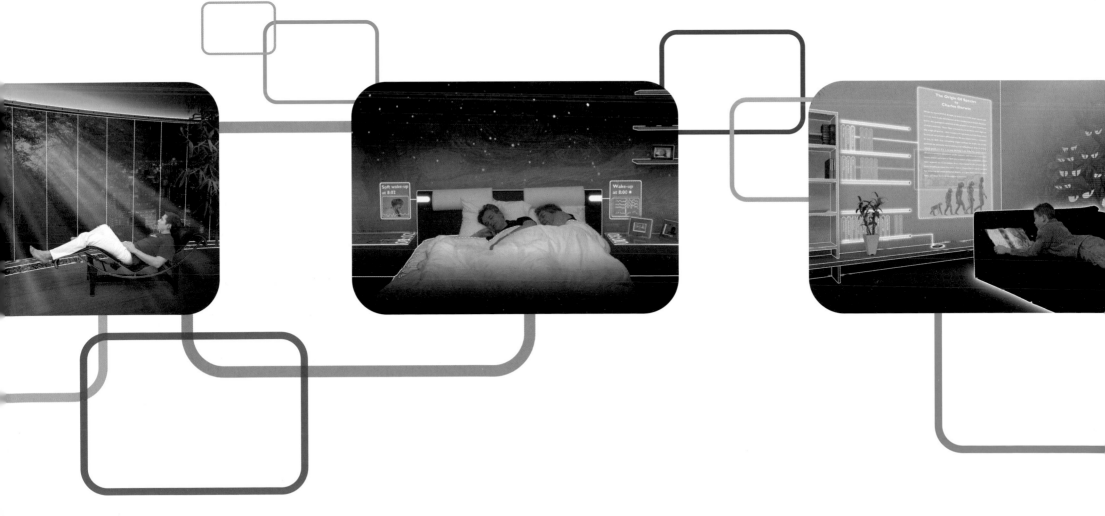

700
AMB

Foreword

The opening of HomeLab back in 2002 was a great event for all of us. It marked the start of a new chapter in the history of Philips Research as research scientists were engaging in a totally new field of investigation through what they called user centered engineering. Consequently, they needed to involve ordinary people on a structural basis in their search for innovative product and service concepts requiring new ways of working and new facilities that were markedly different from the resources they had been using within our industrial research setting for almost ninety years. I have been following this novel development with great interest, because it was far from obvious that the novel approach developed for HomeLab was a guarantee for future success, and this, evidently, is the ultimate concern every research manager has at the start of a new research direction. We, however, took the chance because the momentum that our vision of Ambient Intelligence was generating at that time revealed beyond reasonable doubt that new and unconventional ways of research were required for the actual realization of the vision, and we did not regret it!

After five years of HomeLab research I can safely admit that HomeLab has become a great success. Apart from the many new technologies and prototypes that emerged from it, it also has delivered something that does not come out of most technology laboratories and which is of great value, and that is experiences for people. When our scientists conceived the idea of Ambilight TV and explained the idea to the development groups, many did not believe people would like it. "I don't want disco lights in my house," was a frequently heard reaction. But, when they actually experienced it, opinions changed and the idea was welcomed with great enthusiasm. Nowadays, the Ambilight TV is a great business success and especially in the United States the product has helped to substantially increase Philips' brand image.

Real user insights, real understanding of how people want to be served by technology, that's the value of HomeLab. During its five years of existence this has become a proven fact. As we intend to continue our research on new technologies related to lifestyle and well-being, the significance of experience and application research will increase. Consequently, the expansion of HomeLab into ExperienceLab by the addition of the two experience laboratories CareLab and ShopLab for well-being and retail studies only comes as a logical next step. Especially, in the well-being area, user insights will be even more essential, because this is about technology that does not just work on our surroundings but on our selves, so it should better be good. But also the domain of retail opens many new options for experience and application research because of its direct business impact.

So, in hindsight I can conclude that starting HomeLab was a great success; congratulations to the HomeLab team on the their successes and good luck with ExperienceLab, their next challenge. I'm looking forward to what's new to come!

Rick Harwig
CTO of Royal Philips Electronics

Experiencing Ambient Intelligence

Ambient Intelligence (AmI) is about smart everyday technology that makes sense. The concept refers to electronic environments that are sensitive and responsive to the presence of people. The paradigm relates to a vision for digital systems in the years 2010-2020 which was developed by Philips in the late 1990s and which has become quite influential worldwide in the development of new concepts for information processing, in a multi-disciplinary approach combining fields such as electrical engineering, computer science, industrial design, user interface design, and cognitive sciences.

Ambient Intelligence

The AmI paradigm provides a basis for new models of technological innovation within a multi-dimensional society [1]. The essential enabling factor of the AmI vision is provided by the fact that current technological developments will enable the integration of electronics into the environment, thus enabling the actors, i.e., people and objects, to interact with their environment in a seamless, trustworthy, and especially natural manner [2,3]. In addition, the past few years have revealed a growing interest in the role of information and communication technology to support peoples' lives, and this not only refers to productivity but also to health care, well-being, leisure, and creativity. A major issue in this respect is given by the growing awareness that novel products such as devices and services should meet elementary user requirements such as usefulness and simplicity. So it is generally believed that novel technologies should not only increase functional complexity, but even more should contribute to the development of *easy to use* and *simple to experience* products and services. Obviously, this

statement has a broad endorsement by a wide community of both designers and engineers, but reality reveals that it is hard to achieve in practice, and that novel approaches, as may be provided by the AmI vision, are needed to make it work.

Trends

A novel vision is never a disruptive development on its own; it is always connected to trends in society, technology and economy. Below we will elaborate on these aspects.

Society

What started in the 1980s as an early attempt to connect the scientific world through a network supporting the exchange of scientific documents and results among researchers had developed by the end of the past century into a truly world-wide network allowing not only researchers but also ordinary people to have access to digital information in the broad sense [4]. Access percentages in the Western world started to exceed 50% and it soon became obvious that the Internet would grow into

Emile Aarts, Elmo Diederiks

a truly ubiquitous access network. Furthermore, the Internet had reached a point in its development where it became evident that the long proclaimed convergence of mobile computing, personal computing, and consumer electronics would become effective. Nowadays this promise has become reality as many Internet providers offer what they call *triple play*, which is the use of (mobile) telephony, television, and data access over the Internet through a single subscription, and the next step will be the development of the seamless handover between these services among different wirelessly connected devices.

The Internet has changed society in the broadest possible sense. It enables people to communicate with each other at any time and in any place. It supports freedom of action and nomadic behavior. It supports new ways of living and doing business. In many cases it even triggered completely new economies. Elements like *blogging, gaming, skyping, pod casting, googling,* and *ebaying* are just a few examples of activities that occupy people in their daily lives and provide them with means to express themselves in their own way and let them do their business in their own way. The impact on society is unprecedented and one should realize

that many of these terms did not have a meaning at all just a few years ago, and some of these words even can not be found in a dictionary today.

Moreover, these novel developments are not restricted to Western society: they have started a globalization process that involves the entire world. Developing regions such as China, India, and several countries in Latin America have attracted the attention of the rest of the world for their fast societal and economic developments. The developments in these regions are having an enormous effect on Western societies and this has led to a view on the development of societies in general that should support a sustainable future. Society is changing to an age in which people take a central role; people are the actors in society and they determine their own rules based on their personal beliefs and objectives in life. There are no longer any regional or geographical limitations or boundaries. The world has become flat, as Thomas Friedman [5] describes it. In his compelling book he identifies ten *flatmakers* that are changing our society in a way that is irreversible. The result will be a new society in which local cultures will be integrated into a global structure. We will think globally and act locally.

Technology
Probably one of the most compelling trends in technology results from developments in the semiconductor industry. It is generally known and accepted that this domain follows the generalized Moore's law [6], which states that the integration density of systems on silicon doubles every eighteen months; see Figure 1. This law seems to entail

a self-fulfilling prophecy because the computer industry has now followed this trend for four decades. Moreover, other characteristic quantities of information processing systems, such as communication bandwidth, storage capacity, and cost per bit of input-output communication, seem to follow similar rules.

Recent technological developments have opened the way to new product breakthroughs. The introduction of the blue laser in digital recording technology (DVR) has resulted in consumer devices that can record several tens of hours of video material, thus enabling true time-shifted television watching. Solid-state storage technologies have resulted in portable music jukebox devices that can store thousands of songs. Poly-LED technology made it possible to construct the world's first matrix addressable display on a foil measuring a few microns in thickness, thus enabling the development of flexible ultra thin displays of almost arbitrary size. Developments in materials science have enabled the construction of electronic foils that exhibit paper-like properties.

These so-called electronic paper devices introduce a new dimension in the use of electronic books or calendars. LCD projection allows very large high-definition images to be displayed on white walls from a small invisibly built-in unit. Advances in semiconductor process technology have made it possible to separate the active silicon area from its substrate, and to put it onto other carriers, for instance glass, thus enabling the integration of active circuitry into any conceivable material, such as wearables. Solid-state lighting is a new technology with unprecedented possibilities in the

design of novel concepts for lighting. Light sources can be made whose color and intensity can be adjusted electronically. Large area luminaires can be designed that are only a few millimeters in thickness. The beam shape of light sources can be made electronically adjustable. Light can be integrated into cloth, as is done in *photonic textiles*. Advances in digital signal processing have made it possible to apply audio and video watermarks that enable conditional access, retrieval, and copy protection of audio and video material. There are many new efficient and effective standards for wireless communication. Novel communication

protocols support authentication, partial information, and multiple media in a secure way. Novel media compression schemes building on MPEG-4 and MPEG-7 enable effective transmission and compositionality of video material. Recent developments in speech processing and vision technologies enable new interaction concepts that can be used in conversational user interfaces, thus allowing a first step towards the development of natural interfaces. And this is just a list of recent technology examples. A more detailed overview of Ambient Intelligence related technology developments can be found in the book *AmIware* [7].

Following the lines of thought imposed by the different developments of Moore's law one may conclude that the design and manufacturing of electronic devices has reached a level of miniaturization which allows the integration of electronic systems into our background. In more concrete terms, it implies that it has become feasible to think of integrating electronics into any conceivable physical object, i.e. clothing, furniture, carpets, walls, floors, ceilings, buildings, etcetera. This opens up new opportunities for electronic

devices, because it implies that we can leave the age of the box and enter a new age in which functionalities such as audio, video, communication, and gaming, which were confined to boxes up to now, may become freely available from the environment, helping people to have free access to their functionality and enabling natural interaction with them. So these trends have led to a point in time where it has become feasible from a technology perspective to develop environments that are Ambient Intelligent.

Economy

By the end of the past century, socio-economic investigations revealed that a new wave of business development was emerging based on mass customization, leading to a new economic order, from which an answer could be obtained to the question of whether Ambient Intelligence could contribute to the development of new business and greater wealth for everyone in the world. In their compelling bestseller, Pine & Gilmore [8] describe a new economy, which they call the *expe-*

rience economy. They position this economy as the fourth major wave following the classical economies known as the commodity, the goods, and the service economy. The general belief of the experience economy is that people are willing to spend money on having experiences, and from certain enterprises such as the holiday economy one may indeed conclude that this might very well be true. A salient property of an experience is the fact that it can feel real, irrespective of whether it has been generated by a real or a virtual cause; what counts is the gut feeling. Personal reminiscences that bring back good old feelings are nice examples of such experiences.

Richard Florida [9] takes the idea of the experience economy a step further by sketching a world of urban centers in which people create a living by working as artists in the way they create new products and services. These so-called *creative industries* fully exploit the concept of experience design and provide a new economy, supplying local-for-local markets. From an economic point of view this is a very promising growth area that is only in the early stages of its development, offering huge possibilities for high-tech companies, such as Philips, if they can manage to become part of the ecosystem that is the typical governing organizational structure of the world of creative industries.

Prahalad & Ramaswamy [10] use similar concepts to the experience economy to propose a new way of value creation for the 21st century based on the co-creation and development of novel goods and services that satisfy the greater need of customers. Their views also follow a line of thinking that is related to the development of a sustainable society in which markets in developing countries and regions are considered as serious economic factors in a global economic setting.

All of these socio-economic ideas open up major possibilities for making money in markets that exploit the concept of Ambient Intelligence, thus providing the necessary economic foundation for its further growth and development.

Advances in design
The development of Ambient Intelligence following the insights provided by the macro trends mentioned above has opened the way to a new approach to the design of novel products and services. This had led to a broadly endorsed view of design that involves end users in the design process in a well-structured and systematic way. This novel design concept, which is called *Experience and Application Research (EAR)*, is quite well suited for the research and design of AmI concepts because it supports the systematic use and application of novel technologies for the purpose of generating end-user experience. The meaning and impact of this novel design concept can best be understood by looking at some of the historical developments.

The late nineties of the past century also showed a general development that was following up on the profound desire to have more things that were simply useful, and to move users or people in general into the center of our activities. In other words the information society had resulted in an overload of products and services for which the user benefits were unclear. There was a call to design things that were easy to understand and simple to use. Negroponte [11], Norman [12], and Winograd [13] are all examples of designers who were fiercely opposed to the existing means and concepts for user interfaces and man-machine interaction, and who were desperately in search of novel paradigms that would make the interaction with electronic systems more natural. It was generally believed that the social character of the user interface would be determined by the extent to which the system complies with the intuition and habits of its users and this led to a number of groundbreaking insights. One of these developments is that of a novel research area which is called *affective computing*, which is characterized by a multidisciplinary approach to man-machine interaction that combines different methods from psychology and computer science [14]. Another angle is provided by the approach followed by Reeves and Nass [15], who state in their *Media Equation* that the interaction between man and machine should be based on the very same concepts as the interaction between humans, i.e. it should be intuitive, multi-modal, based on emotion and compliant to social rules.

The development of the AmI vision has been largely influenced by these design developments because they clearly articulated the need for a user-centric approach to the design of novel electronic environments. They also contributed to the understanding that the use of AmI environments can only be measured by the user benefits that are ultimately achieved by them, irrespective of their intricacy and sophistication. Central to the development of the

AmI paradigm is the notion of *experience*, reflecting a user benefit beyond the classical requirement of functionality. Realizing experiences, however, is less well understood compared to meeting functional requirements. For experience research and development, novel approaches are needed that position the end user in the center of the design of novel AmI applications. In addition we need new methods and facilities to carry out such investigations. In addition we need new methods and facilities to carry out such investigations.

The *Experience Application Research* approach refers to a way of working in which the experience designer develops a prototype on which he iterates over a number of cycles. The whole process is based on user insights and during each cycle the experience prototype is improved by applying refined user insights. These are obtained by evaluating the experience prototype with end users, which can be done in various ways. In this way prototyping involves users from the start, improving the effectiveness and efficiency of the design process. To gather the user insights, facilities are needed that reflect as closely as possible the natural environment in which the experiences are generated. Philips' ExperienceLab is such an Experience and Application Research Center, which is fully equipped to conduct feasibility and usability studies with ordinary people in a real-life setting.

Ambient lifestyle - From concept to experience

In this book we report on five years of work in the domain of Experience and Application Research in the context of the realization of the Philips Ambi-

ent Intelligence vision. The book considers the effort of generating experience prototypes as the conversion from concept to experience and views HomeLab and the later ExperienceLab as the place where this work is done. The book follows the line of three different parts, which are described as follows.

Context provides a general scope for the results presented in this book. It elaborates on a number of specific trends and developments in society, technology and economy that are related to the vision of Ambient Intelligence. The chapter *The People Age* presents new insights into the development of our society from a people perspective. *AmIware* presents an overview of recent technological achievements that are relevant for the development of Ambient Intelligence. *New Senses* describes trends in business development at Philips from a brand perspective. The chapter *Experience and Application Research* presents a novel conceptual approach to the research, design and prototyping of Ambient Intelligent products and services.

ExperienceLab provides a detailed description of the resources and the way of working that are applied to implement the Experience and Application Research approach. The chapter *Facilities* provides a detailed description of the infrastructure of ExperienceLab. *Probing* deals with the methods and tools used in the intricate process of collecting information from users who are involved in ExperienceLab in the evaluation and co-creation of novel design concepts. *New Business* presents a number of real-life practices obtained from the process of

developing business from experience prototypes conceptualized in ExperienceLab.

Showcase is the central part of the book and provides a wealth of examples of experience prototypes developed at Philips' Experience and Application Research laboratories. The chapters are sequenced on the basis of the chronological order of and the relation between the projects that led to the resulting prototype. It starts off with *WWICE*, which is viewed as the seminal project in a long series of experience prototypes. This is followed by the prototypes developed in the former HomeLab and it is concluded with *work in progress*: the prototypes that are researched in the current ExperienceLab. The chapters roughly follow the same structure, providing information on the user insights used, the concept created, and the evaluation results obtained. Throughout the book, a set of keywords is used that present for each chapter the basic features to which the content can be related.

Figure 1: *The WWICE living room; the predecessor of HomeLab and ExperienceLab.*

Navigating the book

The graphics used in the book assist reading in a number of ways. The three parts, *Context, ExperienceLab,* and *Showcase,* are represented by colors that are used throughout the book. In addition, a number of keywords are used to interrelate the content of the different chapters. They can also be used to identify specific elements of a more global significance, as indicated by the keyword itself. Finally, the last page of the book presents a map of projects called *The Conversion Tree* which provides an overview of all projects over time and insight in the relation between the projects.

References

1. Aarts, E.H.L., H. Harwig, and M. Schuurmans (2001), Ambient Intelligence, in: J. Denning (ed.) *The Invisible Future,* McGraw Hill, New York, NY, USA, pp. 235-250.

2. Aarts, E.H.L., and S. Marzano (eds.) (2003), *The New Everyday: Visions of Ambient Intelligence,* 010 Publishing, Rotterdam, The Netherlands.

3. Aarts, E.H.L., and J. Encarnaçao (2006), *The Emergence of Ambient Intelligence,* Springer, Berlin, Germany.

4. Berners-Lee, T. (1999), *Weaving the Web,* Harper Collins Publishers Inc., San Francisco, CA, USA.

5. Friedman, T.L. (2005), *The World is Flat: A Brief History of the Globalized World in the 21st Century,* Farrar, Straus, and Giroux, New York, USA.

6. Noyce, R. (1977), Microelectronics, *Scientific American* 237(3), 63-69.

7. Muhkerjee, S., E.H.L. Aarts, M. Ouwerkerk, R. Rovers, and F. Widdershoven (eds.) (2005), *AmIware: Hardware Drivers for Ambient Intelligence,* Springer Verlag, Berlin, Germany.

8. Pine, J., and J. Gilmore (1999), *The Experience Economy,* Bradford Books, New York, NY, USA.

9. Prahalad, C., and V. Ramaswamy (2004), *The Future of Competition,* Harvard Business School Press, Cambridge, MA, USA.

10. Florida, R. (2002), *The Rise of the Creative Class,* Basic Books, New York, NY, USA.

11. Negroponte, N. (1995), *Being Digital,* Alfred A. Knopf Inc., New York, NY, USA.

12. Norman, A. (1993), *Things That Make Us Smart,* Perseus Books, Cambridge, MA, USA.

13. Winograd, T. (ed.) (1996), *Bringing Design to Software,* Addison-Wesley, Reading, MA, USA.

14. Picard, R. (1997), *Affective Computing,* The MIT Press, Cambridge, MA, USA.

15. Reeves, B., and C. Nass (1996), *The Media Equation,* Cambridge University Press, Cambridge, MA, USA.

Contents

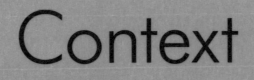

Context

The People Age

Just as the industrial era was characterized by consumption, so the next era will be characterized by context. The industrial era is giving way to a new economy, based more on knowledge and context than on material assets and consumption. While some call this the Knowledge Age, perhaps it would be simpler and more sense-making to call it the People Age. The democratization of information, production and power means inevitably that people are becoming the principal drivers and actors of their own futures, aided and abetted by the flexibility and adaptability of the new technologies. It is people who generate knowledge, and not only knowledge, but also creativity, imagination and sense of purpose, all qualities that we need as we go forward. As people, rather than the economy or technology, drive the future, so the emphasis in terms of why we do things, what we do and how we do them is shifting [1].

In our quest to empower people and contribute to more meaningful qualities of life it is important for us as a company to understand this shift, together with the evolving relationship between people and technology. Our research into society and cultures, through Philips Design, and our research with people offer us insights into the why, the what, and the how.

Josephine Green

What really matters

Ever more technology, productivity and efficiency have helped drive the industrial-consumer economy, but at too high a cost to the environment, the poor and personal happiness. Global warming and the depletion of natural resources, the growing gap between the 'haves' and the 'have-nots' and personal levels of stress are making us re-think what we mean by quality of life. Is it about more money, more goods, or is it about something less tangible [2]? Meanwhile, while the richer regions are asking themselves what happiness is, other regions in the world are struggling with little and too often with hardly anything at all. Yet the material dream dreamt by the few cannot be the dream dreamt by all: the planet cannot sustain it and the dream itself appears to be fading! More people, as our research indicates, are re-defining their well-being, less in material terms and more in terms of health and wellness, community and relationships, personal growth and development and control over their own lives. It seems that what makes people happy, over and above a certain basic standard of living, is more intangible than tangible, and that the belief that more makes you happier is a myth rather than a reality.

The Context Economy

So as a new age seeks new values and new solutions to well-being and prosperity, the new technologies can contribute to supplying them. The dematerialization of happiness is matched by the ability of the new ambient technologies to dematerialize benefits. In a relationship where the technology is embedded in our everyday environment we no longer 'consume' the technology but live side by side with it, as it supports and facilitates our daily living. Through this more intimate co-existence our identity becomes less about needs, "what do I want", and more about expression and experience, "how can I best take advantage of what I want to do in the way I want to do it", in any specific context, be it a home, a car, a public space, a hospital or a school. Intelligence, by changing the paradigm between people and technology, takes us beyond consumption. Given this, we need to re-frame the questions we ask. Rather than asking what people will consume, ask what people will value. Value rather than consumption has the potential to open our minds and our technologies.

Beyond consumption to deep customization
In the Context Economy the space, the activity and the experience become important and passive consumers become active producers of their own lives, as they search for and value ways to interact with, control and create their environments. People co-create their own content and experience and value anything that enables personalization, self and collective expression and creativity. How we light our environment or monitor a health condition will be up to us. Through speech, gesture or touch we can interface with a display, a hand-held device, or an intelligent wearable garment. What becomes increasingly important is the quality of the interaction and accessing and receiving the information we want in the way we want it and being able to interpret and act upon it appropriately. This is about a deep customization [3], based on a live-in relationship with technology, based on an ecosystem of information, services, experiences and solutions, in which interaction and access are the issues rather than ownership.

Beyond products to systems
Co-existing with technology in a more intimate way also opens up a more holistic approach to living. Stand-alone products give way to connected and networked environments, enabling a more systems-based delivery of value, for example in the area of health. Long-term chronic lifestyle-related illnesses, such as diabetes, obesity, or Alzheimer's, and greater health awareness are placing great strain on present health delivery. More ambient technologies can enable a more home-centered health system, in which we become the center of a system connecting us to our different circles of care, from family/friends to support professionals, expert patients, doctors, hospital, etcetera. Such a user-centered system, based on an intuitive relationship between people and their technology, encourages the full engagement of people in their own healthcare as active participants along a continuum from prevention to care [4]. It also emphasizes not only technology research and innovation but also social research and innovation [5]. By creating more structural and socially relevant solutions to today's new problems and unmet needs in areas such as health, education, transport, neighborhoods, etcetera, we are also truly freeing up the new technologies to drive prosperity and well-being. Such systems solutions are relevant to both advanced and developing regions, given that the former need to re-invent new ways of delivering benefits and the latter need to leapfrog old solutions.

Beyond growth to sustainability
A context and systems approach to delivering value also allows us to consider a more sustainable model of development and growth. The dematerialization of the Context Economy based on customization, service and experience allows innovation to go beyond a model of continued obsolescence in material terms. A context-aware society also leads to a higher consciousness of interdependencies and interactions, which in turn fosters more sustainable thinking and behaviors.

A context approach also facilitates more local and distributed economies in which local communities, using local knowledge and local resources, including energy, create and sustain their own livelihoods. By developing more local economies based on local resources and know-how, there is a greater possibility of safeguarding environmental and social qualities through the use of traditional knowledge. A closer proximity of production and consumption also protects the environment and collective community structures. Examples of local sustainable livelihoods are growing, from the surge in organic produce in the West to traditional medicine in India. This more local, decentralized and distributed approach to value rather than global production and consumption promises to be more sense-making and sustainable for the future in that it generates or regenerates local contexts and livelihoods [6]. The Context Economy of the future will push towards an ecosystem of people and technology and an ecosystem of production and consumption and, in either or both cases, offer new value and a more sustainable model for both the developing and developed regions. Our challenge is to research and understand how Ambient Intelligence can empower and enrich individuals and communities in context.

Co-creating the future

The way we do this is changing. The emergence of people as authors and creators of their own environments, through and with the ambient technologies, means that they are becoming participators in our research and innovation. This is necessary because not only are experience and customization subjective and therefore not covered by more classical market research approaches adopted by focus groups and segments but also in an increasingly commoditized world users are a greatly under-used resource. Moving from observing and researching people to engaging with them and involving them actively in our research and design not only makes sense but is also sense-making, as the outcome of our research and design has a greater likelihood of being relevant [7]. Users, designers and researchers working together enable us to fulfill our promise of Sense and Simplicity.

Drawing on future studies, cultural studies, the social sciences and ethnographic research, observing people in their everyday lives, we are now increasingly using these insights to "play" with users in an iterative manner, through experience demonstrators and application prototypes, within the context of so-called experience labs. These environments enable us to learn about and to interact with users and our ambient technologies in an experimental and co-creative way. It is in this context that HomeLab has meaning. So whether we are thinking about a new health system or an interactive home environment the contextualization of future technologies and solutions is reshaping how we innovate and with whom we innovate.

Inclusive innovation

Philips Design and Philips Research have over the last years been exploring and implementing a more integrated innovation approach. Initially this involved carrying out both technology and socio-cultural research and bringing the complementary knowledge and insights into a 'multidisciplinary innovation' approach, involving technology researchers, social and human science researchers, designers and business people. This has progressed towards a more 'open innovation' approach both within Philips, across the Product Divisions, Research and Design, and outside the company, with other university and research centers, customers and companies. We are now experimenting with a higher degree of co-creation through an 'inclusive innovation' approach in which users are involved throughout the research and innovation process. Ambient Intelligence and a Context Economy demand that people become the center of our innovation process, from identifying opportunities to developing demonstrators to finalizing solutions. In the final analysis, Ambi-

ent Intelligence, both in its content being personal customization and user-centered systems, and in its process of co-creative open innovation, is ultimately empowering. The People Age is becoming reality.

References
1. Green, Josephine (2005), *Thinking the Unthinkable: In the Long Run,* Klaus Burmeister and Andres Neef..
2. Haidt, Jonathan (2006), *The Happiness Hypothesis,* Basic Books, William Heinemann.
3. Anton Andrews (2006), *The Open Lifestyle Home,* Positioning Paper, Philips Design.
4. Design Council UK (2005), *Health - Co-Creating Services,* Red Paper.
5. The Young Foundation (2006), *Social Silicon Valleys.*
6. Rocchi, Simona (2006), *Unlocking New Markets,* Positioning Paper, Philips Design.
7. Rameckers, Lucille and Stefanie Un (2006), *People Insights at the Fuzzy Front End of Innovation,* Positioning Paper, Philips Design.

Towards a New Reality

In 2001 Philips opened HomeLab: the first experience laboratory on the premises of its research organization. By making it possible to test the feasibility of new technologies as well as their usability, an old dream came true: placing people center stage in the innovation process. This chapter details the origin of that effort and clarifies how it is related to Philips' current branding efforts.

Customer First!

In the early nineties Philips experienced a financial crisis leading to serious downsizing, sizeable cost reductions and restructuring. 'Operation Centurion', as the change effort was called, also came to include positive messages: "Your work isn't meaningful on its own; we work for our customers together" and "Customer First!". The attempt was to refocus the battered organization with a clear priority: it is in the market place where we, all together, have to make our money. To get this message across to absolutely everybody, 3 full-day events ('Customer Days') were organized between 1991 and 1995 and broadcast globally via satellite to all employees, who had gathered in a joint effort to determine locally how to improve their way of working, bearing the customer in mind.

Despite the enormous efforts to make Philips as a whole more customer-focused, the existing cultural characteristic of not being sufficiently consumer-minded prevented the communication efforts from being truly effective. On all three Customer Days Philips employees spent their time with each other – not with customers. Jan Timmer, CEO of Philips at the time, gave a speech in which he said: "We

will become customer-focused. With these great products [pointing at a collection of design audio-video products]!" – contradicting himself by using a product feature, i.e. design, to stimulate customer focus. The Dutch Philips organization made a sign, 'cUstoMEr 1st!', presenting 'U' and 'ME' as customers, rather than colleagues working for customers. Most efforts represented a serious attempt; most of them failed to illustrate a shifted mindset.

Let's Make Things Better

Under the next CEO, Cor Boonstra (1996-2001), a significant step was taken by a global implementation of the 'Let's Make Things Better' campaign; see Figure 1. For the first time in its history, Philips globally deployed one campaign throughout all its Product Divisions. To avoid global monotony and to be able to remain market-specific, since selling CD players to consumers is slightly different from providing Nokia with excellent power management systems for their phones, Product Divisions retained some degrees of freedom, e.g. regarding photography, and each division had its own color scheme. The Semiconductors division for instance executed Let's Make Things Better in purple.

Although 'Let's' meant a big leap forward in

Figure 1: *A visual used in the Let's Make Things Better campaign.*

Sense and Simplicity

As one of his first actions after he became CEO of Philips, Gerard Kleisterlee contracted Andrea Ragnetti and appointed him Corporate Marketing Officer (CMO); Philips had never had a CMO before. Ad Huijser, Chief Technology Officer, was involved in this process. This meant that, as a new boost for the brand was being prepared, a connection existed early on between the place where new products were invented (Philips Research) and the people developing the best way to present them to the markets.

Sense and Simplicity, Philips' new brand campaign (see Figure 2), built upon the globalizing efforts of 'Let's' and used that precedent to deploy a much stronger brand identity, legitimized by the new president's general principle of 'One Philips'. Sense and Simplicity was communicated to employees as those products and/or services that rest on three pillars: (1) designed around you; (2) easy to experience; and (3) advanced. The fact that the third pillar was 'advanced' is significant: 'advanced' is a judgment made by a user. The original term for the third pillar was 'innovative', which, as a product characteristic, would have still signaled a lack of consumer or customer focus. Although it is too early to determine the extent to which Sense and Simplicity will be successful, it is clear that, in a number of ways, Philips has improved on its previous efforts; see also Table 1.

The significance of ExperienceLab

Over the past 15 years, Philips has devoted a lot of attention to the words 'customer' and 'consumer'. Nowadays, however, more attention is given to

terms of efficiently strengthening Philips as a global brand, the effort also had some flaws. Philips president Boonstra had a strong focus on advertising, leading him to appoint agency professionals, thereby adding competence but without an inside network. As a consequence, the deployment of 'Let's' within Philips (i.e. explaining the philosophy to Philips employees, engaging them in the effort, providing the tools for them to help make things better) suffered. The focus on advertising also caused 'branding' to be focused on consumers (as most advertising at Philips was aimed at consumers). Business-to-Business divisions were,

to a large extent, ignored and left without ways to apply 'Let's' to their non-consumer environment.
At the beginning of the new millennium, a small number of brand-related linguistic artifacts had significant behavioral consequences. The word 'customer' was used to talk and think about colleagues, fuelling a drive to increasingly substitute contractual relations for collegial relations. Branding was approached as advertising. No shared effort was made to develop a branding approach consistent across consumer audiences and Business-to-Business markets. Philips people were not intensively involved in making sure the brand delivered.

Figure 2: Launch of the Sense and Simplicity campaign in Amsterdam.

the customers than to merely using the word 'customer'. In 2001, at what is currently called the High Tech Campus Eindhoven, Philips Research (set up in 1914, making it one of the world's oldest institutes for industrial research) opened HomeLab. It was built as a home, providing a facility to host people in order to observe them trying out new technologies in a natural setting. HomeLab has since been expanded by the addition of two further labs: ShopLab (to test the impact of Solid State Lighting in the public domain) and CareLab (to research how people want to experience personal care at home). Together these three labs form ExperienceLab.

ExperienceLab introduces consumers to researchers' work on an almost daily basis. Customers, in this case key decision-makers at industrial partners, also influence researchers' work more frequently, as the numbers in which they visit the annual Corporate Research Exhibition (CRE) has increased to well over 300 (since 2001). The word 'ExperienceLab' itself testifies to the fact that people's perceptions, the way they make sense of products and services, have now become a starting point for researchers trying to invent new technologies and applications.

The existence of ExperienceLab is significant. Its

effectiveness, however, lies in its use. So how much of the work being done there finds its way to other parts of Philips? A number of possible answers to this question are hinted at by the projects that are described in this book. In this regard, as hinted at by the description of Philips' 'brand voyage' over the past 15 years, expectations about the speed of organizational learning should perhaps be tempered. Organizational learning is a slow process.

Perhaps you would expect email and intranet to accelerate it, since they give people more access to more information? I would argue the possibly counter-intuitive opposite: with more access, communication actually becomes less meaningful (in line with Gossen's first law of the satiation of wants: more of the same diminishes the marginal utility of each new item [2,3]). Organizational learning is not strengthened by email and intranet: with the huge increase in emails and web pages, their individual significance diminishes. Electronic media make people learn less, not more.

In that light, it may actually be seen as quite an achievement that, within 5 years of opening HomeLab, the research, design and industrialization organizations at Philips joined together to present innovations as an experience at the 2006 Corporate Research Exhibition. The trend towards more meaningless communication and even slower organizational learning is being countered by an organized shared effort to 'learn by doing' by trying to achieve innovation jointly as an experience.

A vision of the future
ExperienceLab provides researchers at Philips with a platform to communicate with future users of

	Customer First!	**Let's Make Things Better**	**Sense and Simplicity**
Brief description	Revitalizing the company	Consumer advertising	Delivering on the brand promise
Internal ownership	President and departments driving the change programme	President and Global Brand Management	Corporate Marketing Officer backed by the Board of Management
Rationale	To recover from our problems we need to focus on who to serve in the market	To become stronger in the market we need to become partners with our customers to make their lives better	Reality is becoming increasingly complex. People will pay us for solutions that help them make their lives easier.
Intended effect	Acceptance of change	Perceived unity	Growth
Achieved effect	Substituting contractual arrangements for collegial relations	Re-articulated differences between Product Divisions	Increasing dynamic of shared efforts to satisfy customer/-consumer needs
Main strength	A globally repeated effort to reach all Philips employees with clear messages	A global harmonization of fragmented marketing communication efforts	Deploying a strong brand identity globally across all divisions and providing all employees with brand pillars to base their behavior on
Main weakness	Not effective in making the customer the center of people's work	Focused too much on advertising, not turning promise into reality	(not yet visible)

Table 1: *A comparison of the past three Philips brand campaigns for different performance characteristics.*

their inventions. For Philips, ExperienceLab represents in a way a final chapter of a 15-year effort to turn a traditionally linear production process into an iterative innovation dialogue. By engaging directly with consumers and customer, aiming to present innovations designed around them in ways easy to experience, Philips' research, design and industrialization departments have already started to develop new ways to learn faster together.

Now the challenge is about to get bigger. How can new developments like Solid State Lighting, Personal Healthcare and Ambient Intelligence (electronics with smart functionality invisibly embedded in people's environments) lead to growth for Philips? Only the future can tell to what extent Sense and Simplicity has created sufficient dynamics for Philips to deliver those innovations that people find valuable.

References
1. Aarts, E.H.L., H. Harwig, and M. Schuurmans (2001), Ambient Intelligence, in: J. Denning (ed.) The Invisible Future, McGraw Hill, New York, NY, USA, pp. 235-250.
2. Gossen, H.H. (1854), *Entwicklung der Gesetze des menschlichen Verkehrs und der daraus fliessenden Regeln für menschliches Handeln.*
3. Jevons, W.S. (1862), *General Mathematical Theory of Political Economy.*

AmIware

Ambient Intelligence (AmI) refers to electronic environments that are sensitive, adaptive and responsive to the presence of people [3]. The concept builds on the early ideas of ubiquitous computing introduced in the 1990s by the late Marc Weiser [12], who anticipated a digital world in which electronic devices are the embedded parts of fine-grained distributed networks. Ambient Intelligence aims to take the integration yet one step further by involving the entire environment and any physical object in the interaction with people, thus improving people's wellbeing, productivity, creativity and leisure through enhanced user-system interaction. Evidently, the focus of this paradigm is not only on the physical integration of electronics, but also on the creation and generation of enhanced experiences and, as a result of this, Ambient Intelligence has major cultural and business-related implications [2,4]. In this chapter we discuss the technology for Ambient Intelligence, which builds on a general concept for a distributed systems architecture consisting of three different types of basic devices according to their power consumption and functionality.

The AmI paradigm

Developed in the late 1990s, the AmI paradigm presents a vision for digital systems for 2010 and beyond [3,6]. In an AmI world, large numbers of distributed devices are embedded in the environment. They operate collectively using information and intelligence that is hidden in the interconnection network. Lighting, sound, vision, domestic appliances and personal health-care products all interact seamlessly with one another to improve the total user experience through natural and intuitive user interfaces. The AmI paradigm provides a basis for new models of technological innovation within a multi-dimensional society. A crucial factor for the realization of the AmI vision is the observation that current technological developments enable the integration of electronics into the environment, thus making it possible for people to interact with their environment in a seamless, trustworthy, and natural manner.

In Ambient Intelligence, the term *ambience* refers to the need for technology to be embedded on a large scale in such a way that it becomes unobtrusively integrated into everyday objects and environments. The term *intelligence* reflects the fact that the digital surroundings exhibit specific forms of social interaction, i.e. the environments should be able to recognize the people that inhabit them, personalize according to individual prefer

Emile Aarts

  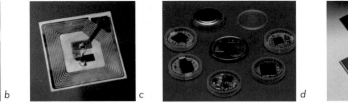 

Figure 1: *Examples of AmIware (AmI technologies).*

a. **Wearable Electronics.** *Electronics integrated into clothing can monitor vital body functions and can autonomously and wirelessly contact communication systems for readout or for emergency rescue.*

b. **Photonic Textiles.** *Interactive light-emitting structures that are woven into fabric open up innovative lighting applications for atmosphere providing illumination and for signage.*

c. **Polymer Electronic RFID Tags.** *Complete radio-frequency identification transponder integrated into an anti-theft sticker.*

d. **Small Autonomous Networked Devices.** *A family of self-empowering electronic devices with a standardized form factor applicable to a large variety of sensor functions.*

e. **Electronic Paper.** *High-resolution Electronic Ink Display with paper-like viewing characteristics, excellent contrast ratio, and clear images that can be seen from any angle.*

The AmI paradigm

Developed in the late 1990s, the AmI paradigm presents a vision for digital systems for 2010 and beyond [3,6]. In an AmI world, large numbers of distributed devices are embedded in the environment. They operate collectively using information and intelligence that is hidden in the interconnection network. Lighting, sound, vision, domestic appliances and personal health-care products all interact seamlessly with one another to improve the total user experience through natural and intuitive user interfaces.

The AmI paradigm provides a basis for new models of technological innovation within a multi-dimensional society. A crucial factor for the realization of the AmI vision is the observation that current technological developments enable the integration of electronics into the environment, thus making it possible for people to interact with their environment in a seamless, trustworthy, and natural manner.

In Ambient Intelligence, the term *ambience* refers to the need for technology to be embedded on a large scale in such a way that it becomes unobtrusively integrated into everyday objects and environments. The term *intelligence* reflects the fact that the digital surroundings exhibit specific forms of social interaction, i.e. the environments should be able to recognize the people that inhabit them, personalize according to individual preferences, adapt themselves to the users, learn from their behavior and possibly act upon their behalf. This implies that embedding through miniaturization is the main systems design objective from a hardware point of view. From a software point of view we distinguish between the following major AmI functionalities: *context awareness, ubiquitous access* and *natural interaction.* The user benefits of the AmI paradigm are aimed at improving the quality of people's lives by creating the desired atmosphere and functionality via intelligent, personalized and interconnected systems and services. However simple this requirement may sound, its true realization is, for the time being, not within our reach.

Enabling Technologies

There are three global factors that enable the development of Ambient Intelligence: technology, global connectivity and socio-economical aspects. Below we elaborate briefly on the technological factors. (We do not consider the other two aspects any further here, but interested readers are referred to [2,4]). For the discussion of the technological factors we use a well-known frame of reference provided by the developments in the semiconductor industry, which is known as Moore's law [9]. This law states that the integration density of systems on silicon doubles every eighteen months. This trend already holds for more than thirty years and provides a clear forecast for the development of semiconductor technology. Recently, some new angles have opened up and, in conjunction with Moore's law, these can be formulated as follows:

- 1D-Moore is the one-dimensional continuation of the classical Moore's law into the sub-micron domain of micro-electronics, resulting in small and powerful integrated circuits that can be produced at low cost.
- 2D-Moore is the development of 2-dimensional large-area electronic circuitry of extremely low cost, possibly using technologies other than silicon, such as polymer-electronics.
- 3D-Moore refers to the development of ultra-highly functional 3-dimensional circuitry consisting of Micro Electronic Mechanical Systems (MEMS) or Systems in a Package (SIPs) that integrate sensor, actuator, computing and communication functions into a single nano-electronics system.

Following the lines of thought imposed by the different developments of Moore's law, one may conclude that the design and manufacturing of electronic devices has reached a level of miniaturization which allows the integration of electronic systems for processing, communication, storage display, and access into any possible physical object, e.g. clothes, furniture, cars and homes, thus making people's environments smart.

For extensive overviews of the various hardware developments that are relevant for Ambient Intelligence we refer to [8, 11].

Basic devices for Ambient Intelligence

AmI environments may consist of three types of devices which are distinguished on the basis of their power consumption. This classification is justified by the general belief that power is the constraining factor in the distribution of AmI functionalities over an AmI environment [5,7]. This leads to the following device hierarchy:

- *Autonomous devices* that empower themselves autonomously over a full lifetime. They extract the required energy from the environment by scavenging light, electromagnetic energy, mechanical energy from vibrations or temperature differences by means of a thermoelectric generator. Examples are all kinds of tags and sensors. These autonomously empowered devices are called μWatt nodes.
- *Nomadic devices* that use rechargeable batteries with typical autonomous operational times of a few hours and standby times of several days. Examples are personal digital assistants, mobile phones, wireless monitors, portable storage containers and intelligent remote controls. These battery-empowered devices are called mWatt nodes.
- *Stationary devices* that have almost unlimited energy resources because they are empowered by a mains network. Examples are large flat displays, recording devices, (home) servers, and large storage and computing devices. These mains-empowered devices are called Watt nodes.

The energy availability as well as the power dissipation of a device may change over time. Different modes of operation may require different energy budgets, which may cause large variations in peak-to-average power dissipation. Evidently, for all of the types of nodes introduced above, energy management is the key factor in the determination of the amount of information processing that can be carried out by the individual nodes. The different nodes may come in different shapes and recent technological developments have given rise to many new devices called AmIware which may become part of an integrated environment, ranging from autonomous sensors and micro-cameras to e-books and 3-D displays; see Figure 1.

Applications and basic AmI functionalities

In an AmI environment electronics may be integrated into any conceivable object, e.g. into clothing, furniture, cars, houses, offices and public places, enabling people to interact with their environment through natural user-interface concepts. Examples of AmI environments in different domains are given in Figure 2.

In all these examples integrated sensors and actuators are used that determine personalized living conditions, such as seating, lighting and airflow, based on the presence of individuals and their activities. Nomadic devices like foldable displays, personal digital assistants and wearable infotainment systems can give users wireless personalized access to audio, video and information. Integrated stationary devices like large displays, info-tables, info-chairs and lighting surfaces, people in a digital environment that supports ambient access and personalized wellbeing through natural multimodal interaction using speech and gesture.

AmI environments contain many different devices that support sensing, actuating, computing, storage, display, communication and interaction. From the AmI environment of Figure 2 we can identify the following three basic AmI functionalities:

Figure 2: *Examples of AmI environments.*

a. Ambient Experience. *An interactive patient room where children can bring their own pictures to be displayed on the walls and ceiling whilst they are being examined.*

b. AmbiLight TV. *An enhanced viewing experience based on ambient lighting effects generated on-line while watching TV or a video.*

c. Intelligent bathroom. *A smart bathroom environment with interactive display mirrors and ambient lighting.*

d. Dimi. *An interactive multi-modal dialogue system that acts as a companion in the home.*

e. Ambient Lighting. *An interactive lighting control environment that uses tangible objects such as colored marbles to determine the appropriate setting.*

- *Context awareness.* The environment uses sensors to determine the context in which certain activities take place. The sensors collect, process and exchange data that can be combined to determine meaningful information on persons and the environment, such as the identity and position of persons and objects. The context information can also be used to introduce actions.
- *Ubiquitous access.* Audio, video and data can be streamed wirelessly to any access device, either portable or fixed, which is present in the environment, thus enabling ubiquitous access to information, communication, services and entertainment.
- *Natural interaction.* Users can interact with their environment through natural modalities such as speech, gesture and tactile movements. Furthermore, the interaction concepts are socially and emotionally intelligent, supporting a personalized, adaptive and pro-active response.

These basic AmI functionalities apply to a large variety of environments like the ones show in Figure 2 and they can implement a variety of applications that are meaningful to people in their everyday activities, such as work, security, health care, entertainment and personal communications. They can be realized by optimally combining information processing technologies distributed over different device types, with the main issue being how to distribute the functionalities over the available nodes. To shed some light on this we elaborate on each of these issues in slightly more detail.

Context awareness

Context awareness is realized in three steps. Firstly, a wireless network of μWatt node sensors is used to sense the environment. Many different sensors may be used to collect mechanical, physical, chemical or biological data. Typical examples of such quantities are position, speed, acceleration, temperature, pressure, brightness, acidity, magnetic flux, skin humidity and heart beat.

Secondly, the raw data are processed to represent relevant contextual information within a given contextual model. Combining the data and classifying it into higher-level data items that represent states of the AmI environment may lead to the computation of new contextual information. This step is often referred to as 'sensor fusion' and requires a computational effort that may be available in the μWatt nodes if the processing is simple, e.g. as in discriminating between day and night or sound and silence. It does, however, rapidly become more demanding if more complex contextual states need to be classified, like the type or level of certain activities. In such a case one has to resort to implementations in mWatt or Watt nodes.

Thirdly, it is necessary to interpret and combine states in order to extract novel information at a high semantic level using contextual models of the environment and people's specific behavioral patterns. This finally may lead to the deduction of the desired pro-active responses of the AmI environment. These tasks generally involve major computational effort, which may only be available within Watt nodes.

Ubiquitous access
Ubiquitous access requires the availability of digital media, such as audio, video, pictures and data at any time, in any place and on any device, either nomadic or stationary. Access involves the retrieval, streaming and playing of media and because these are computationally demanding tasks they require mWatt or Watt nodes.

Digital media require storage devices, which can either be local or embedded in a broadband communication network. The local storage devices can be mWatt nodes that may use solid-state storage or optical disks. Networked storage devices are stationary server-type systems with large storage capacities and are consequently Watt nodes. Networked terminal access is achieved by streaming data, preferably wirelessly, from a storage device to a nomadic or stationary device.

Streaming high-quality video over wireless communication channels requires sophisticated compression and quality-of-service techniques. If the terminals are nomadic devices, effective power management techniques are needed. Especially in cases where nomadic devices need to display several hours of high-quality video, this imposes major requirements on the performance parameters of mWatt nodes.

Natural interaction
Interaction technology may involve all node types. Tangible objects that implement interaction concepts for the control of AmI environments may be implemented as μWatt nodes. For instance, near-field communication technologies may be used to implement user interface concepts for the control of ambient lighting devices. Inclusion of multi-modal interaction concepts, such as vision, speech and gesture recognition, involves the execution of computationally demanding algorithms requiring mWatt or Watt nodes. If intelligence is added, computational efforts may range up to several Tops, thus requiring Watt nodes for their implementation. Examples of such interaction concepts are conversational interfaces, 3-dimensional interactive video interfaces and emotional robot interfaces.

Trends
The device hierarchy of μWatt, mWatt and Watt nodes introduces four major challenges for the design of AmI environments, which can be related to low-power design, design for distribution, and experience design, respectively. Below, we elaborate briefly on each of these challenges; see also [5,7].

Low-power design
Power limitations are probably going to impose the most demanding and challenging design objectives upon AmI environments, and this holds for all three types of nodes. Watt nodes should use energy-scavenging techniques, applying micro-fuel cells, ultra capacitors, photovoltaic cells, vibrational converters and radio-active power sources

to empower themselves autonomously through physical environmental properties such as temperature gradients, light, wind and air flow, pressure variations, and movement [10].

mWatt nodes require high-duty batteries with efficient and effective rechargeability properties. Current battery technologies using zinc-air, lithium or alkaline chemistry provide insufficient energy density capabilities if they are used to empower nomadic devices that should be capable of playing several hours of high-quality video. Furthermore, the embedding of electronics in nomadic devices, such as wearables, tangible objects and small items of furniture, calls for batteries with non-conventional form factors that support foldable and bendable applications.

As AmI environments will contain between several dozens and hundreds of stationary Watt nodes, classical empowering methods can no longer be used because of the thermal and environmental burden they create. Consequently, novel low-power technologies are needed. Asynchronous design paradigms and on-chip power management techniques are promising approaches but it is most probable that new process technologies will be needed which may be substantially different from the current CMOS technologies.

Design for distribution
Design for distribution will call for novel middleware constructs that enable multiple networked and distributed applications and services to coexist and cooperate. The three main issues in this respect are interoperability, heterogeneity and dynamics.

- 'Interoperability' refers to the ability to exchange devices and application code in networked systems. The issue also includes the development of communication protocols that support plug-and-play, such as HAVi, IEEE 1394, Bluetooth, UpnP and IEEE 802.11.
- 'Heterogeneity' refers to the ability to run software applications on devices with markedly different performance characteristics, i.e. static versus mobile or general purpose versus dedicated. This calls for middleware that is scalable to deal with different footprints and operating systems. It also calls for bridging and gateway concepts that support data exchange between networks that apply different communication protocols.
- 'Dynamics' refers to the ability of networked systems to adapt themselves to changes in the environment, such as position, context, configuration, data and others.

To be able to cope with the issues mentioned above, AmI middleware needs to support the following functionalities: device abstraction, device detection, resource management, streaming management, content and asset management, personalization, multi-modal interaction, context awareness, and security.

Evidently, design for distribution calls for the development of a middleware layer that is capable of bonding together the various nodes in an AmI environment. The following major challenges can be formulated for the individual nodes. For μWatt nodes an operating system is required that can handle wireless distributed networks of sensor and actuator nodes. For mWatt nodes communication middleware is needed that supports device discovery and interoperability. For Watt nodes streaming management and asset management are the key issues.

Experience design
The design of AmI environments differs markedly from the design of classical single-box systems. AmI environments introduce new options for services and applications. The fact that boxes will not be present anymore introduces the need for novel interaction concepts that allow the user to communicate with their electronic environment in a natural way.

Requirements engineering for AmI environments can no longer be seen as a task that can be accomplished through the development of scenarios and the translation of use cases into system requirements. System functionalities that generate true user experiences can only be determined in a reliable way from feasible prototypes that provide proofs of concept. These are called experience prototypes, and they can be developed by means of a user-centered design approach that applies both feasibility and usability studies in order to develop a mature interaction concept. More specifically, this means that laboratories are needed which contain infrastructures that support fast prototyping of novel interaction concepts and resemble natural environments of use. Moreover, these experience prototyping centers should also be equipped with an observation infrastructure that can capture and analyze the behavior of people who interact with the experience prototypes.

Philips' HomeLab is an example of such an experience and application research facility. It combines feasibility and usability research into user-centric innovation, leading to a better understanding of the technologies that really matter from a user perspective [1].

Conclusion
Ambient Intelligence is a novel paradigm for future embedded electronic environments that are sensitive to the presence of people, create a personalized interaction, adapt to people's behavior and possibly even anticipate some of their preferences and whishes. Technological advances, such as increased miniaturization, novel lighting and display technologies, and advanced interaction concepts, enable the large-scale integration of electronics into people's environment. Initial evidence of the validity of this concept is available, showing that a paradigm shift in electronic equipment and devices is indeed feasible and desirable. However, the true value of the concept will arise from the extent to which we are able to prove the user benefits of such environments in general, and to do this a great deal of additional research is required into the creation of experience prototypes that can be co-created and evaluated in genuine user environments.

References

1. Aarts, E. and B. Eggen, (2002), *Ambient Intelligence Research in HomeLab*, Neroc Publishers, Eindhoven, The Netherlands.

2. Aarts, E. and J. Encarnaçao (eds.), (2006), *True Visions: Tales on the Realization of Ambient Intelligence*, Springer, Berlin.

3. Aarts, E., H. Harwig, and M. Schuurmans, (2002), Ambient Intelligence, in: J.Denning, (ed) *The Invisible Future*, McGraw Hill, New York, pp. 235-250.

4. Aarts, E. and S. Marzano (eds.), (2003), *The New Everyday: Visions of Ambient Intelligence*, 010 Publishing, Rotterdam, The Netherlands.

5. Basten, T., M. Geilen, and H. de Groot, (2003), *Ambient Intelligence: Impact on Embedded System Design*, Kluwer Academic Publishers, Dordrecht, The Netherlands.

6. ISTAG, *Scenarios for Ambient Intelligence,* (2001), European Commission, ftp://ftp.cordis.lu/pub/ist/docs/istag-scenarios2010.pdf.

7. De Man, H., (2005), Ambient Intelligence: Gigascale Dreams and Nanoscale Realities, *International Solid State Circuits Conference, Digest of Technical Papers*, pp. 29-35.

8. Muhkerjee, S., E.H.L. Aarts, M. Ouwerkerk, R. Rovers, and F. Widdershoven (eds.), (2006), *AmIware: Hardware Drivers for Ambient Intelligence,* Springer, Berlin.

9. Noyce, R.N., (1977), Microelectronics, *Scientific American*, 237(3), pp. 63-69.

10. Rabaey, J. Ammer, T. Karalan, S. Li, B. Otis, M. Sheets, and T. Tuan, (2002), Pico-radio for Wireless Sensor Networks: The Next Challenge in Ultra Low Power Design, *International Solid State Circuit Conference, Digest of Technical Papers,* pp. 200-210.

11. Weber, W., J. Rabaey, and E. Aarts (eds.) (2005), *Ambient Intelligence*, Springer, Berlin.

12. Weiser, M. (1991), The Computer for the TwentyFirst Century, *Scientific American*, 165(3), pp. 94-104.

Experience and Application Research

The search for 'Creative Options' and 'Innovation' in a world dominated by the science of quantitative and the art of qualitative methodologies coupled with the cultural mind-sets of the 'Analytical' and the 'Synthetical' is throwing up new and strong creative possibilities in the way we interpret and transform our emerging world.

The innovation dilemma

It is an accepted 'truth' that only about 20% of the R&D expenses of a large technically orientated company like Philips contributes to a successful product in the market. This number can be made to look better by quantifying indirect benefits such as know-how generation. However, expressing these benefits in hard cash is a difficult and hazy approach, and the fact remains that 80% of mis-investment is a striking figure. If only we knew beforehand what technologies and projects to put our money on. If only we could predict the future.

In an era where companies can no longer rely solely on technological breakthroughs and incremental product development, innovation is high on management agendas. At the same time, innovation has increasingly become a complex activity in which products, services, user needs, and technologies need to be integrated, while bringing a lot of different stakeholders together. [6]

Innovative solutions today increasingly address a complex web in which products, services, technologies and user needs are interwoven. This in turn means that innovation is increasingly dependent on agreements within a larger group of stakeholders.

This carries an inherent risk of slowing the innovative process down - precisely at the time it needs to speed up in the face of an ever more dynamic and volatile market. At the same time, traditional markets are becoming increasingly saturated, educated and brand-wary. Companies can no longer rely solely on technology breakthroughs and incremental product development. Effective differentiation and real added value for the consumer is achieved by incorporating end-user insights in product innovation. Indeed, we believe this is vital in order to truly define and reshape the market. [2]

So, here we are faced with an innovation dilemma. Our Research and Development departments generate countless technological options. Any well-educated person would think that there should be a gem hidden in all these bright ideas and that it would be a waste of money not to use all these options. The result is that many new products are launched each year. And of course, some of these products turn out to be a success, but why?

Senseo success

The Senseo coffee maker shown in Figure 1 is an example of such a success. Many people would like to have or serve friends a quick but good cup of coffee, without making a full pot in which the

Elmo Diederiks, Steven Kyffin

Figure 1: The Senseo coffee maker.

coffee quickly becomes less tasty. The Senseo offers exactly this, and with the wide range of coffee pads a very interesting recurring revenue business model could be put into place. The underlying end-user insight was known, but Philips happened to be able to realize a product technically and thus own the business model together with Douwe Egberts.

Unfortunately, the majority of the products that result from our stack of technical options do not generate substantial cash flow and even harm the brand value because end users are confronted with products that do not really serve their needs or resonate with their desires.

A short story of technology push and brand value

The Perfective steam iron is a concept using anti-crease refill flacons; see Figure 2. It was supposed to leverage on a recurring revenue model like

the Senseo. To assure sufficient revenues the iron would only function if a refill flacon was inserted. However, it turned out that there was no clear end-user insight or need for this product proposition: it was a pure technology and business push. Moreover, the Perfective would be much more expensive over its lifetime compared to a normal steaming iron. Subsequently, the Philips partner, realizing this issue, pulled out. The dilemma now was that about 200,000 pieces needed to be sold to cover investments while the refill flacons were no longer available. The result was that 200,000 loyal Philips customers bought a useless iron and will probably never buy Philips again. Philips took over the distribution and sales of the refill flacons, but the initial damage to the brand value is evident.

Additionally, we suffer, or are going to in the near future, from fierce cost-driven competition from low-labor-cost countries like China. Often we apply a cost-down policy to increase our margins, but this is not our true strength and actually this is not where the true end-user added value is.

It is clear that something should be done to move away from cost-driven competition and focus our research efforts and product portfolio. Maybe we should try to do the impossible and predict the future…but what should we use as our foundations in such predictions?

Application and Experience Research

The good news is that we can say something sensible about the future, and the key is the end user, i.e. we the people, our culture, our societies, our values, and our beliefs. These factors all contribute. If we truly understood the end users we would

Figure 2: The Perfective steam iron.

know what they would put their money on so we would know where to put our investments. However, it does not suffice to try and force-fit our stack of technical options to the user's needs, wishes and emotions in hindsight. Deep end-user understanding should be the starting point of the product creation process; it should be the starting point for research.

To end users it is not the technology that is of interest, but the applications and experiences that are elicited by these applications. This takes on an added significance when developing applications and solutions for the emerging connected, digitally enabled world. Products and services increasingly overlap, everyday products are more intelligent and adaptive, and the talk is of 'systems' rather than stand-alone devices. Additionally, user needs evolve over time. Maintaining simplicity and understanding the user in such a landscape becomes a challenge. Ideas for innovation can quickly be hampered by technical limitations, incomplete use of user insights or lack of fit to existing business models. Therefore, it should be investigated what applications and experiences truly resonate with end–users' needs and wishes. And, of course, a match must be found between applications and technical solutions. In other words, end-user needs are the basis for sensible applications that are enabled by technical solutions and innovations.

It is therefore vital that we, as drivers of the 'new' ideas, incorporate human values, needs and desires from the very beginning of the innovation process. Our innovation activities need to be fed by a more flexible and collaborative approach than ever before. We need to align the way we innovate across disciplines, creating collaborative platforms to rapidly interconnect design ideas, technology solutions and business models.

Based on our experiences in many projects, both at Philips Research and Philips Design, we suggest that innovation in this climate requires design, technology and business to be brought together in an interdisciplinary way. Most importantly, we suggest that it needs to be consumer driven. We believe that such a process should effectively and mutually engage the stakeholders around a common, tangible focus. It should simultaneously support and catalyze the contributions of each participant, enabling a collaborative exploration of potential futures that can be translated to each partner's individual perspective. This is essentially the core of what we might call *Experience and Application Research* (EAR), a multiple stakeholder approach.

The Application and Experience Research approach is an extension of the user-centered design (UCD) process [7] into the research phases preceding product development. It is an iterative process in which each cycle comprises the following phases: Analysis, Creation, Realization and Evaluation; see Figure 3.

In UCD, very simply put, the analysis phase comprises co-creative user research, typically resulting in user requirements: a 'specification of the expected qualities' of the experience being enabled. In the creation phase these user requirements are translated into an articulated design idea, including a product design, interaction or behavioral architecture or user interface solution. Subsequently, a prototype or mock-up is made in the realization phase. During further iterations, recurring prototypes or mock-ups are evaluated and enriched with end users, which in turn gives rise to additional or refined desired qualities of experience and user requirements and a new cycle is started. In this way and in multiple cycles an appropriate solution is realized.

As mentioned before, this multiple stakeholder approach puts the end user in a central position in the innovation process. By incorporating end user insights from the start, it leads to solutions that both make sense to people's lives and leverage the technology assets. Ultimately, this will help any business deliver on its brand promise and further the company's competitive position in its emerging market. The partner's collective rationale for forming this collaboration is seen as three-fold:

1. To use end-user insights and a focus on user experience to steer technology-based innovations, maximizing the chances that they will

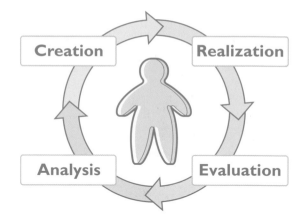

Figure 3: *An iterative cycle in the UCD process.*

deliver on the Philips 'Sense and Simplicity' brand promise;
2. To maximize consistency in innovation by focusing on synergies in related design and technology developments;
3. To create room for potential new business opportunities and Intellectual Property Rights (IPR) portfolio generation by jointly exploring new territories [2].

The EAR process

Any creative process that sets out to synergize the efforts of multiple stakeholders requires a clear structure and powerful creative tools. We have made our approach effective in practice by introducing a sequence of three core tools to support the EAR process, to facilitate collaboration, idea-sharing and cross-fertilization: 'Personas', 'Experience Targets' and 'Slice of Life Experience Prototypes'. More simply put, the EAR process typically comprises three iterative cycles: insights, ideas and concepts; see Figure 4.

Elmo Diederiks • Steven Kyffin

Experience and Application Research

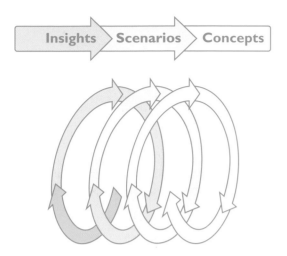

Figure 4: *The three cycles in the EAR process.*

The basis of the EAR process is formed by end-user insights. The insights phase starts with an analysis phase, which is more of a discovery: contextual research is conducted to build end-user understanding. User needs and desires in the social and physical context are investigated through observations and interviews, but also based on social trend and market analysis. In the subsequent phases, end-user insights are distilled from this information and formulated in such a way that they can be validated with end users.

To drive the forming of insights we co-create Personas, a hybrid of real and fictional relational people. Because it is difficult to predict how technology will be used in daily life, the involvement of user insights from the beginning of the innovation process is crucial in the development of solutions that make sense. We have developed a

unique approach to embedding user insights by using Personas. Personas are fictional characters based on real-life data (in-depth interviews, observations and home visits) and people research (co-research, socio-cultural trends research).

The richness of information they bring is useful throughout the innovation process for direction setting, solution creation and concept testing. In a typical innovation project we would expect to create at least three Personas from interviews during field studies from across the expected market region, such as Europe. These are used, not only as individual people but also in the fictional relationships they have with each other, to provide qualitative consumer insights and identify key user needs and experience challenges over time and imaginary history. [2]

Experience Targets

There is a need to 'place' such general insights in the realm of an actual experience so that designers and researchers can translate them into actual solutions and application ideas that reflect the qualitative desires that make those experiences meaningful and relevant. We have achieved this through a complementary innovation tool: Experience Targets.

Experience Targets also signal a shift away from merely wrapping a consumer experience around a predefined solution, focusing instead on building relevant solutions around key end-user experiences. In such a collaborative environment we enable the partners to jointly define a spectrum of early 'sketch' use cases relevant to their development roadmaps and to their businesses. Qualitative end-user insights captured in the form of

Personas are then set in the context of technological developments and socio-cultural trends to create an overall picture of potentially 'key' connected consumer experiences. By formulating these into so-called 'experience targets' [2], measurable objectives and common goals for innovation are set for all partners. The targets provide a common focal point for generating compelling user experience solutions. They become landing zones for technology research results, design solutions and new business models, facilitating the creation of future solutions, next-generation product platforms and new design paradigms. [2]

In the idea phase, the validated insights are the basis for idea generation sessions. The resulting ideas are usually too abstract to evaluate with end users. The ideas are therefore molded, combined and shaped into scenarios. Such scenarios do not actually detail a final solution, but rather address a use case. A scenario illustrates the use, functionality and purpose of an idea in an envisioned real-life situation relating to people and their activities [3]. It describes the experience across devices and locations. A 'slice of life', as we might also call such a scenario, therefore does not include in-depth details of any device or application, but only what is relevant to the activities in question. Each moment of user activity should make sense on its own and illustrate a compelling moment of user experience. It should also show how technologies can benefit users when applied in an ingenious way. [2]

In fact, these scenarios are a first intermediate stop on the journey from end-user insight to solution in the market. The scenarios are evaluated with potential end users to identify potentially good ideas, but especially to deepen user understanding and to fine-tune the end-user insights. In addition, discussions with technical experts and business people result in selection criteria from their perspectives. The careful assessment of all three points of view leads to the proper selection of the best scenarios.

Experience Prototypes

After the scenario cycle, the selected scenarios are taken into the next stage. The functions and interaction are defined in more detail, and possible technical solutions are investigated and worked out. These concepts are implemented in such a way that people can actually interact with and experience the proposed solution in a realistic context: an Experience Prototype.

To ensure that the Experience Prototype is believable and that the prototyped 'user experience' is achievable within the given time frame it is important to identify the right level of prototyping for each use case in the 'slice of life'. This also serves to ensure that the user experience remains the focus and that concessions are not made because of technical limitations. Where possible, a decision is made to integrate real working technology and platforms into the Experience Prototype to stress its feasibility. In some cases, where integration effort would outstrip value to the demonstrator, the use cases are 'simulated to specification'. As a result, each of the use cases maps to technologies that are either already available or on the roadmap of at least one of the partners. This is where our so-called 'ExperienceLab' [1] comes into play. The

evaluation of these prototypes with end users results in more detailed end-user insight with respect to the concept under investigation. User feedback is gathered through the early testing of the tangible concept prototypes. It is important that the testing of tangible concepts is not confused with usability testing or product testing. The objective here is to receive feedback on the principles of the solution rather than the solution as presented, since it is not a finished product proposal. As a part of this, the validity of the Experience Targets defined in the earlier stages can be tested [2]. At this stage, it has become quite clear whether a concept is viable, what the conceived user benefits and requirements are and what a proper product proposition should comprise. It is now time for the business and its product development departments to adopt the concept, including the insight that it is based on, and build a good product proposition.

The proposed EAR approach seems quite extensive and it is often argued that it only takes additional time and money to involve end users as early as the research state of the Product Creation Process (PCP). However, the opposite is true: yes, it costs time and money to involve end users, but the subsequent phases (in the entire PCP) are more focused, which actually saves more time and money. More importantly, the proposed technical options are embedded in applications that fit a true end-user need or desire, which increases the chance of success considerably.

Innovation is often defined as: '...new ideas, successfully exploited'. We strongly believe that the two most important drivers of innovation within such a

definition are the need for better ideas (ideas are easy, but relevant or good ideas are hard to find) and successful exploitation or a reduced time to market. The latter is in our view solely dependent on rigorous and disciplined collaboration across the participating stakeholders. Driving any form of innovation along a single track rarely 'sticks' or resonates for much longer than the initial craze or trend hype.

A good example is AmbiLight[tm], which was conceived through an EAR process. It took only one year to move from idea to experience demonstrator and only one additional year to realize a very successful product in the market [5].

End user insight driven innovation and the qualities of experience

As described in the previous paragraphs, the EAR process starts with the generation and validation of end-user insights through understanding the qualities of any given experience, but what exactly is an end-user insight and how does it relate to the quality of an experience?

An end-user insight is basically the first concrete expression of a deep user understanding. It describes a context for a specific target group and it describes a problem (need) and possible improvement (desire) for that situation, without implying a solution direction. An end-user insight is more than an observation (the need or desire as such), since it comprises the emotional values and reasons for a certain need or desire. A good end-user insight resonates with a specific target group and makes the people in this target group feel truly understood.

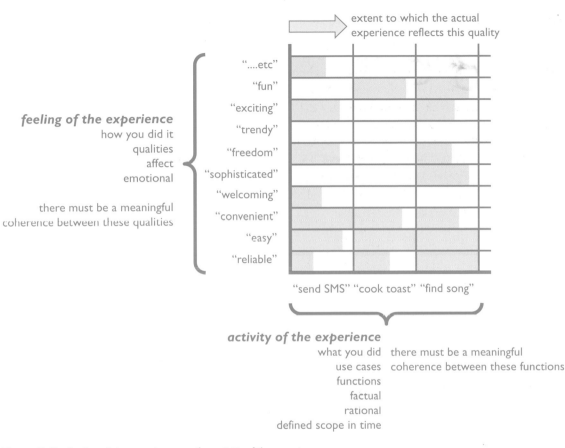

feeling of the experience
how you did it
qualities
affect
emotional

there must be a meaningful
coherence between these qualities

extent to which the actual
experience reflects this quality

"....etc"
"fun"
"exciting"
"trendy"
"freedom"
"sophisticated"
"welcoming"
"convenient"
"easy"
"reliable"

"send SMS" "cook toast" "find song"

activity of the experience
what you did   there must be a meaningful
use cases   coherence between these functions
functions
factual
rational
defined scope in time

Figure 5: *The feeling of the experience vs. the activity of the experience.*

These have been called the 'rational' and 'emotional' dimensions of an experience. Both of these dimensions need to be considered when describing or defining an experience. They are necessarily related in that sometimes a feeling will result simply from the fact that certain functions are available. More often, the feeling will be determined by the way in which that function is made available [4]; see also Figure 5.

Being aware of these dimensions is incredibly important when describing experiences and working with stories. It is important that a story does not just capture the factual happenings, in the correct order. In order to be useful in terms of experience design, stories need to capture both the fact of the activity and the feeling of the activity [4].

Using stories or scenarios to describe what the experience is like, or what it evokes, helps designers find key words and concepts that capture the essential qualities of the experience. These are concepts that capture essential aspects of the feelings and emotions this experience should evoke. In our example, below, the Philips-Alessi key word qualities might have included: peacefulness, slowness, indulgence, quietness, family togetherness and laziness.

Philips-Alessi and the 'cozy Sunday morning breakfast'

The Philips-Alessi reference to "a cozy Sunday morning breakfast" was used internally as the project kicked off to orientate and align all stakeholders, including the designers. It created an orientation for the entire project team at the earli-

An end-user insight is therefore a good start for focused innovation and it is important to maintain and take along the insight throughout the product creation process. In this way, the end-user insight can help focus development, design, product proposition definition as well as marketing and sales, so that in the end a clear and consistent message is communicated to the end user.

Concerning the application, there are two important and distinct dimensions to describing an experience:

• describing the 'what' of the experience – what you did
• describing the 'how' of the experience – how it felt when doing it.

est stage – enabling them to talk about qualities that were going to be evoked and qualities of the objects that would be created. The language of this design process was used almost directly (with some interpretation) to drive the communication process. It must have resonated with the way in which people themselves would have described what was valuable to them about the experience of using these things. The 'cozy Sunday morning breakfast' did not just resonate with designers; it proved to be more than a design tool.

The specification of these 'qualities of experience' may come from research into fundamental, current or future human needs, directly from the 'story of the experience', from a definition of the brand values, historical associations of the company, from the person leading the project or from a positioning relative to other alternatives in the market.

Apart from describing the qualities of experience verbally, designers often use a wide array of visual references and aids, such as mood boards, etcetera, to express the qualities of the intended experience. These are used to help translate the abstract idea of an experience into very tangible aspects of a product and its supporting materials.

These 'qualities of experience' form the standard against which decisions about the product will be made. If a certain decision has to be made between various design options, designers will be able to evaluate the options against these objectives and decide how to proceed. These 'qualities' are not about making an overall value judgment ('is the experience good quality?') but identifying what type of experience is enabled or made possible through this. Quality of experience needs to be given not just valence (good or bad), but also a kind of 'direction'. Designers ask 'does it achieve the quality of …', 'the feeling of…', 'does it evoke responses that are similar to the feeling of …'. Designers have often created a scale related to that quality. Typically the scale will range from one quality to its opposite, e.g. from 'boring' to 'exciting' or from 'fast' to 'slow'. We can evaluate where a certain design lies on this scale, and in particular how it compares to other designs [4].

Insights, experience targets, scenarios or slices of life and experience prototypes are realized as a main result of each of the three aforementioned cycles in the EAR approach. These three intermediate results are essential to get end-user feedback, but it is important that the scenarios and the experience demonstrators explicitly incorporate the end-user insights that they are based on. In this way, all three results are very useful in communicating with stakeholders inside and outside the company and in making sure that the project team remains focused as the project evolves from high-level insights to concrete solutions while end-user understanding deepens with each iterative cycle.

Why work together?

There are a number of clear advantages to working together within Philips as proposed by the creatively collaborative approach. Often individual businesses focus on their existing roadmaps and need help to 'break out' and notice new opportunities. New directions are especially interesting when backed by technologies and platforms that ensure timely development and help give new and exciting products a jump-start. Working in this manner has helped the partners to involve ventures into new business directions in a number of ways.

Creating new user experiences
Working as a team across technology, design and business assists the identification of new key scenarios relevant to technology research and business development. By focusing on end-user experiences, opportunities can be prioritized. And by designing solutions that show technology in context, the 'human' value of technology is underlined.

Protecting future businesses
By designing user interfaces, interactions and products that show technical innovations in a context of use, new directions for business are explored. The technologies considered for use can be protected by a focused portfolio of IPR. This gives a head start to the creation of a competitive advantage for Philips. In addition, a consistent set of application-orientated and related technology-focused IPR will serve to protect new business.

Early exploration of markets
Early experimentation with novel applications based on early or emerging technologies allows for the advanced development of 'high potential' application areas. This helps increase 'confidence' in the new technologies and creates awareness of new business opportunities. It also helps the business focus on starting up further initiatives that support the introduction of new innovations.

Delivering on the brand promise
By designing and engineering solutions for real-

life situations, based on the Personas, it becomes clear how technology can offer new value for people in compelling ways. It also helps Philips deliver on the brand promises of 'Designed around you', 'Easy to experience' and 'Advanced'; the three pillars of Sense and Simplicity. [2]

Concluding remarks and implications

A people focus, or more specifically perhaps, an end-user focus is essential to be able to move away from cost and technology-driven competition in a saturated market and towards true added value and transformational growth. Of course it is not a guarantee for product success, but it does help to focus our research efforts and limit our product portfolio to products that have a high chance of both cultural and commercial success.

To bring a successful product to the market it should be based on end-user insights: on true user needs and wishes. But in addition, there should also be a viable technical solution and the company should be able to bring it to the market and sell it with an acceptable margin. In other words, the user perspective should be balanced with the design, technology and business perspectives.

This implies that the many disciplines involved in the product creation process should be working in the same direction and focused on reaching the same goal. The end-user insight is the basis for this joint goal and focused work. This holds for the business-to-consumer as well as the business-to-business arena, although for the latter the end-user insights, of course, also need to be translated into customer needs and wishes. In any case, the

EAR process with its end-user insight driven characteristics has three main complications for the method of working in research.

Often the contextual research, end-user insight formulation and end-user insight validation are done by the businesses' market intelligence departments. By incorporating end-user insights from the start, the collaborative approach leads to solutions that both make sense to people's lives and leverage our technology assets. Ultimately, this will help Philips' business to prioritize opportunities that can deliver on the Sense and Simplicity brand promise. Also, by emphasizing context of use and cultural relevance, the 'human' value of technology is underlined and any risk that 'technology-push' strategies might occur out of human context is minimized at the earliest stages. Creating appropriate solutions for these insights is a creative process that requires a level of intuition for the issues at hand. In this respect, it simply helps enormously for the research team to witness the end-user issues in the end-user context at first hand. Therefore this work should be done in a strategic cooperation between research and the market intelligence departments.

A second implication for the research process is that all intermediate results, not only the insights but also the scenarios and the experience demonstrators, should be used to communicate with the business stakeholders. Not only to keep them up to date on project progress, but especially to maintain a joint focus. Philips' innovative collaborative approach has enabled a 'free flow' of information across partners from design, research and business and has helped facilitate a shared 'language'

by focusing on a tangible articulation of new digital solutions. This has resulted in a shared and realistic vision for innovations that is in line with technology research roadmaps and digital product platform development and, most importantly, is based on consumer insights. Indeed, by working together for the future, Philips Design, Philips Research and our product development labs are maximizing the opportunity to create highly desirable and human-focused new solutions that provide added value differentiators for Philips.

A third implication is that research should work together with the business stakeholders to assure appropriate absorption in this business. This boils down to sitting down together to formulate a first product proposition based on the end-user insight, the concept solution as well as the lessons learned from the various user evaluations in the EAR process. We should be sharing the vision. A key aspect is the joint development of tangible Experience Prototypes as vision demonstrators to mutually engage the partners around a common goal. This creates a rallying point around which partners can discuss ideas, technologies and user insights in a very concrete context. It also enables projects with different timeframes to work together, align mutual interests and inspire each other. As a synergetic outcome that combines design, technology and business roadmaps, the experience demonstrator is considerably more powerful in projecting the ideas of all the contributing partners than presenting them individually.

Enriching our competitive position and unlocking creativity: a fourth implication suggests that working together generates considerably more progress in each of the otherwise separate research domains. By combining advances in emerging technologies and user-led design, it has been possible to propose new applications that point out the 'human value' of Philips' technology IPR and create inspiring insights for next-generation product development. This combined approach allows the early discovery and protection of realistic opportunities that have the potential to add a competitive edge to Philips' business.

We suggest that by working together in this way and by prototyping our intended experiences we actually intensify the working relationships between the disciplines by identifying and agreeing on the goals of the projects at the earliest stage. This releases more creative possibilities and options, which in turn can be rigorously tested from all standpoints without the fear of being rejected on the grounds of 'not invented here'. [2]

References
1. Aarts, E and M. Groten (2006), *Moving from HomeLab to ExperienceLab: The next phase in experience research*. In: T. Lashina, J. Hoonhout, E. Diederiks (eds.): New Business through User Centric Innovation: A key role for Philips' ExperienceLab, Philips Research Europe, Eindhoven, pp. 17-21.

2. Andrews, A., L. Geurts, and S. Kyffin (2005), *TO:DO: Collaborative Experience Driven innovation*, Philips Design Eindhoven, The Netherlands.

3. Caroll, J.M. (ed.) (1995), *Scenario-based Design: Envisioning Work and Technology in System Development*, Wiley, New York.

4. Cass, J., et al., (2004), *Experience Design: A positioning paper for Philips Design*. Philips Design Eindhoven, The Netherlands.

5. Diederiks, E.M.A., and J.H. Hoonhout (2005), *From Picture Quality to Viewing Experience*. In: C.J. Overbeeke, et al. (eds.), *Proceedings of Designing Pleasurable Products and Interfaces*, Eindhoven University of Technology, Eindhoven, The Netherlands, pp 467-475.

6. Gardien, P., et al. (2006), *Breathing New Life into Delicate Ideas*, Positioning Paper, Philips Design Eindhoven, The Netherlands.

7. Norman, D.A. (1986), *User Centered System Design: New Perspectives on Human-Computer Interaction*, Lawrence Erlbaum Associates Inc., New Jersey.

ExperienceLab

ExperienceLab

Facilities

Evert van Loenen • Boris de Ruyter • Vic Teeven

Facilities

ExperienceLab offers a unique environment, both physically and intellectually, for researchers and their partners inside and outside Philips to give concrete form to the Ambient Intelligence vision. By developing and integrating advanced technologies in the area of Ambient Intelligence, ExperienceLab is an innovation center for the development of novel consumer products and services, and it therefore makes a substantial contribution to the implementation of the Philips strategy in the domain of Lifestyle and Wellbeing. In this chapter we present ExperienceLab's infrastructure. We start off with a discussion of HomeLab, as this has been the center for experience and application research for more than five years. Next we move on to ExperienceLab, which is an augmentation of HomeLab through the addition of two other facilities, CareLab and ShopLab, for studies in the consumer healthcare and retail domains respectively. The discussions are centered on the two key elements of experience and application research, which are feasibility and usability studies. Before we discuss the ExperienceLab facilities in detail, we will elaborate briefly on the concept of user-centered research, which is a key element underlying the design and development of the ExperienceLab.

Evert van Loenen, Boris de Ruyter, Vic Teeven

User-centered research

Nowadays, the technological possibilities for enhancing peoples' life are vast; to quote the prototypical engineer: "tell us what you want and we can make it". But, what do people really want? Once we better understand people's needs and desires, the output of a structured idea generation process is expected to yield product or service concepts that show an increased potential to truly enhance living and being at home. Of course, such claims should be validated by evaluating the anticipated user benefits before a selection is made to bring certain concepts into a subsequent research and design cycle. In a subsequent iteration cycle, more detailed user requirements need to be uncovered and fed into the generation and implementation of concrete design solutions. Next, conducting carefully planned user tests can check the utility and usability of the proposed solutions. This iterative process, which is carried out by multidisciplinary teams and in which user involvement plays a crucial role, is called user-centered research. ExperienceLab is designed to be the place where researchers and designers can team up with end users to create a shared and tangible vision of the future of in-home electronic systems.

Multidisciplinary approaches

Advanced technology is readily advertised as enhancing the quality of future home life. For example, the introduction of network technology in the home is said to reduce the functional redundancy found in current homes and increase efficiency and ease of use so as to save time do the things one really wants to do (quality time). But, how are future electronic products going to use these networks to achieve the anticipated user benefits, and what user-system interaction knowledge is required to bring about a true paradigm shift from 'operating devices' to enhanced and new 'interactive experiences'? To find answers to these questions we need to study the physical, social and cultural context in which technology will be used and its implications for daily life. ExperienceLab offers a unique environment that is optimized for conducting research in these areas. Multidisciplinary teams of researchers together with potential end users explore the advantages and disadvantages of prototypes of future electronic systems in a realistic home setting.

User involvement

Although ExperienceLab provides a fully functioning home environment where people can stay for a considerable period of time, initially people will participate in interactive ExperienceLab sessions that typically last only a couple of hours. During these sessions researchers can directly interact with the participants and the systems being studied, or people can explore the Ambient Intelligence environment on their own while unobtrusively being observed by researchers using the ExperienceLab observation facilities. ExperienceLab is well

equipped to support both types of user behavior research. The interior decorating and the possibilities for flexibly re-arranging or moving furniture around the house make it easy to adjust the house to match the particular lifestyle of intended target groups, making the 'inhabitants' of ExperienceLab feel safe, happy, at ease, and stimulated. ExperienceLab has two observation rooms that, in combination with 34 cameras distributed throughout the house and controlled by the ExperienceLab control system, provide the right infrastructure for performing observational user studies. The type of user studies that can be facilitated ranges from observations of user (and system) behavior to 'traditional' usability tests. Below some imaginary examples are described.

Studying human behavior

The possibility of observing participants during their stay in ExperienceLab is one of its primary functions. A tailor-made ExperienceLab control system has been developed in-house to collect and analyze observational data. The system controls the cameras and the routing of the video and audio signals. Human activities, postures, facial expressions, social interactions, but also sensor output and user-system interactions can be recorded and digitally stored to study patterns, trends and relationships. Results will be used to improve products, to eliminate imperfections and to explore new applications. The main observation room offers a place for an observation leader and four observers. The observation leader is responsible for the data collection and will be the director of the ExperienceLab interactive session. The observation leader modifies camera setups, routes video and

audio signals, and monitors the capture stations. The main task for an observer is to concentrate on monitoring the behavior of the participants. This can be done by viewing a video monitor that can be connected to any of the observation cameras in the house. The behavior of a participant is 'scored' in terms of events that characterize the observed scene. The scored events are time-stamped and appended to the video data.

Though real-time scoring is valuable in some cases, researchers sometimes prefer a different setup. A selection of 4 video and 8 audio signals can be captured on hard disk stations. An additional toolset within the ExperienceLab control system has been developed to enable the researcher to process his recorded data in a more efficient way. The reason is simple. An experiment consisting of 20 or more separate sessions with participants may result in many hours of video. The possibility of quickly navigating through the recorded material and skipping the irrelevant scenes makes this method attractive to use. Making a compilation is easy, even for newbie. And scoring can now be done off-line in a less time-consuming way.

Sensors play an important role in HomeLab, and therefore sensor data can be handled in a similar way to scored events. For example, a researcher is doing an experiment at HomeLab and he is interested in knowing the movement of his participants in the house. He will use cameras in room A, room B and room C. Sensors in doors will signal when they open and this information will be registered on the recorders, together with the video. With the toolset it is now easy to watch only the situations where doors opened. And for the researcher it is easy to score who left or entered which room at what time. Export functions in the toolset allow the score data to be used in specific behavioral analysis programs (e.g. Pattern Analysis [3]).

In this way the ExperienceLab control system both offers an accurate and efficient support tool for making observations and facilitates a flexible system for exploration and analysis of the acquired data.

HomeLab

HomeLab can be seen as the first of the three current ExperienceLab facilities. The early plans to develop an advanced laboratory that could be used to conduct feasibility and usability studies in ambient intelligence within Philips Research date back to the year 2000. After two years of design and construction, Gerard Kleisterlee, president of Philips Electronics, opened HomeLab on April 24, 2002. On the occasion of the opening an international technology seminar was held which officially marked the start of ambient intelligence research at HomeLab. Since then HomeLab has attracted a great deal of attention from the press and has been featured over fifty times on radio and television around the world. More than 500 press articles have been published in a wide variety of journals ranging from *Focus* to *The Wall Street Journal*. People have shown an overwhelming interest in the facilities and it has been a real challenge to ensure that HomeLab was able to adhere to its original objective of being a research facility rather than becoming a showcase for novel and promising consumer electronics products and services. At that time we knew that we were one of the first in the

Figure 1: The HomeLab front door.

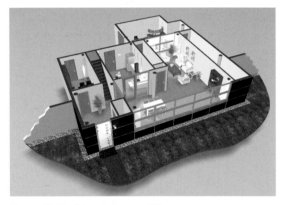

Figure 2: The HomeLab ground floor.

world to implement *co-creation* as a novel strategy for product innovation, but the reactions from the outside world were overwhelming and reassuring and consequently they stimulated us to carry on with this novel approach for the years to come.

The home

Standing in front of one of the new buildings on the High Tech Campus, you will notice a part that

clearly differs from the rest; see Figure 1. It has a front door made of glass, with the sign 'HomeLab' on it; it is built in a different style and has a different appearance. Going through the front door you will discover something that you would not expect: you are entering the hall of a normal house. It is a completely furnished environment, including the objects found in real homes. People can stay here and interact with concept demonstrators of future in-home electronic systems developed by researchers and designers.

The HomeLab floor plan in Figures 2 and 3 shows that it is an ordinary two-storey house with a living room, a kitchen, two bedrooms, a bathroom and a study. Interior decorators have created an atmosphere that matches a modern single family home as closely as possible. At first glance the home does not show anything special, but a closer look reveals the black domes in the ceilings that conceal cameras and microphones. These cam-

Figure 3: The HomeLab first floor.

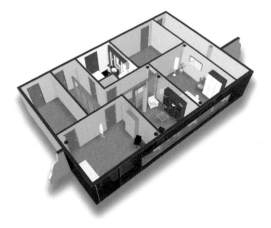

eras and microphones form an integral part of the house and are designed to quickly disappear in the background of people's minds.

The lab
Adjacent to the home there are two observation rooms. The video signals captured by hard disk recorders can be monitored on the many flat screens available in the main observation room. Another, smaller observation room is located on the second floor. In the early days of HomeLab one-way mirrors were used to allow a direct view from the observation rooms into some of the rooms in the house. But we have found that cameras are sufficient to obtain a good view of the progress of the experiments.

The technical infrastructure
HomeLab has more to offer. Abundant network connections (wired and wireless) are available all over the place to connect parts of the HomeLab infrastructure to the High Tech Campus network. It is possible to connect HomeLab to the outside world with Next Generation Internet facilities. If cables are required, false floors provide nice hiding places. Most cupboards and drawers in HomeLab, but also the corridors adjacent to the rooms, accommodate the equipment that researchers and developers need to create and control their systems and to process and render audio and video signals for the large flat screens in HomeLab; see Figure 5. This equipment consists largely of by powerful PCs, since many of the applications and functions that are being researched are not yet integrated on silicon. It is the intention to have it tested with participants in an unobtrusive environment, no perceptible high tech in the home at all.

A power control system features remote controllable light settings and power switches. But participants can still simply turn the lights on and off by using 'ordinary' switches. Future intelligent systems that aim to enhance people's emotions and experiences by means of lighting will be able to interface with the HomeLab power control system.

From HomeLab to ExperienceLab

Five years of experience research in HomeLab has provided Philips with a wealth of consumer insights that have led to novel product concepts. The bathroom with its context aware relaxing atmospheres controlled by *Interactive Mirrors*, and the living room with its *Active Ambilight™ TV*, *Living Light*, *Dream Screens*, and *Adaptive Lighting* are just two examples of ambient intelligent rooms that were realized at HomeLab and have led to major business successes. A good overview of the outcome and added value that the research work at HomeLab has provided over the past five years is given by the HomeLab publications that were released for the various Philips *Corporate Research Exhibitions* (CREs)

Figure 4: The HomeLab main observation room.

Figure 5: The HomeLab communication infrastructure

Figure 6: ExperienceLab is an extension of HomeLab.

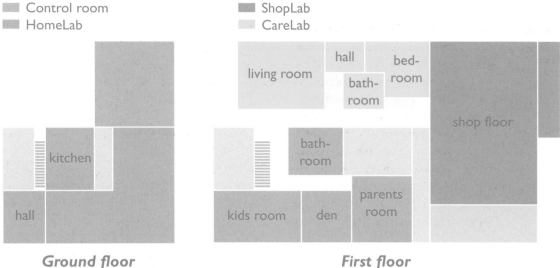

Ground floor

living room hall bed-room bath-room shop floor bath-room kids room den parents room kitchen hall

First floor

Figure 7: *The ExperienceLab floor plan.*

that were held during that period [2,3,4,5,6]. Now we are keen to extend the experience research concept of HomeLab to a broader domain that includes healthcare and retail. CareLab and ShopLab are the resulting extensions of HomeLab and the combination of these three research environments constitutes the novel ExperienceLab.

New areas for experience research
The vision of Ambient Intelligence, which was developed in the 1999-2001 timeframe [1], has been the driving force underlying the experience research programme carried out at HomeLab over the past five years. The investigations were aimed at creating compelling experiences and intelligent environments that interact upon the presence of people. The creation of experiences has been focussed on the Lifestyle domain, is based on applying state-of-the-art technologies, such as

video and sound processing, and adds elements that can truly create the experience. We are moving away from sheer functional quality, like picture and sound quality, and towards creating differentiating experiences that add value for end users. The HomeLab research programme has over time delivered many examples and demonstrators of these experiences. These developments have led both to a better understanding of end user insights and to novel product concepts.

Research at HomeLab has concentrated on defining compelling experiences, developing the technical solutions that elicit those experiences, and finally validating the experiences with end users, with the emphasis being on the Lifestyle domain. The end user insights thus obtained have been developed and shared with business partners pre-

dominantly in the areas of consumer electronics and lighting. The newly created technologies and products were transferred to our business partners, including the validation methodologies that were developed to quantify experiences. Based on the success of HomeLab and in line with the Philips strategy, CareLab and ShopLab have been developed as two new experience laboratories adjacent to HomeLab. The conglomerate of HomeLab, ShopLab and CareLab is called ExperienceLab; see Figure 6. The floor plan of Figure 7 shows how the two new facilities are positioned close to the existing HomeLab facility. The three experience research facilities will focus on the following fields of interest.

HomeLab
The HomeLab research programme will continue its main effort in the consumer electronics area, with the emphasis on novel concepts for products and services in the Lifestyle domain. Extensions of *Active Ambilight*™ into immersive home-cinema experiences and the development of novel end-user-programming driven concepts for home-media editing are novel directions for research. In addition, HomeLab will be used to explore the innovative power of social presence and ambient narratives in the development of novel concepts for wellbeing, gaming, and education. Another major effort at HomeLab will be dedicated to the exploration and co-creation of new lighting applications in the domain of ambient experience. The availability of new lighting technologies enables the development of novel lighting concepts that add the immersive feeling of ambient experiences to classical 'functional' lighting. More specifically, the

HomeLab research programme will study the use of light as a third modality that can take on the role of a mature and self-contained type of media in addition to the two existing types of media, audio and video. This domain is extremely challenging as it opens the way for studies in unexplored fields of cognitive science and experience design.

ShopLab

The ShopLab research programme builds on the vision that personalized ambient atmospheres will increase the shopping experience. On the other hand many retail chains want to maintain their house style for branding reasons. This introduces the challenge of combining these two major aspects, and one approach to this could be that one atmosphere design will be sent to all stores and slightly adapted there to meet local conditions. Tuning these atmospheres requires controlling several hundred lamp settings, introducing a complex overall control challenge. Adaptation of the ambient shop atmospheres also requires input from smart environments that detect people's presence and product interests while they are in a shop. Lighting systems that are able to fulfill these requirements are being studied. A first version was demonstrated at CRE of 2006. Furthermore, an interactive shopping display window will be demonstrated with enhanced explicit and implicit interaction styles.

CareLab

The CareLab research programme will focus on 'elderly care'. A senior apartment block has been built, equipped with an advanced distributed sensor infrastructure that can extract context-aware and personalized information from the inhabitants for a variety of use cases. The sensor information is then processed and combined to extract higher-order behavioral patterns that can be related to activities and states such as the presence of people, their activities, the state of the home infrastructure, etc. Applying the appropriate data mining techniques as well as knowledge representation and reasoning technologies, conclusions may be drawn on safety and well-being issues and aspects of elderly people in their homes, which is generally referred to as their *Activities of Daily Life* patterns and beyond.

Outlook

ExperienceLab applies the user centric research approach to experience research with a clear focus on generating added value for the end users in their context. One common approach underlying the vision relating to the activities in all three experience research facilities is that electronics and intelligence are embedded in the environment and not at all visible or noticeable by the end users. This calls for extremely easy-to-use, intelligent interaction solutions that can cope with these complex integrated environments and their users in order to create a positive experience.

We anticipate that ExperienceLab will serve the purpose of developing novel concepts for products and services for the forthcoming years, as HomeLab has done for the past five years. We are looking forward to supporting the development of new experience prototypes and their user evaluation by making use of the advanced research facilities provided by ExperienceLab.

References

1. Aarts, E.H.L., H. Harwig, and M. Schuurmans (2001), Ambient Intelligence, in: J. Denning (ed.) *The Invisible Future*, McGraw Hill, New York, NY, USA, pp. 235-250.

2. Aarts, E. and B. Eggen (eds.) (2002), *Ambient Intelligence Research in ExperienceLab*, Philips Research and Neroc MediaWare, Eindhoven, The Netherlands.

2. Ruyter, B. (ed.) (2003), *365 days' Ambient Intelligence Research in HomeLab*, Philips Research and Neroc MediaWare, Eindhoven, The Netherlands.

3. Diederiks, E. (ed.) (2004), *Understanding Well-being: Philips's HomeLab* Philips Research and Neroc MediaWare, Eindhoven, The Netherlands.

4. Diederiks, E. (ed.) (2005), *1000 Days HomeLab*, Philips Research and Neroc MediaWare, Eindhoven, The Netherlands.

5. Lashina, T., J. Hoonhout, and E. Diederiks (eds.) (2006), *New Business Through User Centric Innovation: A Key role for Philips' ExperienceLab*, Philips Research Europe and Creada, Eindhoven, The Netherlands.

Probing

The introduction of Ambient Intelligence (AmI) [1] has brought about a paradigm shift in User - System Interaction (USI). An example of this shift is provided by the AmI requirement to "separate functions from boxes" [1,2]. Such separation leads to new challenges in the design of interactive systems: how will users interact with a system that has disappeared into the background? In addition, consider AmI's emphasis on a rich end user experience when interacting with AmI environments. Such user experiences cannot be assessed in controlled laboratory settings but require near real-life settings and advanced research methodologies to study end user experiences, which are by their very nature subjective.

User experiments

The possibility of studying user experiences of test participants during their stay in HomeLab or one of the other ExperienceLabs is one of the primary functions of these labs. A tailor-made control system has been developed in-house to collect and analyze observational data. The system controls the cameras and the routing of the video and audio signals; see also Chapter 2.1. Human activities, postures, facial expressions, social interactions and user-system interactions can be recorded and digitally stored to study patterns, trends and relationships; see Figure 2. Results will be used to improve applications of innovative technologies, to eliminate imperfections and to explore new applications.

From usability to user experiences

Nowadays, the technological possibilities for enhancing home life are vast; to quote the prototypical engineer: "tell us what you want and we can make it". But, what do people really want? Once we better understand people's needs and desires, the output of a structured idea generation process is expected to yield product or system concepts that show an increased potential to truly enhance living and being at home. Of course, such claims should be validated by evaluating the anticipated user benefits before a selection is made to bring certain concepts into a second research and development cycle. In a subsequent iteration cycle, more detailed user requirements need to be uncovered and fed into the generation and implementation of concrete concept solutions. Next, the utility and usability of the proposed solutions can be checked by conducting carefully planned user tests. This iterative research process, which is carried out by multidisciplinary teams and in which user involvement plays a central role, is called *Experience and Application Research* (EAR); see Chapter 1.4.

In general, four phases are identified in the one iterative cycle of the EAR process: analysis, con-

Boris de Ruyter

HomeLab is designed to be the place where researchers and designers can team up with end users to realize a shared and tangible vision of the future of in-home electronic systems. Given the application domain of the home environment (i.e. networked information, communication and entertainment) and the ubiquitous character of the interactive systems there is a need to extend the traditional utility measures (such as effectiveness and efficiency) towards user experiences. Established organizations such as the Usability Professional's Organization have recognized the need for new approaches to usability testing [3].

The real user benefit of AmI environments will be found in their impact in terms of the user experiences they generate. For this, the HomeLab offers a complete environment for the analysis, conceptualization, implementation and evaluation of Ambient Intelligence systems that provide true user experiences.

Various types of user research and user evaluation are conducted during the EAR process. In the initial stages it is important to gather contextual knowledge: how people behave in a certain context or how they use certain products. This type of user research is characterized by its qualitative nature. Typical methods used are: observations, probes, focus groups and open (or semi-structured) interviews. In the later stages of the EAR process it becomes clearer what the envisioned solution could be. The result of this is that the user evaluations have a more quantitative character. Researchers now use methods and tools such as task analysis, structured interviews, questionnaires and even physiological measurements.

Figure 1: *The HomeLab observation system.*

ception or improvement, implementation or realization, and evaluation through user testing. To bring a user-centered approach into user interaction research, the following principles should be applied to these phases:

- *Early user involvement.* This includes the usage of user knowledge in the form of guidelines or models.
- *Empirical measurement.* At some stage of the design process an empirical validation of the design assumptions is needed. Without actual empirical measurement (for example by building on guidelines only) one cannot claim to adhere to the UCD approach.
- *Iterative design.* Throughout the conceptualization and implementation process new insights will be gained on the basis of empirical measurement and iteration will be necessary.
- *Multidisciplinary teams.* To create usable systems different disciplines are needed to combine knowledge about users, technologies and context of use into requirements for the conceptualization and implementation of interactive systems.

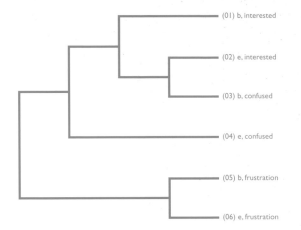

(01) b, interested
(02) e, interested
(03) b, confused
(04) e, confused
(05) b, frustration
(06) e, frustration

Figure 2: *A pattern indicating the relationship between the behaviors being interested, confused and frustrated as registered during an experimental session in HomeLab.*

During the entire process the focus is on the user's behavior and especially on the reasons for this behavior. It is vital to truly understand this motivation of people to behave in a certain manner, since this helps us to better understand the user and thus to better gear our solutions to true user needs and wishes. Application and Experience Research Centers (EARCs) like HomeLab are essential tools for collecting the required behavioral data.

The collection of behavioral data

When setting up an experiment to collect behavioral data at HomeLab, the researcher designs a coding scheme for the observation session. A coding scheme lists all the prototypical behaviors that are expected to be observable during the session. These behaviors should be structured as an orthogonal classification system: during the classification

of behavior it should not be possible to classify any behavior in more than one category. The observers mark the occurrence of these behaviors during the HomeLab session by pressing keys on a keyboard. In addition, more and more behavioral events are registered automatically through the use of sensors. Once the coding scheme has been developed it is saved into the scoring system. Very similar to questionnaires, the coding schemes are standardized and reused. For example, coding schemes for *problem-solving behavior* or *user-system interaction in voice-controlled environments* have been developed and reused over several experimental sessions.

If applicable, a detailed user profile for test participants is established in collaboration with a consumer marketing intelligence department. The user profile is then provided to a recruitment agency for test participant recruitment. As a rule these participants are recruited externally to ensure that they have no affiliation with Philips, as such affiliation could influence test results. Depending on the focus of the research question a test methodology is designed. If this methodology so requires, test participants will spend hours or days in HomeLab. Although HomeLab is a fully functional home environment, the aim is not to maximize the stay there. If longitudinal data collection is needed we set up field trials during which the experimental systems are installed in end users' homes.

Data analysis can vary from a simple frequency analysis to a sophisticated data mining analysis for finding hidden patterns in the data set. This latter technique has been adopted in other research

areas and is now being deployed in the area of user – system interaction research [4]. In our research at HomeLab we use the software package called 'Theme', as distributed by Noldus. This software tool is capable of detecting repeated patterns that are invisible to observers and very hard or impossible to detect with other available methods. It is particularly suitable for analyzing behavioral data.

Conclusions and future challenges in USI research

The design and assessment of interactive systems that are targeted to be introduced into the market within a timeframe of five to ten years remains a methodological challenge. More specific the evaluation of futuristic AmI environments with end users living in today's reality can raise questions with regard to the validity of these assessments. There is a need to validate the potential response bias created by using a HomeLab-like assessment instrument.

As more automated data collection techniques (e.g. sensors) become available there will be a need for more suitable data analysis techniques to make sense of the rich datasets that will be collected in AmI environments. The use of T-pattern techniques has produced some very promising results in the analysis of complex behavioral patterns as collected in AmI environments.

Although large amounts of data can be collected through observational techniques the challenge of collecting data on subjective user experiences remains. Today we are using standardized questionnaires to assess the user experience, which by its very nature is subjective. The future challenge will be to deploy psycho-physiological techniques to complement or even automate the assessment of subjective user experiences.

References

1. Aarts, E., R. Harwig, and M. Schuurmans (2001), Ambient Intelligence, in: Denning, P (ed.), *The Invisible Future: The Seamless Integration Of Technology Into Everyday Life*, McGraw-Hill, New York, pp. 235-250.

2. Aarts, E.H.L., and B. Eggen (eds.) (2002), *Ambient Intelligence in HomeLab*, Philsip Research and Neroc Media-Ware, Eindhoven, The Netherlands.

3. Branaghan, R.J. (2001). Design by people for people: essays on usability, Usability Professional's Association, Dertouzos, M. (1999), The Future ot Computing, *Scientific American* 281(2), pp. 52-55.

4. Jonsson, G.K., S.H. Bjarkadottir, B. Gislason, A. Borrie, and M.S. Magnusson (2003), Detection of real-time patterns in sports: interactions in football, in C. Baudoin (ed.), *L'éthologie appliquée aujourd'hui,* Volume 3, Levallois-Perret, Paris, France.

New Business

It goes without saying that HomeLab is a wonderful building. It offers fantastic research facilities as well. And yes, it is a very attractive setting in which to organize demos. But it is even more than that: HomeLab is also a powerful enabler for business innovation.

HomeLab has been set up as a lab for studying human-technology interaction and for testing new ambient intelligence concepts. As such, it enables both the development and evaluation of innovative applications and user interaction solutions by means of a user-centric design process. In order to achieve this, there are multidisciplinary project teams consisting of interaction and technology researchers and cognitive psychologists. The laboratory offers an advanced observation and data analysis system for conducting studies with users. Advanced methodologies are used and new research tools are developed to analyze the participants' reactions.

The above factors create a firm foundation for scientific research into consumer preferences. Does a new concept appeal to a user? Does it create a desirable user experience? What user benefits does it offer? Is there anything we have overlooked? What could be improved?
By providing this information about consumers, HomeLab lays a firm foundation for product innovation. However, this on its own is not enough. A new product concept often requires – or enables – new business models. True break-through, end-user-driven technology innovation requires business innovation as well. To achieve this, other players in

a business value chain have to be called in. Discussions about new concepts and newly acquired end-user insights can give rise to new opportunities throughout the entire business arena. Together with business partners we can use HomeLab as a valuable asset for business innovation.

An inspiring example of a product resulting from an HomeLab project is the Miravision™ mirror TV. At first sight it would seem logical to start with the aim of the project, since that is an essential ingredient for a good, clear storyline. However, this poses a dilemma. Should it be a slick success story, showing how brilliant our vision was and how we marched with military precision to achieve this aim? A tale of a solid plan that would inevitably lead to success? Or should it be the true story? That we just started out, utterly naïve, completely missed the point, changed plan at least three times, stumbled on an invention and ended up with a very nice concept, but not at all what we had envisioned? To ask these questions openly is to answer them. The inspiration was in the expedition, the journey of improvisation….

The starting point was a project at the Philips Research Personal Care Institute on "Intelligent Personal Health Care", an exploratory research

Joost Horsten

project of the kind of which at the outset only the title is clear. At a certain point the project focused on "Diet Coaching". Some time later a sophisticated model was developed that could predict a person's future weight. This was intended to act as a deterrent to the person concerned At least potentially, since in its early form it was just a graph on a PC, which is easily ignored by the target group. So the application required a user interface that was really confrontational and embedded in the daily routine. So after some experiments we decided to include the application in the HomeLab bathroom. An LCD screen was placed behind the mirror and the application was triggered by weighing scales integrated in the floor. No possible escape. Soon we recognized that this setting opened more opportunities: when it was implemented in the HomeLab bathroom it became clear that both the technology and the context of use enabled many other applications, such as personal infotainment and beauty care. Thus, we added more applications (such as a tooth brushing coach). As a consequence, the project scope was changed to "Intelligent Personal Care Environment".

So far, so good. Several user tests and many demonstrations to visitors showed that these applications were very much appreciated by different consumers. A performance issue, however, was that the screen image was rather dark and difficult to read. This changed suddenly when one of the engineers in the team stumbled upon on a mirror-like plate from some old display. To our surprise this material gave a much brighter screen image, while hardly affecting the reflected mirror image. Not being display experts ourselves, we consulted

some colleagues in other groups and they told us that we had found a reflecting polarizer, not uncommon in LCDs, but unknown in the way we used it. So we had coincidentally made an invention. Further user tests confirmed its superior quality.

As a next step, discussions with several major bathroom suppliers were held, together with Consumer Electronics, all starting with a demonstration and discussion of the HomeLab bathroom concept. The response was overwhelmingly positive: "great product concept", "it's definitely going to happen", although some also said "it's too soon for us". And, once again, we quickly realized that the possibilities of the concept were much broader than our original set of applications: car rear-view mirrors, shop displays or, simply, TVs. This is the place to confess that we had discarded the Mirror TV idea originally as being "far too simple". How wrong we were proved to be. That very same simplicity was what ultimately triggered and accelerated the conception of the Miravision™ mirror TV by Philips Consumer Electronics. The "Intelligent Personal Care" concept had a very high appeal to almost everyone who was exposed to it. But in the end, at least for now, it was too far stretched, both in terms of product complexity and consumer proposition. A plain, old television, disguised as a mirror, was the low hanging fruit.

The Miravision™ product was launched in 2004. It generated an overwhelming wave of press coverage, received many design awards and was listed by Fortune and Time Magazine in their overviews of "Best 25 Products of the Year" and "Most Amaz-

Figure 1: The Miravision™ mirror TV.

ing Inventions of 2004". Notwithstanding its niche status, and consequently modest volume, it has been a profitable product from the outset.

What is to be learned from this? Not that plans or visions are useless. The vision kept us going and released a lot of energy in our environment. But it tells that not all innovations can be planned. Early visions may turn out to be unrealistic, and unexpected challenges may arise. But the very same challenges can be turned into opportunities. As such, innovations can arise out of the unexpected. Innovations arise at the cross-sections of disciplines, in our case personal care, displays and user research. It's a struggle, an expedition. Sometimes you are walking with your head in the clouds, and sometimes you are brought back to earth with a bump. Imagination and pragmatism walk hand in hand.

Another similar example is the combination of AmbiLight TV and amBX. These two concepts started out as a cross-fertilization between several research groups and are now finding their way to the market. Both concepts add additional sensorial experiences to AV content and bring entertainment from the screen into the room. AmbiLight TV does so by adding light effects based on an automatic analysis of the screen content. amBX goes further by adding multi-sensorial effects (lights, rumbles, fans, etc.).

These concepts are in fact quite complementary, each with its own strengths. Extensive end-user studies have confirmed their appeal. Subsequent discussions with representatives of consumer electronics and the movie and gaming worlds, amongst others, have gradually helped to define the best market entry strategies for both concepts.
As a result, the AmbiLight TV is currently on the market and is a powerful discriminator in the Philips high-end TV line. Also amBX gaming peripherals have been presented at the 2006 Simplicity Event. In both cases early user studies in HomeLab

played a key role in obtaining consumer insights and selecting solutions with the highest value for end users.

The three cases discuessed in this chapter – the Mirror TV, AmbiLight TV and amBX – illustrate that HomeLab is instrumental in showing the way along the hazardous path of business innovation.

University for the Creative Arts

Item Title	Due Date
Tools for living : a sourcebook	20/02/2012
Snow	20/02/2012
Graphis product design 3	09/02/2012
Design meets disability	23/02/2012
Food Design	24/02/2012
Ecodesign : the sourcebook	24/02/2012
Ambient lifestyle : from con	13/02/2012

Indicates items borrowed today
Thank you for using self-service.

University Library Farnham
libraryfarn@ucreative.ac.uk
1252892709
www.ucreative.ac.uk/library

University for the Creative Arts

Library Borrowed Items 08/02/2012 16:?

XXX5418

Item Title	Due Date
Tools for living : a sourcebook	20/02/2012
Snow	20/02/2012
Graphis product design 3	09/02/2012
Design meets disability	23/02/2012
Food Design	24/02/2012
Ecodesign : the sourcebook	24/02/2012
Ambient lifestyle : from con...	13/02/2012

Indicates items borrowed today

Thank you for using self-service.

University Library Farnham

libraryfarn@ucreative.ac.uk

1252892709

www.ucreative.ac.uk/library

Showcase

Showcase

Windows to the World of Information, Communication and Entertainment

The WWICE project (Windows to the World of Information, Communication and Entertainment) was started in 1996 as one of the first projects at Philips Research to explore integrated digital Audio/Video systems for Information, Communication and Entertainment functions throughout the home for the 2000 to 2005 timeframe. The project was a joint initiative of Philips Sound and Vision (now Consumer Electronics) and Philips Research and aimed to identify the architectural requirements of such systems. It can be considered a ground-breaking activity in the exploration of ambient intelligent home environments.

Content anywhere and anytime with the WWICE tokens.

Huib Eggenhuisen

As Peter returns from school he opens his backpack and takes out the disc he got from a friend who recorded a compilation of classic 90's songs for him.

He stores the disc in the living room media archiver.
Peter goes to his bedroom where he commands the system to play back the music.

While lying down he listens to the music, occasionally skipping a track he doesn't like, or turning up the volume on other tracks.

As he skips a track, the system slowly builds up a profile of Peter's musical habits and preferences.

When Peter has spent an hour or so listening to the music, he gets up and walks over to the bathroom. Tonight he has a date with Susan, one of the school team's cheerleaders.

"Continue music" Peter says, as he undresses. The music he was listening to in his bedroom is now played over the bathroom speakers.

Just as he starts to get sleepy from the soothing warm water, the telephone rings in the bathroom. It's Susan, and as the call is for Peter, it is automatically routed through to the bathroom phone.

"Oh my god, it's Susan", Peter thinks as he answers the call. "Hi Peter. You're not using the videophone?" "Well um.. I'm just taking a bath, so ... uhm.." Peter stammers.

Susan interrupts with a big smile. "I just called to check what time you'll be picking me up tonight."
As they finish their conversation, Peter gets out of the bath and gets dressed.

Figure 1: *The Follow Me scenario, with activities that follow people as they move through the home.*

Exploratory studies

In 1996, video was predominantly analogue and broadband to the home was envisaged but far from a commonplace reality. However, the transition to digital audio and video was in progress and one could foresee all digital systems in the home. The hypothesis was that functions of these systems would not be restricted to small clusters but would rather be available throughout the home via an in-home digital network. For one of the first times at Philips Research, a scenario-based user-centric approach was adopted to identify what people would want to use the future technology options for. An initial workshop with Philips Design yielded some 50 scenario fragments. The workshop was primed with technology projections and with previous studies carried out by Philips Design, such as *Quo Vadis Audio* and *Vision of the Future* [2]. The fragments were filtered and clustered to capture the key user requirements that emerged. The four condensed scenario stories were:

- 'Follow Me': media activities that follow a person in the home,
- 'Entertainment Apart Together': various functions in a social setting,
- 'Birthday Surprise': manipulation of media and content, and
- 'Product Marriage': additions to the configuration.

The Follow Me scenario, depicted in Figure 1, was subsequently used as a carrier for the project because the freedom to access and seamlessly continue media activities throughout the home was identified as an important user benefit.

A preliminary user test was performed in a living-room setting and a dining-room setting in two separate laboratory rooms. An operator, invisible to the 24 participants, simulated the fact that the participants could carry around activities, such as listening to a specific piece of music and viewing a specific TV program. The results showed that people did indeed have some awareness of mobility restrictions in the home before the experiment, but after exposure to Follow Me they were in doubt about how useful it was.

Realistic experience prototyping

In order to provide a more realistic setting, an apartment-like structure was built in an empty part of a loft in a building at Philips Research Eindhoven. The schematic in Figure 2 shows the layout with a

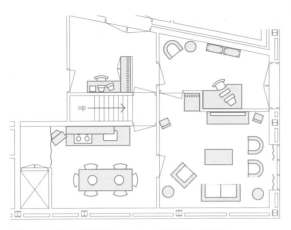

Figure 2: *The WWICE Apartment (1998 – 2001).*

Figure 3: *The WWICE tokens.*

living room, a kitchen and a study, and with a plain but effective observation station in the top left. The first functions integrated into the apartment included watching live TV, simple web browsing and video communication. These functions could be used simultaneously within a single screen/audio environment in each room. For example, one could watch a TV program and have a video communication at the same time. These combined activities could be taken from one room to another with tokens, as shown in Figure 3, or transported with a screen-based 'house map' interaction. In one of the iterations voice control was introduced using microphones hanging from the ceiling.

The system was demonstrated extensively on many occasions and proved to be a very strong medium for communicating the vision of future home environments. User tests showed that people recognized the usefulness, found it fun and easy to learn, and felt in control – despite the relatively complex

combination of functions that was offered [3]. The feasibility part of the project showed that yes, the system could be built, but not without considerable effort. The home networking technology (IEEE 1394) was not really mature at the time and the software was taxing the processing infrastructure (PCs were used for the prototype implementation). The design also identified the requirements on interoperability between the devices in a home network.

In retrospect

In hindsight one can conclude that a single, activity-oriented system environment for the user, with a coherent UI and unified interaction concept, has not really established a firm position in consumer homes yet. Certain elements are becoming commonplace with the penetration of broadband Internet, digital video, digital TV, (mobile) video communication and wireless in-home network technology. However, these enabling elements

have taken time to achieve penetration because of many factors, including cost and the dynamics of society and industry. It is for this reason that it took some years for the Follow Me concept to hit the market. The 'Music Follows Me' feature was introduced in Philips' wireless audio stations in 2005 [4].

The early WWICE project did catalyze and inspire a number of further activities and visions at Philips. HomeLab was built and opened in 2002 using the experiences gathered in the WWICE apartment. A number of projects that took further steps towards the vision are described in other chapters of this book. The partial, early vision has now been taken to a completely new and more encompassing level with the formulation of Ambient Intelligence [1].

References

1. Aarts, E., R. Harwig, and M. Schuurmans (2002), Ambient Intelligence. In: P. Denning (ed.), *The Invisible Future: The Seamless Integration Of Technology Into Everyday Life*, McGraw-Hill, New York, pp. 235-250.

2. Baxter, A., R. Bird, K. Feiz, K. Gilbert, G. Hilde, S. Marzano, and A. McAra (eds.) (1996), *Vision of the future*, Philips Corporate Design and V+K Publishing.

3. Sluis, R. van de, B. Eggen, J. Jansen, and H. Kohar (2001), User Interface for an In-Home Environment. In: M. Hirose (ed.), *Human-Computer Interaction – INTERACT'01*, IOS Press, pp. 383-390.

4. Philips Consumer Electronics Press Information (online), *Access CDs from anywhere at home with Philips Streamium Wireless Music Centers*, September 2005, http://www.press.ce.philips.com/apps/c_dir/e3379701.nsf/0/8EDAEAB3CF2E0128C125705900400964/$File/Press%20Release%20Wireless%20Music%20Center.pdf.

The Experience of Being Connected

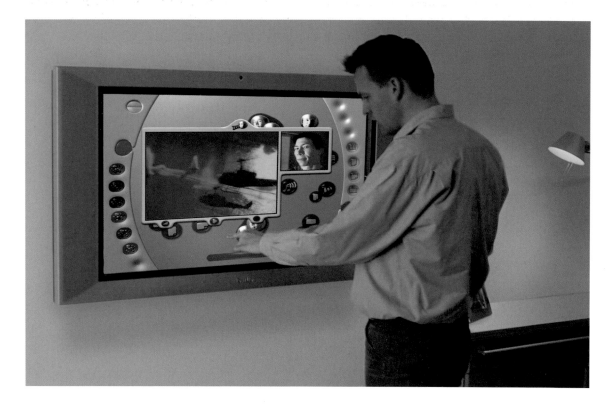

Network Technology
System Architecture
User Interaction

Sharing is essential for social communities:
a shared activity on a large screen

The WWICE project addressed the concept of home networking from the point of view that digital television would drive the emergence of home networking; see chapter 3.1. During the later stages of this project, it became clear that digital television was taking up much more slowly than expected. On the other hand, developments like broadband Internet and wireless connectivity were developing rapidly.

Mark Verberkt

As the name suggests, the WWICE-2 project was the direct successor of the WWICE project. WWICE-2 was started in 2000 to explore new applications, user interaction concepts as well as the underlying system architecture for home networks and that are driven by always-on broadband Internet. Again, a user-centered way of working was adopted and the project started off with an analysis of social and cultural trends in the world. Based on these trends, user scenarios were developed and analyzed carefully to ascertain their attractiveness for end users. From these scenarios two applications were selected, for which the user-interaction concepts and technology were developed in parallel.

Spaces and linking

Two important needs were observed in the trend analysis. The first is the basic need of social belonging. The second is the need for people to have freedom of movement, especially in the home.

Social belonging

People have a strong basic need to express themselves by associating with or dissociating from certain social groups. Important social groups could for instance be the family, a group of friends, sports companions or colleagues. In the real world, social interaction within groups is often facilitated by specific physical locations. For instance, people generally meet up with their family at home, with their colleagues at work, with their friends in the pub, etcetera. Broadband networking could enable social interaction in such a group despite the members of this group being in different locations.

The concept of *Spaces* meets the requirement for networked social interaction. A space can be considered as the virtual counterpart of a physical place and it enables people from a certain social group to share content, to meet other group members and to share experiences in real time. A member of the group can add content to a space, after which this content item is accessible to the other members of the group, from any location in

the world; see Figure 1. 'Meeting each other' in a space is made possible by means of real-time communication, typically video conferencing. Finally, in real-time sharing of experiences the people involved have a synchronized experience of the content, in combination with a video conference. For instance, in a shared video-watching activity, all of the people involved see the same video at the same time combined with a video conference between all of the people involved.

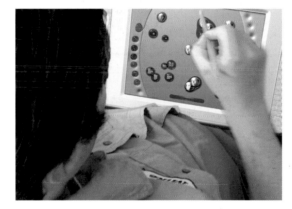

Figure 1: *The Spaces concept on a portable device.*

Freedom of Movement

Besides the need for social interaction, people also have a need for freedom of movement, which fuels the development of wireless and portable devices. People want to experience content to the full, within the possibilities of the equipment in their current context and they want continuity in their activities. For instance, if a user is listening to music via the speakers in the living he should be able to control this activity using his PDA. If he now wants to continue in another location, e.g. in the car, he should be able to do so in an easy way.

The *Linking* concept supports mobility by building on the idea that each room in the home should operate as a coherent cluster of devices, allowing the user to interact with the 'room' instead of with all separate devices. For instance, if a portable screen is brought within viewing and listening distance of a stationary device cluster, e.g. a big screen, an option for linking is presented; see Figure 2. The user carrying the portable screen can then decide whether or not he wants to link the portable device. Confirmation of the link suggestion establishes the link between the portable device and the cluster, after which the portable is considered to be part of that 'device cluster'. The linking concept allows the user to start and control activities in the cluster and to transfer activities from the portable to the cluster and vice versa. [1]

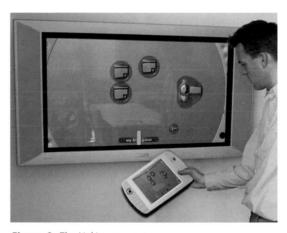

Figure 2: *The Linking concept.*

System architecture and prototype

To enable the applications and interaction concepts described in an easy way the system complexity should be hidden from the user. Heterogeneity is an important issue in the Spaces and Linking concepts. There may be devices with different capabilities, such as MPEG-2 or MPEG-4 decoding, different content formats and different types of networks, but the user only wants to select content and experiencing that specific content on the devices that are available. Consequently, the system has to hide this heterogeneity from the user. The application management and user interaction systems developed handle this heterogeneity. If, for instance, the user wants to watch the 8 o'clock news, the application management sub-system chooses which source to take the 8 o'clock news from, e.g. satellite or the Internet, and which application to start, based on the available decoders, network bandwidth, interaction device, etcetera. The user interface sub-system allows the application that has been started to specify its user interface in an abstract, device-independent manner. In this way, applications can be made device independent.

In the Spaces concept, transparent access to content is of key importance. Users are able to share information with other users who may even be outside the home. As a result, a user can access information that is located in somebody else's home. Care should be taken to ensure that it is not possible for unauthorized people to access content despite security measures, such as firewalls. To ensure this, we introduce proxies, which are similar to the proxies in firewalls, except that in this case they are for accessing content from the outside. The access rights of the user to the content in question are checked during the process of instantiation and in the proxies themselves.

In order to support the linking concept, two further technologies had to be developed: context awareness and distributed interfaces. The context awareness sub-system determines which devices are in close proximity to each other and which devices are in the proximity of which user. To determine this information it uses RF-ID, fingerprint sensors, the Cricket positioning system and computer vision. Because individual sensor measurements do not provide the required information reliably, the context awareness sub-system combines sensor measurements and draws conclusions from these. In the linked situation, the user interface of an application is distributed over the interaction devices in the cluster. The user interface sub-system provides mechanisms to allow applications to distribute their UI. Alignment of the distribution of the UI of different applications is handled by the UI-Shell system application.

A functional system prototype that implements the application, interaction and system concepts described has been built and installed in HomeLab. The system stack has been implemented on different platforms, including a system-on-chip platform such as Philips NexperiaTM [3]. The system incorporates both wired (100Mbps Ethernet) and wireless (IEEE802.11b) network technologies. Different interaction devices were used, including large stationary screens – both with and without touch input – and lap-top-sized portable screens. The system prototype supports live television watching, stored movies, pictures, picture albums, music, and video conferencing on all devices. The system automatically transcodes the MPEG-2 content from satellite into MPEG-4.

User evaluation

Ten couples who are friends or family members and who tend to adopt technology at an early stage but are not experts in the field were invited to HomeLab and exposed to the Spaces concept. They found sharing of content to be the most interesting feature of the Spaces concept. Photos proved the most important content to be shared, both for sharing the content and for sharing the experience of watching them. All participants were positive about the concept and regarded the Spaces concept as a way to increase and enhance social interaction with friends and family members.

Acknowledgements
The author would like to thank the WWICE-2 project team, and in particular: Heribert Baldus, Markus Baumeister, Elmo Diederiks, Holger Gappisch, Srinivas Gutta, Mi-Suen Lee, Patrick Niessen, Joost Reusel, Mariana Simons-Nikolova, Richard van de Sluis, Leon van Stuivenberg, Ramon van de Ven, and Koen Vrielink(er).

References
1. Diederiks, E., R. van de Sluis, and R. van de Ven (2002), Sociability and Mobility Concepts for the Connected Home, in: N. Carbonell, and C. Stephanidis (eds.), *Universal Access: Theoretical Perspectives, Practice , and Experience, 7th ERCIM International Workshop on User Interfaces for All*, Paris, France, October 24-25, pp. 442-457.
2. Balakrishnan, H. (Online), *The Cricket Indoor Location System: An NMS Project @ MIT CSAIL*, http://cricket.csail.mit.edu/.
3. Philips Semiconductors (Online), *About Nexperia*, http://www.semiconductors.philips.com/products/nexperia/about/.

3.3 69

Creating Social Presence through Peripheral Awareness
Boris de Ruyter • Claire Huijnen • Panos Markopoulos • Wijnand IJsselstein

Creating Social Presence through Peripheral Awareness

○ User interaction
○ User Research
○ New Applications
○ User Evaluation

Peripheral visualisation of remote friends
(artist's impression).

Boris de Ruyter, Claire Huijnen,
Panos Markopoulos, Wijnand IJsselstein

Although the current trend towards interconnected consumer electronics devices originated as a result of the availability of technologies for wireless interconnectivity, there are nevertheless many benefits from an end-user perspective [1]. One such benefit arises from our need to be socially connected, our need for *social presence*, i.e. the sensation of 'being together' that can be experienced when people interact through a telecommunications medium [2]. As connectivity permeates our daily lives, so we expect network infrastructures to become enablers for social interaction. Although communication media, such as e-mail, telephony, text messaging for mobile phones, etc., are common, there is more to system-mediated communication than exchanging information. Research was conducted to assess the potential affective benefits of attaining social presence by maintaining a peripheral (visual) awareness of a connected person or group of persons outside the context of communication/information exchange tasks.

Usability aspects

An experiment was conducted with 34 participants, all of whom were Dutch males. The persons were recruited as groups of 3 friends who enjoy watching soccer games and who do not have an intimate relationship, since such relationships could bias the measurement of group attraction. The friends were split up (2-1) and taken to two different rooms. (There were two groups of only two friends. In those two cases each of the two participants was located in a different room). During the experiment all participants watched the same soccer game.

A mixed experimental design was adopted. Firstly, two kinds of viewers were distinguished: a single viewer, i.e. only one person in a room, and a group viewer, i.e. two persons in a room. This was a between-subject condition. The information provided about the remote friend(s) was a within-subject condition. Each subject is subjected to each condition for approximately 30 minutes. The different conditions are: the control condition, the silhouette visualization and the full video condition. In the control condition all participants watched the same match on TV at remote locations. However, the persons could not see any visualization of the remote participant(s). They were told that their friends were watching the same match at the same time. This condition is a baseline for comparing the visualizations. It may be that people experience a certain level of social presence when they know that they are both engaged in the same activity at a given time.
The second level of visual information was a black and white (silhouette-like) image of the remote match viewers that was updated in real time when the persons in that room moved. The processed visual representation of the persons in the remote location was projected onto the wall behind the screen/onto the TV screen people were watching, to provide the image of the remote friends at the periphery of the test participants' field of attention. In the third condition the participants were shown full-size, live video images of their friends watching the match. In this visualization more detail was shown and the people in the visualization were always visible. This is the opposite of the silhouette visualization, where people only see silhouettes when there is a change in activity.

Lessons learned

The present study investigated whether social presence can be established by providing a visual display of remote friends who are watching the same television program. By presenting different visualizations of the physical activities in the remote locations in parallel with shared TV content, an experimental condition was created in which the amount of social presence and group attraction could be measured. The results from this study indicate that a low bandwidth visualization of the physical activities from remote locations is capable of establishing a sense of social presence.

Furthermore, the feeling of being part of a group, i.e. *group attraction*, was increased. When the single viewers did not receive any representation about their friends' location, they had a low feeling of belonging to and being an accepted member of the group. The group viewer, on the other hand, did have the feeling of belonging to the group in the control condition. When the minimal representation is introduced to the single viewer, this person did feel like an accepted member of the group. The difference between the two kinds of viewers disappeared with the introduction of visual media.

The silhouette visualization was just as distracting as the full video but it made the participants feel less like they were being observed. This latter aspect of the visualization could be of great importance for creating social-presence-enabling systems for the home environment. Although the full video visualization created a stronger feeling of being together and being part of a group, the low bandwidth visualization using silhouette representations of physical activity is probably more acceptable because it respects the user's privacy. Further research needs to be conducted to establish the optimum level of social presence: the present study did not consider whether the amount of social presence created by the experimental visualization was sufficient to be of value to users. Test participants indicated that they would prefer different levels of social presence for different kinds of TV programs. People prefer to watch sports and movies in the presence of others, whereas they prefer to watch news and documentaries alone. For entertainment programs, viewers enjoy creating a cozy atmosphere and experiencing other people's reactions. More research is needed to investigate the context in which people prefer less or more social presence.

Additional research is required to assess whether the effects can be generalized for different types of relations. It may be the case that people prefer different levels of social presence depending on the

Creating Social Presence through Peripheral Awareness

Boris de Ruyter • Claire Huijnen • Panos Markopoulos • Wijnand IJsselstein

'interaction/communication' partner. Moreover, different kinds of activities need to be investigated. It may well be that different kinds of activities elicit different levels of social presence. Moreover, it could be interesting to asses the level of enjoyment of the participants during interaction with different systems. Finally, further research is needed to assess whether any differences exist between men and women.

References

1. Aarts, E., R. Harwig, and M. Schuurmans, (2001) Ambient Intelligence, in: Denning, P (ed.). *The Invisible Future: The Seamless Integration Of Technology Into Everyday Life,* McGraw-Hill, New York, pp. 235-250.

2. Ruyter, B.E.R. de, C.A.G.J Huijnen, P. Markopoulos, and W.A. IJsselsteijn, (2003). Creating social presence through peripheral awareness, in C. Stephanidis and J. Jacko (eds.), *Human-computer interaction : theory and practice Vol. 2 of the proceedings of HCI International 2003,* June 22-27, Crete, Greece, pp. 889-893.

Memory Browsing in a Connected Home

Sharing memories with others is considered by many as a more fundamental consumer need. One of the first projects in HomeLab, called 'Phenom' and running from 1999-2003, aimed to investigate and create concepts and technologies that address this consumer needs for personal memory browsing. It started with the development of a solution for instant access to digital photo albums anywhere in the home in order come to guidelines for the development of a product that supports people in sharing memories with others. The resulting product prototype was obtained through a sequence of three user-centric application research phases.

Network Technology
New Applications

Firstly, an intelligent *Photo Browsing* system was developed that provides users with the freedom to access photos anywhere at home and to show these photos to others on TVs in their vicinity. Photos can be accessed either by searching in albums, browsing associatively, entering into dialogue with the system or simply by placing a souvenir that is associated with a certain photo album on a nearby table.

Secondly, this concept was extended to a *Photo Sharing* system, in which favorite photos are also available outside the home and can be copied to a friend's collection. Novel methods have been implemented that deal with the multi-user and multi-device issues involved.

Thirdly, studies have been conducted to determine which cues (photos, videos, sounds, smells and text) can be used most effectively in a system that supports people in *Memory Sharing*. These studies were prompted by the observation that people

Evert van Loenen

have a basic need to retrieve or re-live memories of important events in their life and to share these memories with others, for example by telling stories.

Scope

The development of the Phenom photo and memory sharing concepts was motivated on the one hand by an extensive user study into what people find important in their homes [1] and, on the other hand, by a vision of the evolution of Ambient Intelligent environments [2]. One of the major conclusions of the user studies was that "photographs are irreplaceable representatives of the memories that people have" and "they are the undisputed number one in the ranks of important objects". Many people mention the need to share their memories with others, for example by showing them their photos and telling them about the experiences they had at the time. With the advent of digital photo and video cameras it has become much easier to create and store valuable memories, but the same cannot be said for retrieving and sharing them. Indeed, quite the opposite is true. Digital photos are usually not stored in the location where they will be needed to show to others (the living room), and it has become increasingly difficult to find the relevant photos quickly in a large collection.

Photo browsing

In the first phase of the project these issues were addressed by developing a Photo Browser that uses context awareness methods and wireless connectivity to enable instant access to personal photos anywhere in a smart home [3,4]. This system has the following main features:

- *Wireless displays.* Private browsing and selection of photos can be done on 'Sepias': portable touch-screen devices, such as tablet PCs, like the Fujitsu Stylistic, or wireless monitors, like the Philips DesXcape. These are wirelessly connected to the 'HomeBase': a PC or other multimedia server.
- *Use of displays or printers in the user's vicinity.* Photos can be sent to any display or printer connected to the home network using simple gestures ('Drag-and-View', 'Drag-and-Print').
- *User interface.* The user interface is designed for touch-screen, consumer-type devices, with simplicity as the main focus. When the Sepias are used in a smart environment, such as HomeLab, they know where they are located and use this information to minimize the number of icons visible on the screen.

Photos can be accessed in various ways. Firstly, they can be selected from all albums in the home network. These are shown as thumbnails in a continuously moving photo roll.

Figure 1: *Impression of the photo browsing user interface on a 'Sepia'.*

Secondly, a Browsing Assistant allows users to browse through collections associatively. It continuously provides a selection of photos relating to a similar location, date, event or topic as the photo currently selected.

Thirdly, a *Conversational Interface* was developed to allow the user to find specific photos quickly through a dialogue with the system. A fundamental aspect of the interface is the concept of *souvenir interaction*, which involves the use of tangible objects to retrieve photos. Tangible icons are considered to be by far the easiest and most natural solution to the retrieval problem in question. Albums of particular events can be retrieved instantly simply by placing a related souvenir on a nearby table. This concept is radically different from other browsing solutions in that it uses personal objects belonging to the users that have inherent meaning, in this case souvenirs are inherently linked to memories. It is no longer the user who has to learn how to use a system's objects, but the system that has to understand the meaning of each of the user's objects. Tangible Shortcut has been implemented by tagging relevant souvenirs with a small RFID tag and fitting the tables with RFID readers.

Photo sharing

In the second phase of the project this concept was extended into a Photo Sharing system that allows users to access and share photos, both at home and while on the move. This system has the following additional features:

- *Context awareness.* The Sepias have embedded sensors [5] and are aware of their own orientation. For example, when they are rotated from landscape to portrait orientation, the UI adapts automatically. The system also has built-in intelligence for tracking the position of all devices throughout the home using an RF/Ultrasound technology.

- *Sharing user interface.* Particular attention has been paid to keeping the Sharing UI as simple as the successful Browsing UI, even though this second version has many more features. The only difference is the appearance of an additional screen icon when a second Sepia is detected. Photos can be moved to this second Sepia using the same drag-and-view actions that are used to move photos to nearby TVs.

- *Off-line use and synchronization.* Favorite collections can also be made available when the user is on the move or visiting other homes. Digital photos can be exchanged and solutions have been developed for synchronizing the changes with the main collection when the user returns home.

- *Color-changing devices and tables.* The color of the Sepia's casing adapts to the favorite color of the current user (Chameleon casing). In multiuser situations the system provides clear indications of who is currently in control of which table (Chameleon table) and screen by changing their respective colors to match that of the current user's Sepia. This is accomplished by embedding RGB LEDs in the casings and tables.

- *Photo-frame mode.* When they are not being used for browsing, the Sepias automatically turn into decorative photo frames.

Software architecture

A dedicated software platform was developed to deal with discovery and ad hoc connectivity of stationary and portable devices. This platform, called the 'Empire', is very flexible: new functionality can be added by plugging in software modules called 'servants'. A range of servants has been developed to provide increasing intelligence to the system. An example is the servant that keeps track of favorite photos for each user and minimizes waiting times by showing the favorites more often than other photos in the film roll. Other examples are servants that keep track of the location, orientation and color of the devices in use.

Lessons learned and next steps

Initial user evaluations in HomeLab have shown that the Phenom system is appealing and that it indeed addresses existing consumer needs. One insight obtained is that collecting and browsing photos is only one expression of this fundamental need to retrieve or re-live memories of important events in one's life, and to share these memories with others. (Telling stories is for example an alternative way to fulfill this need). Therefore, the project continued to investigate the importance of memories to people and into what cues (photos, videos, sounds, smells, text) are the most effective for use in a system that supports people in Memory Sharing.

Acknowledgement

The author gratefully acknowledges the other members of the Phenom project team involved in this work: Nick de Jong, Elise van den Hoven, Esko Dijk, Yuechen Qian and Dario Teixeira, as well as those who were involved for part of the time: Doug Tedd, Yvonne Burgers, Miguel Ferreira and Esa Tuulari.

References

1. Eggen, J.H., G. Hollemans, and R. van de Sluis (2002), *Exploring and Enhancing the Home Experience. Cognition, Technology and Work*, Springer-Verlag, London.

2. Aarts, E., R. Harwig, and M. Schuurmans (2002). Ambient Intelligence, in P.J. Denning (ed.), *The Invisible Future*, ACM Press. pp. 235-250

3. Loenen, E. van, N. de Jong, E. Dijk, E. van den Hoven, Y. Qian, and D. Teixeira (2003), "Phenom", in: E. Aarts and S. Marzano (eds.), *The New Everyday, Views on Ambient Intelligence*, 010 Publishers, Rotterdam, The Netherlands, pp. 302-303.

4. Dijk, E., E. van den Hoven, E. van Loenen, Y. Qian, D. Tedd, and D. Teixeira, (2000), *A Portable Ambient-Intelligent Photo-Browser*, Philips Research Technical Note NL-TN 2000/257, Eindhoven, The Netherlands.

5. Tuulari, E., and A. Ylisaukko-oja, (2002), SoapBox: a platform for ubiquitous computing research and applications", *Proceedings of Pervasive 2002*, Springer, Berlin, pp. 125-138.

New Applications
Smart Sensors
Interaction Technology
User Research

Dreamscreens: Towards Virtual and Augmented Windows

The vision of Ambient Intelligence anticipates a world of many intelligent devices that are integrated into the surroundings, thus bringing the user to the foreground by allowing natural interaction with smart electronic environments. Since the very beginning, large displays have played a central role in the development and implementation of the vision. One of the major challenges is the design of large interactive screens that support ambience creation in a home environment. DreamScreen refers to a project in which we conducted exploratory studies in this field with the emphasis on the creation of interactive visual experiences.

Objectives

The DreamScreen project aims to create beautiful immersive experiences by augmenting or replacing the view of otherwise transparent window screens. In the first phase of the project, an inventory was created of user, system and interaction requirements for a broad range of applications in the professional, public, automotive and home domains. A clear trend in each of these domains is the need for ever-larger display areas. In the professional domain, for instance, this is driven by the need to combine and compare increasing amounts of information in a single view, e.g. diagnostic images. In the home domain it is driven primarily by the wish for more immersive home theatre and gaming experiences.

One of the main barriers, apart from cost, standing in the way of the application of ultra-large displays is simply lack of space: existing solutions either take up a lot of room (bulky projection TVs) or require a lot of desk or wall space (beamers, monitors, FlatTVs). Windows with a display capability (DreamScreens) would solve this problem, because windows are typically large, free areas. The TV/monitor simply disappears when the windows are switched back to their normal, transparent view.

Research challenges

Our goal is to find out as early as possible what value propositions can be created that address the needs, wants and wishes that exist in the different domains, to provide requirements for the technologies that are needed to realize them, and eventually to create complete prototype systems, including appropriate interaction solutions. The approach is a user-centered one: even though transparent display technologies are not yet available in the sizes typically needed for DreamScreens, user and sys-

Evert van Loenen

Figure 1: *DreamScreen Underwater View.*

tem requirements can already be determined by studying how users respond to DreamScreen experiences, simulated with projection techniques.

A first project demonstrator shows various relaxing atmospheres, created by projecting 9-meter-wide semi-dynamic scenes. These scenes consist of a static background with animated elements rendered on top. It has been found that such scenes are already quite impressive and relaxing, but the question remains of what users' perception will be over time.

A key challenge is to find easy-to-use interaction solutions for such DreamScreens. Having very large-area views does open up the possibility of combining much more information in a single view, but without appropriate counter-measures interaction with such large overviews can become highly complex.

Interaction concepts

Both implicit and explicit interaction concepts were investigated in a second iteration of the project demonstrator. In this implementation an interactive underwater view was displayed on the windows of HomeLab; see Figure 1. The application shows an animated movie of a deep-sea scene with swimming fish and crawling sea creatures of many different species, moving water plants and pulsing coral. The scene has a shipwreck lying on the bottom of the sea as its main focus. The fish and water movements produce sounds that are directed into the room by beam-forming arrays of loudspeakers; see Figure 2. In front of the display there is a touch-sensitive floor that can determine the position of a spectator.

Figure 2: *A beam-forming array of loudspeakers under construction*

The underwater sounds are directed towards the spectator by the beam formers. Spectators can interact with the sea creatures by simply walking up to or away from the windows. In the research demonstrator this is enabled by sensors incorporated in the floor. People can explicitly interact with, for instance, some dolphins by walking purposely up to and along the front of the windows. The dolphins will follow the spectators and try to get as close as possible. The animations were generated pseudo-randomly and consequently did not follow

a script. The movements were typically slow and smooth, and there were no abrupt scene changes.

First observations

Evidently the prototype created in HomeLab was primarily aimed at proving the feasibility of large-screen interaction concepts. Creating a realistic large-screen animated scene was in itself quite an effort. In particular, the problem of generating a sufficiently large screen resolution for the animated video and the synchronization of the different displays required quite some engineering effort. From a usability point of view, the preliminary user tests revealed quite a number of new insights. It can be concluded that it is indeed possible to generate a positive immersive experience in this way. After some exposure time spectators were really absorbed by the attraction of the displayed scene and became part of it. The attention span was fairly long, indicating that spectators remained fascinated for quite some time, ranging from a few minutes to an hour. Most spectators found the experience rather relaxing and some compared it with the experience of gazing into an open fireplace or looking at a panoramic landscape. The implicit interaction was also appreciated and the recommendation was to keep it as indirect and shallow as possible, i.e. the user should not always get his own way in attracting the dolphins' attention. Most test persons could imagine having such an application at home in their living room.

Conclusion

DreamScreen has been a very fascinating project for the study of immersive user experience generated by large interactive screens. It has increased our understanding of such applications in terms of their system complexity and user requirements. It will probably take another generation of display technology to bring the cost of display screens down by an order of magnitude before such applications can be successfully introduced into a high-volume consumer electronics market. Some areas are however conceivable in which such interactive applications could be introduced much earlier, such as retail and hospitality.

Entertaible

Ambient Intelligence relates to environments and systems that are sensitive and responsive to the needs of the people who inhabit them. It goes without saying that gaming should be included in the topics addressed by research into Ambient Intelligence. There is a clear consumer need for entertainment, part of which is fulfilled by gaming.

Electronic board games

Advances in electronics and networks have enabled rapid and exciting developments in gaming, e.g. the PlayStation and the Xbox. The Internet provides an opportunity for large groups of gamers to become involved in online role-playing [1] and electronic games in general enable gamers to connect through a network and to play together. Despite these opportunities to play together, gamers still have a natural need for direct human and social interaction, as is shown by the gamers meetings that are often organized to give gamers a chance to meet 'in real life'.

The social and direct human interaction is well supported in traditional board games such as *Monopoly, Risk* [2] and *Settlers of Catan* [3]. However, apart from a few exceptions, such as *King Arthur* [4] and *Cluedo Live* [5], there is a gap between the world of electronic games and the world of board games. Evidently, there is a space here for the electronic board game, a concept that combines the attractiveness of the two worlds. The interactivity and dynamics of electronic games together with the direct social interaction and the physical objects used in board games enables a whole new class of games. The aim of the Enter-

taible project was, therefore, to develop the concept of electronic board games and to explore its potential.

Concept realization

To realize Entertaible, as the concept is called, a standard 30" LCD panel was mounted on top of a table and used as the board; see Figure 1. The large viewing angle of present-day LCD panels provides all of the players around the table with a good viewing experience. For natural game play it is desirable for the players to use physical playing pieces (e.g. pawns), just as they are used to doing. This means that a touch-detection technology is needed to record the position of objects on the board (the LCD panel) and the inputs made by the players using their hands and fingers. Furthermore, all of these inputs need to be handled simultaneously.

The current touch-detection solutions that also allow multiple inputs at the same time were not adequate for Entertaible. Camera-based solutions require carefully controlled lighting conditions, a requirement that conflicts with the setting in which Entertaible will be used, e.g. at home, in bars or casinos, etcetera. Conductive or capacitive touch-

Gerard Hollemans, Sander van de Wijdeven,
Tom Bergman, Evert van Loenen

Figure 1: Entertaible.

detection solutions require that the game pieces are at least conductive, and in most cases a history needs to be maintained to know where the playing pieces are when the players are not touching them.

A new touch-detection technology was invented and used for Entertaible. This technology uses infrared LEDs and photodiodes, which are mounted dis-

cretely around the perimeter of the LCD. By intelligently processing the data that are generated by this setup, it is possible to determine the location of up to 40 objects or fingers simultaneously.

The combination of display and position detection for multiple objects simultaneously enables the use of interactive pawns. The simpler pawns change color: transparent pawns transport the light from

the display underneath the pawn to the top of the pawn using the principle of total internal reflection. When the color of the display changes, so the color of the pawn changes too. Furthermore, the state of the pawn can also be controlled by the display. For example, the pawn can blink when it is the player's turn. More advanced pawns can be activated and controlled by the display. Using a photodiode, the pawn can read (color) codes from the display underneath it. With some processing, these codes can be interpreted as commands, e.g. to control small motors in the pawn and move it across the display.

YellowCab

The games that can be played on Entertaible run on a computer that is connected to it. In theory, any gaming platform can be used to drive Entertaible and the computation needed to run and render the game can also be embedded in Entertaible itself. To illustrate some of the new possibilities for board games that are enabled by Entertaible, a new game was implemented, called *YellowCab*.

When playing a game of Yellow Cab, each player is a taxi driver in Manhattan and has to pick up passengers from the sidewalks and take them to their destination in order to earn points. The taxis are represented by pawns, a map representing Manhattan is displayed on the LCD, and matching sounds accompany the actions in the game, e.g. the sound of cars driving, car doors slamming, etcetera. Other cars that drive on the board, wear and tear on the road, traffic lights and police chasing cars that have jumped the lights showcase some of the newly enabled dynamics and interactivity. These represent some of the daily challenges faced by a taxi driver: gridlock, roadblocks, traffic congestion and (potentially) fines. The winner is the player who has picked up and delivered the most passengers by the end of the game.

Presentation to the world
After Entertaible had been presented successfully at the Philips in-house research exhibition, it was tested informally by a large group of children as part of a public event. Given the choice between watching a movie, playing a game on a video game setup with 3D graphics or playing Yellow-Cab on Entertaible, most children played for hours on Entertaible, explaining to newcomers how the game worked. No explanation of the concept or how to interact with the table was necessary. Even though technical glitches sometimes meant that the game had to be restarted to ensure it worked at its best, the children were reluctant to let the researchers do this because they wanted to continue playing.

Entertaible was shown publicly at the CES show in Las Vegas in January 2006. Hundreds of people visited our booth and reacted very enthusiastically. The international press also showed a keen interest in it. The TV and both online and printed press covered the story and the number of hits in Google peaked at 800,000 a couple of days after the show. Most importantly, a considerable number of companies and individuals showed an interest in entering into a partnership to get Entertaible onto the market.

Acknowledgement
The authors wish to thank Vincent Buil, Rene Cortenraad, Michel Decre, Jettie Hoonhout, Nick de Jong and Tatiana Lashina for their invaluable and continuing contribution to the Entertaible project.

References
2. http://www.wordiq.com/definition/Computer_role-playing_game/.
2. *Monopoly* and *Risk* are games by Parker Brothers.
3. *Settlers of Catan* is a game by Mayfair Games; see also http://www.mayfairgames.com/.
4. *King Arthur* is a game by Ravensburger, see also http://www.kingarthur.de/.
5. *Cluedo Live* is a game by Parker Brothers, see also http://www.boardgamegeek.com/game/8069.

Mark van Doorn, Warner ten Kate,
Herman ter Horst, Natasha Kravtsova

Your Media Environment

The Your Media Environment project investigated the use of Semantic Web technology [1] for reasoning about content and context information in a generic way by making knowledge explicit on the Web. Two demonstrations were built. The first demonstration showed how Semantic Web technology could be applied to adapt the choice of music on an Internet-enabled audio mini set according to the situation and the presence of users. The second demonstration explored how Semantic Web technology could be used to select content from different content providers, which each provided metadata in different formats. These two applications are discussed below.

Context-aware music selection

Everybody knows what it is like when you just want to sit down somewhere and listen to music that matches your mood. As part of the Your Media Environment project a system was developed that allowed context-aware music selection. The system consisted of a query formulation procedure that uses as input context information represented on the Semantic Web and generates as output a query that is appropriate for the user's current situation; see Figure 1.

In the prototype the query asks for a music recommendation in the form of a play list. The context information includes information collected by sensors about the people and objects present, rules for reasoning about the context, and context-dependent user profiles. The reasoning rules are used to determine from sensor data the nature of the relevant user situation. The query is submitted to a separate retrieval system, which recommends songs that are then played on an Internet-enabled

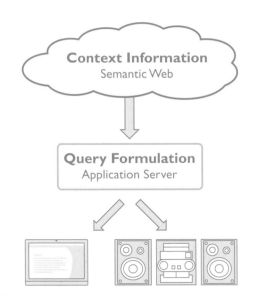

Figure 1: Context-aware music selection using the Semantic Web.

home theatre system. As a result, the environment becomes sensitive and adaptive to the presence of people, showing a basic form of ambient intelligence, which is realized using standard Internet

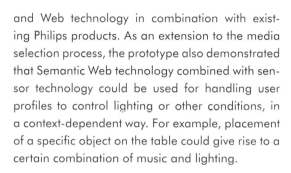

Your Media Environment
Mark van Doorn • Warner ter Kate • Herman ter Horst • Natasha Kravtsova

and Web technology in combination with existing Philips products. As an extension to the media selection process, the prototype also demonstrated that Semantic Web technology combined with sensor technology could be used for handling user profiles to control lighting or other conditions, in a context-dependent way. For example, placement of a specific object on the table could give rise to a certain combination of music and lighting.

Automatic content provider selection

The most common way to search in multimedia content is by means of textual annotations added to content items. These days there are numerous metadata sources on the Internet, but each of these sources uses a different ontology to describe the music. One source may, for example, use the word 'artist' while another uses the word 'artiste' or 'band' to indicate the same concept. How does the end user know which language or ontology to use? As in the case of context-aware music, a query formulation procedure was developed, but this time information about the available metadata repositories offered by different content providers who are represented on the Web was taken as input; see Figure 2. Based on this input information, the query formulation component generates a query that is sent to the appropriate content provider (or multiple queries for multiple content providers). This gives end users transparent access to content from different providers, and system administrators can quickly change the set of content providers based on service agreements with third parties.

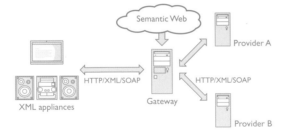

Figure 2: *Automatic content provider selection using the Semantic Web.*

Reference architecture

A second goal of the Your Media Environment project was to create a system architecture in which interactive media applications for a wide-range of different CE devices and user contexts could be customized quickly and cost-effectively; see Figure 3. This system architecture inspired the design of the ambient narrative system discussed in [4]. In Figure 3, feedback from users is collected by several CE input devices and sensors (top left corner) and forwarded to a reasoning component (center).

This reasoning component takes context information, preferences of users and device capabilities to compose a query for one or more search engines (top right corner). The results of this query are aggregated by a presentation generation component (bottom right corner) and transformed in a web-based multimedia presentation language. The final-form presentation is rendered by a distributed media presentation component (center) that controls the timing and synchronization of media elements in the presentation across one or more consumer output devices.

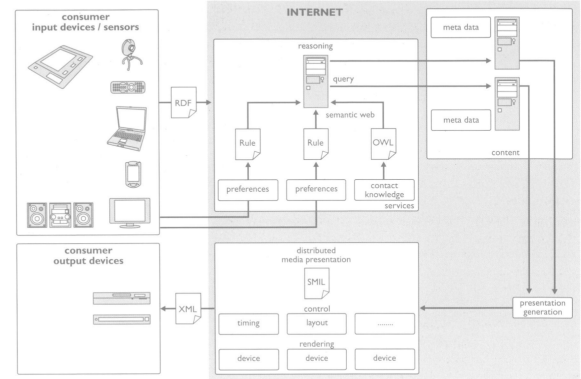

Figure 3: *Reference architecture.*

Usability

The context-aware music selection demonstration was shown in the HomeLab in 2002. People liked to see and experience the way RFID tags are used. By combining user tags, CD album tags and object tags, users could easily create a different music and lighting atmosphere in the room. Simply stacking CD albums with tags to create a play list was also appreciated as a nice option. One remark commonly made related to the rules governing the required behavior. In the demonstration the rules were designed beforehand. This is not representa-

tive of a real-world situation because every individual is different and wants to customize the ambient intelligence environment to suit his own personal preferences.

Feasibility

The demonstrations showed that Semantic Web technology could be used effectively to model and reason about context and media. One of the advantages of Semantic Web technology is that it makes reasoning explicit and this makes it easy to

Your Media Environment
Mark van Doorn • Warner ten Kate • Herman ter Horst • Natasha Kravtsova

add new statements or, using the hyperlink feature of the Web, to refer to existing statements. The query formulation procedure in both demonstrations is quite similar. Since Semantic Web technology is based on deductive reasoning, it requires additional technologies to support reasoning with uncertainty, something that is important when modeling many real-life situations. Greater technical detail about the underlying model and reasoning process has been published in [2].

Lessons learned

The project raised some interesting questions for future work. First of all, we learned that end users should be in control of the ambient intelligence surrounding them, so that they can change the behavior of the smart environment as they see fit. This topic is currently being addressed in the DreamScreen project. Another aspect concerns the accurate determination of the current context of use, i.e. accurate so as to simplify the action required by the user to perform the control. This problem has been investigated further for application in care for the elderly, in which the determination of an elderly person's Activity of Daily Living (ADL) is a central, recurring factor. Secondly, hosting the application intelligence outside the device on a web application server made it possible and easy to add new services relating to features of existing CE Internet-enabled devices. However, when intelligence moves into the network, so does economic value and this, in turn, puts pressure on existing business models. Thirdly, we learned to see devices more and more as multi-application I/O devices, across which the timing and synchronization of media and ambient effects was

an important issue. Last but not least, the lessons we learned about automatic content selection between different content providers were used in several follow-up research projects on intelligent reasoning in content management systems.

References

1. Berners-Lee, T., J. Hendler, and O. Lassila (2001), The Semantic Web, *Scientific American*, 85(4), pp. 35-43.
2. Horst, H. ter, M. van Doorn, N. Kravtsova, W. ten Kate, and D. Siahaan (2002), Context-aware Media using the Semantic Web, in: *Proceedings of the Belgian-Dutch Conference on Artificial Intelligence (BNAIC-02)*, pp.131-155.
3. Doorn, M. van, and A.P. de Vries (2006), Co-creation in Ambient Narratives, in Ambient Intelligence and Everyday Life, *Lecture Notes on Artificial Intelligence* 3864, Springer, Berlin, Germany, (to appear).

Physical Markup Language and amBX
David Eves • Joost Horsten • Jo Cooke • Richard Cole

Physical Markup Language and amBX

Ambient Intelligence – where the objects around us play a dynamic, coordinated and ever-changing role in altering our sensory experience of a space – is a vision made possible by the increasing reality of the 'networked home'. Technical developments in computing and networking could soon see many of us living in homes capable of facilitating Ambient Intelligence experiences.

However, we will never realize the full potential of the networked home and Ambient Intelligence unless we establish some common ground to enable the objects around us to work together. amBX lays out just such a framework, thus bringing Ambient Intelligence to life. In the future we will judge a product not only by its features or specifications, but also by the experience that it enables us to have, according to our expectation that entertainment really should be immersive.

amBX features

amBX is a revolutionary new technology that extends entertainment beyond traditional screens and speakers and out into the living room [1]. Consisting of a description language and a software engine and architecture, amBX enables an alliance of content producers and device manufactures to develop and deliver new kinds of experiences to consumers. The key features of amBX can be described as follows:

- *Enhancing entertainment.* amBX takes the game world beyond your PC screen to make it come alive in the room around you – with monsters seemingly crashing about behind your sofa and bullets ricocheting off the walls. More subtly, amBX enhances movies with 'surround experiences', deepening and widening the level of immersion in a similar way to surround sound. amBX even enables the lighting and ambient atmosphere in a room to change according to your mood throughout the day; see Figure 1.

- *Extending hardware.* The real world experiences made possible by amBX are realized by specially-enabled consumer devices, such as color-controlled lights, active furniture and video and audio devices. amBX provides the support framework that enables manufacturers to develop these amBX-ready products.

- *Empowering creativity.* Filmmakers and games developers can include whatever ambient effects they like with amBX's description language. With amBX, the creative industries have a new brush and a new palette at their disposal.

- *Supporting flexibility.* amBX's architecture has been designed so content creators can specify experiences without having to have any knowledge of the exact environment where they'll be recreated. And it doesn't matter what particular amBX device a consumer has in his home: amBX acts dynamically to make the best of what is available in any given situation.

David Eves, Joost Horsten, Jo Cooke, Richard Cole

- Turning your room into a browser. The many diverse objects around us need to work in harmony if we are to realize the entertainment applications that we are all dreaming up. Existing systems are not adequate: we require new standards and protocols that go beyond the infrastructure to describe the real-world spaces and the experiences of the people living in them.

Figure 1: *Example of an amBX setup for entertainment.*

amBX Development
Philips has developed amBX to enable multiple devices to be coordinated with each other so that the potential of Ambient Intelligence can be realized. amBX also provides content authors with a common language that can be used to describe the experiences that are to be recreated in an Ambient Intelligent environment.

amBX came about as the product of a 'Vision Brainstorming Day' which was held at Philips Research in Redhill back in 2000. The bright idea behind what was at first known as 'Physical Markup Language' (PML) and then grew into the amBX product was: if you can have a markup language for describing a document (HTML) or a virtual world (VRML), then it must be possible to create one that could describe an experience in the real world.

From this initial idea, the PML research team then looked at the items which might be used to create an amBX 'experience' and realized that we are already surrounded by things that provide us with real experiences – heat, light, etcetera – and so the means to deliver such an experience already exists in the home – and elsewhere. At an exhibition held in HomeLab in 2002, the PML team demonstrated the PC game 'Quake', which was enabled in this way – the potential was clear and gaming became a focus for launching the technology under the new name of amBX.

amBX technology
At the heart of amBX is the amBX engine, which will be made available to Philips' development and manufacturing partners for inclusion in the games or as part of the hardware installation. This acts essentially as 'middleware' – an 'experience engine' comparable in many ways to a physics engine in existing computer games.

Developers who incorporate amBX into a game will use the amBX scripting language to embed these scripts into the game, for example to trigger an explosion description as a rocket hits a wall. These instructions take the form of a markup language, which is sent to the software engine which mediates between the author's intention and the capabilities of the devices connected to the PC.

In taking this approach, Philips' intention was to put amBX firmly in the hands of the creative community – people who are ideally placed to describe the 'experience'. The language is in effect no more complicated to use or understand than HTML and, with Philips providing the tools for its use, writing a short amBX script should be virtually as straightforward as designing a web page.

amBX in HomeLab
HomeLab has played a key part in helping us to understand the needs of all parts of the amBX-enabled value chain: content developers, hardware manufacturers, retailers and end consumers. It not only places the technology in context, thus inspiring understanding and innovation, but also provides a situation for user study that will lead to greater expertise in experience creation and a more focused and appreciated product as a result.

At present amBX is being demonstrated with a specific range of experience effects on a select number of PC games; however, its potential is far broader than this. The lighting and physics models of the game can also be linked with script generation, which can be delivered dynamically, bringing the game models out of the virtual and into the real world.

HomeLab brings many projects together, inspiring new applications and acting as a showcase for enabling technologies such as amBX. As a result, there will be a much richer set of future applications that also provide meaningful and engaging user experiences.

Physical Markup Language and amBX
David Eves • Joost Horsten • Jo Cooke • Richard Cole

amBX will be an enabler for experience-based entertainment in a wider range of application areas, both consumer and professional. Even at launch, Philips will have support for applications beyond gaming – including music, video and ambient lighting. It is Philips' intention that this will be a revolutionary technology enabling new scope for creative expression in many fields, such as home theatre, mood lighting, toys, shop and club lighting and many more.

Consumers become 'experiencers'

For the consumer, ambient intelligence means a world of new experiences, augmenting our entertainment and enabling better and more tangible interfaces to evolve – making life more fun and easier to cope with.

Consumers will also be able to create or collate personal content based around amBX's general-purpose language, which can then be shared and experienced with others. Bringing entertainment out of the screen and into the space around us will enable us to inhabit fantasy worlds, to travel through distant locations or to share experiences, even when we are far apart. And it could be used as a way to recreate and share a treasured memory, such as a wedding, by capturing aspects of the experience as a combination of favorite images, sound phrases, lighting and even feelings and emotions.

Most of all, with amBX entertainment becomes more immersive and interactive, integrating with the space that surrounds us. One day everything in a room will be able to contribute intelligently to the moment-by-moment sensory experience of anyone in that room; amBX makes that future possible.

Quotations

To illustrate the success of amBX we mention the following quotations which we took from the open literature:

- "I 'got' amBX the moment I saw it – I really liked the way it added to the visual experience. I also liked feeling the wind in my face, it made the whole game experience more real."
  ChrisTaylor, CEO, Gas Powered Games.

- "I want an amBX system because it adds a completely new type of immersion to my favourite games."
  Adam Oxford, Editor, PC Format.

- "amBX and its enabled peripherals are very much aimed towards growing the experience on-screen and making it more 'real'...it does this in a much more high-concept way than some well-drawn texture. It gives a more involving experience making the atmosphere between you and the game all the more potent."
  Michael French, Editor, Develop Magazine.

- "Linking together all manner of devices from surrounding ambient lighting to hot-air fans and vibrating furniture, it could change the way games are experienced."
  Edge Magazine.

References
1. *amBX* (online), official website, http://www.ambx.com/.

Toons Toys, developing a fun experience

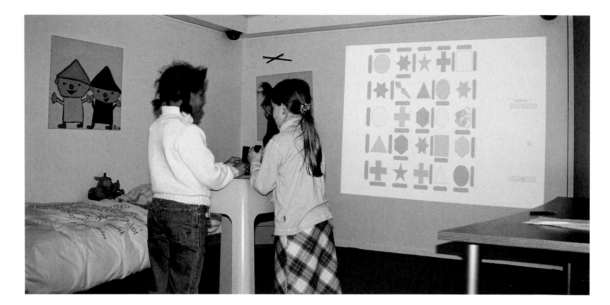

Physical play is important and fun for children.

The vision of Ambient Intelligence poses a number of interesting issues and questions that require thorough investigation. In particular, issues related to how people are going to interact with the ambient intelligent technologies are interesting, as the means provided to do this will determine users' first impressions of the technologies and make a major contribution to the success of Ambient Intelligence. In an Ambient Intelligent environment the hardware associated with the new technologies will be integrated into the background [1], but while the technology will become invisible, users will still need to interact with it. Furthermore, the environment in which the technologies are used implies a different, new set of requirements for the interaction style that will be adopted. The issues that are relevant in a work environment, such as efficient output, are different to the ones that are important in a home or leisure environment. Enjoying the experience of using these new concepts will be more important to the user than the efficiency of the interaction. Besides *ease of use*, we will have to consider *joy of use* as well. In this chapter, the Toons Toys will be presented as an example of how devices can be functional and fun.

Marcelle Stienstra, Jettie Hoonhout

Toons Toys, developing a fun experience
Marcelle Stienstra • Jettie Hoonhout

Toons Toys background

Children grow up today with electronic toys and computer games that might offer them some mental but certainly hardly any physical stimulation. As the development of children should take place at multiple levels, we wanted to develop electronic toys that are fun – and thus motivating to use – while at the same time stimulating cognitive and social learning and physical exercise.

The toys were designed within the framework of TOONS, an interactive TV programme aimed at children aged 8 to 10 [2]. One of the intended functions of the toys was to serve as input devices for the TOONS application, allowing children to interact with the story. But the toys were to be designed in such a way that they could also be used in other settings, e.g. in games.

Three interaction toys were developed. The three toys differed from each other in the motor capabilities the children had to address when interacting with the toys – fine or gross motor skills. One of the questions that we wanted to address in this project is the appeal of these different physical challenges to boys and girls.

Fun requirements

In the design of the toys we adopted a set of design heuristics outlined by Malone and Lepper [3]. They postulate, for example, that for games and software to be enjoyable they should be designed in such a way that they present an appropriate challenge to the user, raise his or her curiosity, let the user be in control, and in their appearance have a touch of fantasy. When more than one user is involved, elements such as competition and co-operation should be added to these heuristics. Although these heuristics are primarily directed at (educational) software design, we considered them to be usable starting points for the design requirements of our interaction toys:

- The toys should provide a cognitive and physical *challenge* to the children, i.e. provide a difficult enough task that will put the child's abilities to the test without becoming too challenging.

- They should raise the children's *curiosity* (by providing novel, surprising, and puzzling, but not completely incomprehensible interface elements) and encourage them to continue with the activity by stimulating exploration.
- They should contain a *competitive* and a co-*operative* element, as the toys were designed for team play. Both elements contribute to a challenging and motivating experience.
- The toys should invite the children to take an *active* attitude, cognitively as well as physically (NB this requirement is not in Malone & Lepper's set of heuristics).

The children were to be cognitively challenged by the fact that they had to co-operate and co-ordinate their actions and by the fact that it was not immediately obvious how the devices should be used.

So they were challenged to explore how the device should be operated and used – calling upon their problem-solving skills – which is considered to be motivating [3].

Figure 1: *From left to right: the keyboard-mouse combination, Stickysticks, Twistyertouch, and Tunemein.*

The interaction toys

The first toy, *Stickysticks*, is a magnetic table that can be operated by two magnetic sticks, one for each child, challenging their fine motor skills. The top of the table is like a chessboard, with five fields by five. A magnet is positioned under each field of the board. The interaction is achieved by positioning magnetic sticks above specific fields. Feedback and feed-forward are given through sound and magnetic force. The board consists of fields filled with colored blobs or grey geometric figures. Each child manipulates one stick that can either be used for the color or the figure fields. It is not allowed to touch the game board with the sticks. The children have to create particular combinations as input for the game by 'activating' a color field and a figure field at the same time, such as a red blob plus a square shape or a blue blob and a star shape.

The second toy, *Twistyertouch*, is a large soft mat. Four cubes measuring 40 x 40 x 40 cm are placed on the base, which measures 160 x 160 cm. Every visible surface of Twistyertouch, horizontal and vertical, is covered with a cushion and functions as a button. The interaction takes place by pushing, jumping, or hitting the centre of the surface, all requiring children's gross motor skills. When a cushion is correctly activated, feedback is given through sound. Co-operation between children is stimulated by the dimensions of Twistyertouch: to achieve a certain outcome as quickly as possible all cushions that need to be activated have to be divided between the two players, otherwise it will take more time. The version of Twistyertouch we used in the study was implemented as a 'color' keyboard: all cushions of the same color have to be activated in order to get the desired outcome. In the game itself children receive feedback on whether they have already activated enough cushions of a specific color. However, as an additional challenge they cannot see which ones are activated.

Tunemein is based on the theremin, a musical instrument developed in 1919 by the Russian physicist Lev Termen [6]. Tunemein is an instrument that consists of a small base with a long aerial sticking out of it. The total height of the Tunemein is 1.60 m. Tones can be produced by moving a hand towards the aerial. The closer you move your hand towards the aerial, the louder the tone will be. It requires a child's fine motor skills to make a very loud tone, while not touching the aerial. Different tones can be produced by moving your hand along the aerial, calling upon children's gross motor skills. Feedback and feed-forward information is provided through sounds and LEDs on the Tunemein's base. For our study we used two Tunemeins to play the game, one for each child, each with 3 unique tones. Each tone is linked to an action, which is only completed if a certain volume is produced. This way one Tunemein can be used to initiate three different actions: two of these actions can also be initiated by the other Tunemein, the remaining one is unique to the specific Tunemein. The children are not allowed to touch the aerial. To add an extra challenge the mapping of the tones on the aerial changes every two minutes.

In addition to the three toys, a game was designed in order to provide a setting in which the toys could be used as interaction devices: 'Rabbitmaze'. The aim of the game is to earn as many points as possible by guiding two rabbit's feet through a maze towards a carrot. When the rabbit reaches the carrot a new carrot will appear in a different position in the maze. This game was used in combination with all toys, with only some slight variations in the visual presentation required for each toy. For instance, in the case of Stickysticks colored figures are positioned in the maze to enable movements through the maze.

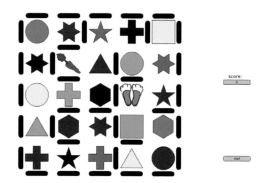

Figure 2: The "Rabbitmaze" version for Stickysticks.

Testing 'fun'

An experiment was set up to determine which of the three toys children found the most fun to play with. In order to be able to compare the children's response to the new toys with their appreciation of more common devices, i.e. to see whether the toys were more interesting and engaging and not too difficult, we used a (laptop) keyboard and a mouse connected to the laptop as a baseline. Nowadays these input devices are familiar to most children. One child had to operate the keyboard, the other the mouse. Actions were divided between the two input devices: the keyboard could only be used for moving up and down and the mouse for moving left and right, both obligatory actions for the "Rab-

Toons Toys, developing a fun experience
Marcelle Stienstra • Jettie Hoonhout

bitmaze" game used in this experiment.

The experiment was divided into two parts. The first part was carried out in the children's bedroom of HomeLab. Children participated either in boy pairs or in girl pairs. They had to play the game 'Rabbitmaze' with the interaction toys. The children always started with the keyboard/mouse, and then they played the game either with Stickysticks and Tunemein or just with Twistyertouch. After each game the children would individually fill in a Fun-questionnaire. The last task the children had to do was to fill in a paired-comparison test (presented with pair-wise combinations of the games, the children were asked to choose the most fun game of each pair), again on an individual basis.

After the HomeLab session in the second part of the study, the children were tested to assess their cognitive and motor capabilities. We did this in order to be able to deduce the challenge the different toys would pose for each child and thus clarify the choices made by the participants. In total 108 children participated in the study.

Findings

The highlights of the results will be presented here: for more details we refer to [4, 5]. The results showed that the toys were more difficult to use, i.e. the children got higher scores playing the 'Rabbitmaze' using the keyboard/mouse than they got when using the toys. Even though the toys were more difficult to use, judging by the scores obtained and the children's reports, this did not have an adverse effect on the degree to which they were rated. On the contrary, despite the keyboard/mouse combination giving the highest score, this device was rated the lowest (and, as was to be expected, more

so by girls than by boys). One of the reasons why the children preferred the new toys was the challenge they offered: according to the children, "playing with these toys is really difficult, and that's what makes it fun" and "it's different from other things and much more difficult, and that's why I like it". The scores from the Fun-questionnaire indicated a similar pattern as reflected by the results from the paired comparison test. The children's rating of Stickysticks was somewhat higher than their rating of the keyboard/mouse. But the rating of Tunemein and Twistyertouch was far higher than the other two. One possible reason for this could be that besides the cognitive challenge presented by the toys the physical challenge offered by Tunemein and Twistyertouch is an important factor contributing to 'fun'. So both boys and girls greatly enjoyed the physical activities required by Twistyertouch. We aimed for devices that would promote active behavior in the children, but we did not expect that being physically active would be valued so much by boys and girls alike. An interesting finding with respect to future electronic game and toy design.

Some striking observations were made during the trial sessions. For instance, most boys were very interested in their own scores. As there was no high score list available on the screen, they would ask the researcher how well they had performed compared to other teams. Although girls were also interested in their own scores, they wanted to hear whether they had done better than the first time. They were not so much interested in how other pairs performed compared to their own performance. So in both cases the challenge aspect was present but expressed differently.

Conclusions

Given the results of the study and the reactions of the children who participated, we believe that the heuristics that we adopted are a promising set of design guidelines for creating games and tangible devices that will offer the user a fun and enjoyable experience. Challenge, curiosity, and novelty definitely play a role, as well as playing together in a team and being physically active. Further studies should help to clarify the respective contributions of each factor to the overall enjoyment of games and toys. And further studies could also help us to understand how we might apply these factors not just for toys, but also in the development of other consumer devices [5] for which "ease of use" is as important as "fun in use".

References

1. Aarts, E., and B. Eggen (eds.) (2002), *Ambient Intelligence in HomeLab*, Neroc, Eindhoven, The Netherlands.

2. Janse, M.D. (ed.) (2000), *Requirements for the selected application and its user interface Deliverable D2 WP1*, Status report of EC-funded IST project 1999-11288 NexTV.

3. Malone, T.W., and M.R. Lepper (1987), Making learning fun: A taxonomy of intrinsic motivations for learning, in: R.E. Snow and M.J. Farr (eds.), *Aptitude, learning and instruction*, Erlnaum, Hillsdale, N.J., USA.

4. Stienstra, M.A. (2003), *Is every kid having fun? A gender approach to interactive toy design*. Ph.D. thesis, University of Twente, The Netherlands.

5. Hoonhout, H.C.M., and M.A. Stienstra (2003), Exploring enjoyability: which factors in a consumer device make the user smile?, in D. de Waard, K.A. Brookhuis, S.M. Sommer, and W.B. Verwey (eds.), *Human Factors in the Age of Virtual Reality*, Shaker Publishing, Maastricht, The Netherlands, pp. 341-355.

6. Thermin, L. (online), http://www.thereminworld.com/learn.asp.

StoryToy

Smart Sensors
Intuitive Interaction Solutions
New Applications

Children are abandoning traditional toys in favor of computer games at an ever-younger age. The user interface of these games is, however, very restricting. The child sits down and looks at a screen. Children would benefit from toys that combine the level of flexibility and interactivity of computer games with the look and feel of traditional toys. The aim of the StoryToy project was to develop such a toy [1].

StoryToy combines physical play, storytelling and digital flexibility.

Willem Fontijn

There were, however, some constraints attached to the final result. The technology used should be advanced but not obtrusive. Ideally it should be invisible. In addition, the toy had to be easy to use, like traditional toys. The children should be able and willing to play with the toy without any instruction. Furthermore, the technology used should be cheap to enable pervasive application without prohibitive cost.

Concept

StoryToy is a storytelling environment that consists of an audio replay engine and a tactile user interface based on a sensor network. However, the scope of StoryToy is not limited to storytelling. The same technology can be used in education, instruction, control applications and even for therapeutic purposes in a health-care setting. For this purpose a platform design was derived from Story-Toy (Edutainment Sensor Platform, ESP) that can be used in a wide variety of stand-alone applications that require a tactile user interface.

Although it is fun to develop toys, the technology has wider implications. Toys and games have a special quality that compels users to interact with them before they really know how to use them. Often one can learn to play a game just by playing it, with little advance knowledge. A study of how this works may reveal principles of user interaction that can be applied to other applications.

The interactive farm

The StoryToy environment comprises multiple characters who, together, can tell a story. The first user interface implemented is in the form of a farm, but more or less any other theme could have

been chosen. All that is visible is a farmhouse, several stuffed farm animals and some marked locations around the farm, like the road, a pond and a stable box. In the first version the active mode of operation is determined by the location of the duck. There are three modes of operation: *free play, reactive play* and *story play*. The mode of operation is selected by placing a duck on specific locations around the farm. With the duck in the stable box the system is in free play mode, which means that the system is turned off and the child can play with it in a 'traditional' manner. The reactive play mode is selected by placing the duck in the pond. In this mode, when an animal is picked up the sound made by that animal is reproduced. For example, when the cow is touched the system produces a mooing sound. If the duck is placed on the story patch the farm enters 'story play' mode and the narrator reads the first line of the story. An example is a linear story in which each story line ends with a reference to one of the animals. The player now needs to touch that animal. If the correct animal is touched the appropriate sound for that animal is reproduced and the story continues. If the wrong animal is chosen, the system will point this out using various responses, such as 'that is not the sheep' or 'that is the calf'. If the user waits too long the system will give a reminder, e.g. 'I am waiting' or 'please pick up the pig'. Several stories and games with different levels of complexity were created and tested on children between the ages of two and six.

Interactive tapestry

The second version of StoryToy still uses the farm but now a wall-mounted tapestry depicting a land-

scape is used to select the mode of operation; see Figure 1. In the sky on the tapestry several locations are marked that can be selected by placing an object in the shape of the sun on that location, where it will stick. In addition, the system is connected to an amBX server; see Chapter 3.8. This server enables light effects to be used in the stories along with the audio responses. If the sun is placed on the left in the sky an amBX script starts running that dims the lights in the room and mimics a rising sun by gradually changing the color of the lamp in the east corner of the room from red to white. The other lamps gradually get brighter. Meanwhile, a game starts where the children have to identify which animals belong to the sequence of noises they hear. Other settings are: 'daylight' – switches the lights to full intensity and switches the

Figure 1: *Second version of StoryToy with on the left the interactive farm and tapestry and on the right the different positions of the sun corresponding to 'morning', 'daylight', 'storm' and 'twilight'.*

farm to reactive play mode; 'storm' – lowers the general lighting level, features the effects of thunder and lightning, starts a story based on a dialogue between the animals over what to do during the imminent storm; 'twilight' – gradually dims the lights until they are switched off. This setup demonstrates that lighting effects can be incorporated easily and that the tangible user interface of StoryToy can also be used as an advanced light switch.

Conclusion and lessons learned

The story mode in particular offers something that other storytelling toys do not. There are multiple characters that can work together. The farm animals can enter into dialogue and are able to react to each other's actions. They can experience an adventure together and the child can play a role in that adventure. The fact that the animals work together without any visible technology makes the farm appear magical.

Apart from being educational, StoryToy is fun to play with. When confronted with the stuffed animals, the children's natural reaction is to pick them up. The fact that the animals respond to this is very appealing to children and immediately draws them into the game.

With the StoryToy platform it is easy to turn simple traditional toys into environments that deliver interactive stories and games that can be quite complex. When stories and games of different levels of complexity were tested with children in HomeLab this showed that by using traditional toys as the input device and just audio feedback it is possible to offer a level of interactivity similar to that provided by computer games for young children. It also showed that with a 'roadmap' of complexity, the same platform can grow with the child.

References
1. Fontijn, W.F.J. and P. Mendels (2005), StoryToy, the Interactive Storytelling Toy, *PerGames workshop, Int. Conference on Pervasive Computing,* May 11, Munich, Germany.

Splashball

Children used to play outside in the backyard or on a playground somewhere much more than they do today. Now many children spend significant amounts of time sitting down and looking at the screen of a computer, game console or television. As a result, children are no longer getting enough physical exercise and this is a major contributing factor to the problem of childhood obesity. However, interest in how to make electronic toys and games more physical and tangible is growing and modern electronics in combination with more traditional game elements can offer interesting options: more flexibility in game flow, less static game situations, personalization of game elements (skinning), and different game levels.

Simple sensors convert a digital game into a fun physical challenge.

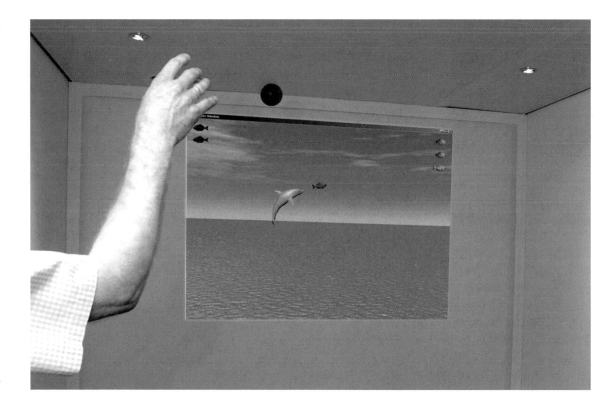

Willem Fontijn, Jettie Hoonhout

The aim of Splashball was to create a gaming platform that was physically stimulating and, at the same time, attractive enough to move children away from their screens [1]. Moreover, the application is not limited to children. Although it looks like a game, Splashball is in fact a motivational tool to improve health and wellbeing. It does so by combining Philips' current strengths, i.e. image processing and camera technologies, with sensor network technology.

Feasibility Aspects

The Splashball platform uses the impact of balls on a wall as a form of point-and-click interface. The basic Splashball setup consists of a beamer and a means of impact localization. The beamer is used to project a playing field, i.e. the game, onto the wall. This is the output screen of a PC that runs the application software. A motion sensor is mounted on the wall plate to detect the impact of a ball on this wall plate. To determine the location of the impact, two cameras are mounted near the two bottom corners of the wall at a grazing angle with respect to the wall; see Figure 1. The centers of the field of vision of the cameras cross near the center of the projected playing field on the wall. The cameras and motion sensor are connected to a second PC that runs the detection software. Detection of an impact triggers the image-processing sub-system to determine the location of the ball upon impact by analyzing the successive frames in the image buffer at around the time of the impact trigger. This requires advanced image processing as, due to the speed of the ball, only a few frames have the ball in them and the image of the ball exhibits substantial motion blur.

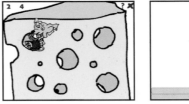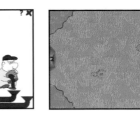

Figure 2: Screen 'shots' from 'mouse game' (left), 'paint game' (middle), and 'rabbit game' (right).

Several games were developed that were sequential in nature to ensure that only one player throws a ball at a time. Three games were tested on adolescents. In the first game a mouse pops up from within a giant piece of cheese. The player gains a point by hitting a mouse wearing a shirt of his color. The object of the second game is to hit a bucket of paint of a given color to prevent a man from carrying it across the screen. The men that reach the other side of the screen pour the paint into a funnel until one of the players collects a certain amount of paint. The third game features a rabbit that has to be chased into a rabbit hole of a given color. To do this, the player must hit the opposite side of the screen from the direction in which he wants the rabbit to run, thus chasing the

rabbit in the right direction. Screenshots of these three games are shown in Figure 2.

Another game developed was based on dolphins, as a reference to a DreamScreen under-sea landscape; see Chapter 3.5. During the game, fish that are either red or green jump out of the water. If a fish is hit by a ball, the dolphin jumps out of the water to catch it in mid flight and then eats it. The player whose color corresponds to the color of the fish that was hit gets a point. The player who manages to hit 5 fish first wins.

Usability Aspects

The games were tested in the recreation room of HomeLab as part of a JetNet activity (Youth and Technology Network Netherlands). JetNet is a cooperation between high schools and multinationals with the aim of promoting technical studies. The participants in the test were adolescents between the ages of 12 and 16. This target group was chosen because it was expected that children of this age group might be less physically active than those in other (younger) age groups. A total of 38 2nd- and 3rd-year high school students participated: 20 girls and 18 boys, in same-gender pairs, who were asked to select their own partner in the test. Participants were positioned between 2 and 2.5 meters

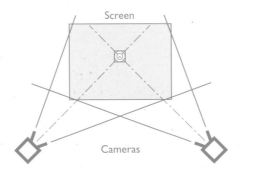

Figure 1: Impression of the camera positioning in Splashball.

Figure 3: *The large picture presents a screen shot from the game 'Catching fish to feed your dolphins'. The smaller picture in the lower right hand corner shows a player in the playroom throwing a ball at the screen.*

from the wall to enable them to see the full projection and so that they would be close enough to hit the wall with some accuracy. They played each game at least once for a total test duration of 1 to 1½ hours. The participants were observed whilst they were playing the game and were interviewed afterwards.

The tests focused primarily on the initial experience of the game. It is essential to gain insight into this stage of the user's experience by testing because designers and developers are often so immersed in the game that they tend to forget what the initial experience is like for someone who has never played the game. A development team usually likes to obtain detailed feedback about game play beyond the initial experience, but this would require a more robust implementation of the impact detection.

Lessons Learned

The vast majority of participants said the Splashball games were fun. What they liked about the games was that they involved throwing balls against a wall indoors. They also enjoyed being able to play a game that involved physical activity rather than being confined to a chair and keyboard. They liked the fact that it was something new and different from other games and that it had been designed for multiple players.

The main complaint was that the games did not always react accurately, although the participants acknowledged the fact that the games were under development. The participants also felt the current games were a bit slow. Furthermore, they suggested that the games could be made more complex, with more variation, greater challenges and unexpected events.

The comments made by the participants in this test were quite promising: they liked the key concept of the game – a physical game with hidden electronics – and made suggestions for improvements that will be feasible to adopt. It is important to point out here that the impact detection and localization have been improved substantially since these tests were conducted.

The test results indicated that Splashball is enjoyable and that it encourages children to be physically active. Based on the observation data and the interview results, it can be concluded that the competitive aspect was indeed a strong motivator. This was also obvious in the feedback that was collected from adult players who were asked to try out the dolphin game on the Splashball platform when it

was presented at an exhibition. Although Splashball is designed for children, it can therefore be used to motivate people of other ages to engage in physical exercise.

Conclusion

The concept of Splashball is very attractive to players, both young and old, but a good implementation in terms of both appearance and accuracy is crucial. If the latter is achieved, Splashball can be an effective means to encourage physical activity, with some degree of competition as a good additional motivator.

Acknowledgements
We would like to thank Clara Otero Perez, Paul Shrubsole, and Kero van Gelder, all from Philips Research, Eindhoven, the Netherlands, and Philip Mendels, from the Technical University of Eindhoven, for their much valued contribution to building the Splashball demo.

References
1. Hoonhout, H.C.M., W.F.J. Fontijn, and L. Smets. (2006), Splashball: Throwing reality at the virtual world. *Proceedings of the first Fun and Games conference*, June 26-28, Preston, England.

Query by Humming

Singing a 'hook-line' of a song to retrieve it from a large music collection, known as 'query by humming', was researched in 2000 as part of the Easy Access project. The project aimed to deliver easy-to-use interaction solutions for navigating through large digital music collections. As a project result, the Easy Access Jukebox provided music access using a mixture of user-system interaction technologies, such as voice control, touch, speaker recognition, speech synthesis and non-speech audio. In a combined voice and menu-driven dialogue, users could easily skip to artists, albums and songs by pronouncing their names or by performing a few finger touches on a visual display [1]. Since it is often difficult to remember the artist or song title [2], users could also retrieve a song by humming, whistling or singing the melody.

User study

The research started with a series of workshops in which ideas and concepts were formed on how users would be interacting with digital music from 2000 onwards. At that time, audio compression and the Internet had just started to persuade people to collect massive numbers of digital music files for personal use. Out of the many ideas put forward, five concepts, including 'query by humming', were picked out as being most promising and were elaborated into a usage scenario in full-blown animations. These animations were used to obtain feedback early in the design process from prospective end users and stakeholders in the project. From the feedback we learned that 'query by humming' was marked as one of the most innovative and most exciting ways of finding music; see Figure 1. This result challenged us to study the singing of the general public, to realize 'query by humming' technologically, and to evaluate and demonstrate its ease and use in a real-world music system.

Singing a melody from memory is more difficult than it might appear at first. It requires individuals to be able to recall the pitches of the melody, to master their vocal apparatus and to listen carefully to themselves in order to control their singing. It is clear that a certain level of singing proficiency is required to become a successful user of a 'query by humming' system, but a certain degree of familiarity with the song to be retrieved is also essential. To study how these factors affect singing performance in real life, we conducted a controlled experiment in which the singing of Conservatory vocal students was compared with the singing of participants who had never had any singing lessons in their lives [3]. All participants were asked to sing the melody of very familiar songs (e.g. a No. 1 hit by the Beatles) and far less familiar songs. The results showed that all participants performed at a similar level when it came to reproducing the overall contour (i.e. the ups and downs) of a melody. Dramatic effects were observed in the way participants sang the finer details of a melody. The trained singers were better

Steffen Pauws

at singing the right notes at the right time than the untrained ones. Familiarity with the song was essential for both groups in order to sing the melody exactly. We also found that everyone started at a pitch of their own personal preference without considering the key in which the song was composed or recorded. Surprisingly, everyone had a fairly good memory of the tempo of the song. All these findings, and many more, were collected and used as insights and requirements for further technology development and evaluation.

Realization

The technology for 'query by humming' involves detecting the pitch and the timing of the query that is sung and using the pitch to search through a large database to find the corresponding melody. As became apparent from the user study, the first step of pitch detection needs to be robust to all levels of singing ability and all singing variations, including humming, whistling, use of nonsense syllables and use of lyrics. The concluding search step needs to be tolerant to various singing errors, such as singing out

of key, incorrect timing, omission of notes or inclusion of extra notes. The time taken to search should not exceed a few seconds, since the user is waiting for the result. The technology should be suitable for music collections of any size and type. Lastly but not least, the technology should be easily accessible to end users in an intelligible way. This all resulted in the Easy Access jukebox in which 'query by humming' was incorporated [4]; see also Figure 2.

Evaluation

User tests were performed in co-operation with the University of Ghent to assess the accuracy and scalability of 'query by humming' technology and to evaluate the ease-of-use of the Easy Access jukebox. The singing of more than 70 participants was used to assess the technology; they had a range of singing abilities and used various ways to produce the melody. A fair chance of 42% of retrieving the correct song from a 10,000 song database is attainable with only a single sung query [5]. When confronted with the Easy Access jukebox in HomeLab, many users ini-

Figure 2: *The Easy Access jukebox.*

tially felt embarrassed and too shy to sing to the system. But after their initial attempt, users were already very taken with its convincing performance and playful interaction. 'Query of humming' is more than just a slick way to find a song, users also enjoyed using it as an interactive gaming experience to see who was the best singer.

References

1. Pauws, S. and G. Hollemans (2002), Easy access to a large digital music collection, *Proceedings of the International Symposium on Consumer Electronics, ISCE 2002*, September 23-26, Erfurt, Germany, G 7.

2. Peynirçioglu, Z., A. Tekcan, J. Wagner, T. Baxter, and S. Shaffer (1998), Name or hum that tune: Feeling of knowing for music, *Memory & Cognition*, 26, 6, 1131-1137.

3. Pauws, S. (2003), Effects of song familiarity, singing training and recent song exposure on the singing of melodies, In: H.H. Hoos and D Bainbridge (eds.), *Proceedings of the fourth International Conference on Music Information Retrieval, ISMIR 2003*, October 26-30, Baltimore, Maryland, USA, pp. 57-64.

4. Pauws, S. (2002), CubyHum: A fully operational query by humming system. In: T. Crawford and D Bainbridge (eds.), *Proceedings of the third International Conference on Music Information Retrieval, ISMIR 2002*, October 13-17, Paris, France, pp. 187-196.

5. De Mulder, T., J.-P. Martens, S. Pauws, F. Vignoli, M. Lesaffre, M. Leman, B. De Baets, and H. De Meyer (2006), Factors affecting music retrieval in query-by-melody. *IEEE Transactions on Multimedia*, Vol. 8, No. 4, August 2006, 728-739.

Figure 1: *An example scenario.*

Joey plays with the Easy Access jukebox that contains his extensive music collection. At last, there is a music system for which he does not need to be an expert user; a few words or finger touches give him the music he wants to listen to.

He remembers that he heard a song at the local pub last night, but he cannot recall the artist or title, so he tries to reproduce the song by singing the melody into the handheld device.

The system uses Joey's imperfect singing as a cue for searching in the collection. It swiftly responds with a list of songs with melodies that come close to what Joey has produced. With a simple touch, Joey finds the song he heard last night.

The Expressive Music Jukebox

System Intelligence

The music business is increasingly embracing the digital distribution model. The various download music stores in the world of personal computing have enjoyed incredible success and the digital download model already represents a considerable share of the entire music market. As a result, Direct to Device (D2D) services are going to provide direct access to music stores for download and subscription in a lean-back mode and, at the same time, music on mobile is set to be a very lucrative business. The logical next step is to integrate music players into mobile phones, since the mobile phone is the one device people already carry everywhere. Major operators are exploring the market for music download services and handset makers are meeting demand by adding more and more music capabilities.

Easy and enjoyable browsing through similar music (artist's impression).

Fabio Vignoli, Steffen Pauws

User needs

The increasing availability of digital music and the ever-increasing transmission bandwidth and storage capacity are creating new challenges and opportunities for music applications. These propositions no longer relate to music quality/availability, but to choice and selection. The aim of the E-Mu project is to focus on differentiating aspects of the music download business. We develop technology for music management in embedded applications and music services. We have identified simplicity as one of these differentiating aspects. Therefore, we are aiming to create simpler but more interesting music applications that will provide users with flexible ways to acquire, select and listen to their music. Ultimately, what matters is that we support the user experience: finding the right music at the right time, creating and listening to inspiring play lists, discovering new music that suits the users' tastes and preferences.

To create this experience, which will eventually distinguish our products from those of our competitors, new applications and services are being researched. In order to be effective, these applications will need to take the following into account:
1. What users know, how they reason and how they express themselves.
2. How users listen to and organize their music.
3. What is known about the music and what can be derived from the music itself through content analysis.

The E-Mu Jukebox

The E-Mu jukebox is based on the concept of navigation through music collections and automatic play-list generation. Navigation through the music collection is traditionally accomplished by using a folder-based structure focused on the genre/artist/album; see Figure 1. This structure is efficient only when users want to perform specific searches (e.g. for artists or songs), but does not support them very well if the requirement is not specific. As the size of the collection increases, so new ways to find the desired music are needed, for example on portable players that can store 40 GB of music but have displays with only a few lines.

User studies have revealed that being able to search for similar artists and for similar songs is one of the most important user needs [1]. The E-Mu Jukebox has been developed from this idea. It features a novel interface structure that combines hierarchical and similarity-based navigation. The jukebox helps the user to search effortlessly for artists/songs that are similar to a given set of artists/songs. Additionally, the user has complete

Figure 1: *The Expressive Music Jukebox*

a) Browsing,

b) Search similar songs: the user can define the similarity function applied to the music collection by dragging the sound/tempo/mood/genre/year adapters on the screen. An adapter that is close to the center is weighted more heavily than one that is positioned on the periphery.

c) Compile a play list: The relative position of the various genres (artists and albums) determines the amount of music for each of the genres (artists and albums). The users can also choose their preferred period of time and the preferred tempo for the music.

control over what musical aspects make up the current definition of similarity. In other words, the user can request any combination of songs that radiate the 'same mood' and that 'sound similar' or songs that have a 'similar tempo' or that stem from the 'same period/genre'.

Creating your own play list is another important user need [6]. It allows users to experiment freely with their music and to really discover their music collection. A play list can be created by manually selecting each song individually. This is not advisable due to the amount of effort involved. Alternatively, this can be achieved by leaving the music selection entirely up to the system. This is not advisable either because of the lack of control. Therefore, the jukebox generates play lists by

meeting selection criteria that are set by the user in the interface. These criteria indicate 'how much' one wants from a specific genre, artist or album, in what tempo range or from what time period, etc. It is quick, requires little thought, only needs a few clicks of the button and can be re-done in an incremental fashion if the play list needs improvement.

The concepts and algorithms in the E-Mu jukebox are enabled by metadata that includes catalogue metadata (i.e. genre/artist/album) from third parties and music-intrinsic features (i.e. tempo, sound texture) from content analysis.

User benefits

User benefits are crucial to the research and the development of the present system. For the E-Mu

The Expressive Music Jukebox
Fabio Vignoli • Steffen Pauws

Jukebox these can be formulated as follows:

- High quality: "I experience my music to the full"
- Low thinking: "I do not have to think much to select my music"
- Low effort: "I do not have to do much to select my music"
- Great fun: "I forget about time passing by"
- Complete control: "I decide what will happen".

The E-Mu jukebox was evaluated with actual users to test both the appeal of the concept and the subjective quality of the results [2,3]. The SiMix concept, together with the algorithms that implement it, enables the user to choose music based on the similarity with a seed song. The specificity of SiMix is such that it allows the user to define the similarity function on the basis of content analysis (e.g. timbre and tempo) and catalogue metadata (e.g. genre, artist name). The test was conducted with twenty-two participants. The main aim of the test was to compare the objective and user-perceived performance of SiMix against two other control systems with reduced user control over the similarity function. The results were measured with respect to: play-list quality, task performance, and perceived ease-of-use and usefulness.

The notion of *music similarity* has been identified as a much appreciated tool to help end users to find their preferred music in large collections. We believe that music similarity involves the comparison of different song features like timbre, genre, mood, tempo and year. Moreover, given that the importance of features is heavily dependent on the relevant context and listening intentions, we pro-

posed a system in which the user has complete control over the contribution made by each feature to the overall similarity. The findings showed that users with a more explorative nature who work with the proposed system are able to make better play lists in less time and with less effort than the control systems. Purely because of the additional effort required to learn to work with the user-driven similarity function the first time the system is used, most users find that the proposed system is not quite as easy to use as the other systems. In conclusion, users preferred to have complete control over their personal definition of music similarity and found this to be more useful than no control.

References

1. Vignoli, F. (2004), Digital Music Interaction concepts: a user study, *Proceedings of International Conference on Music Information Retrieval, ISMIR 2004*, October 10-14, 2004, Barcelona(Spain), pp. 415-420.

2. Pauws, S. (2003), *Evaluating playlist creating with SatisFly assistance*, Philips Technical Note PR-TN-2003/00714.

3. Vignoli, F. and S. Pauws (2005), A Music Retrieval System based on User-Driven Similarity and its evaluation, *Proceedings of the International Conference on Music Information Retrieval, ISMIR2005*, September 10-15, London, United Kingdom, pp. 272-279

Context Aware Remote Control

Mobile devices can frustrate users by disturbing them with non-urgent information at an inappropriate moment or failing to deliver an important message. Most people will at some time have missed a telephone call because their mobile was in their bag. Another typical example is receiving an audible call in a meeting or in the theatre because you forgot to switch the phone to silent mode. These examples illustrate the problem of the burden being on the user to control their mobile devices.

A Context Aware Remote Control makes life easier (artist's impression).

Gerard Hollemans, Tatiana Lashina, Vincent Buil, Sander van de Wijdeven, Fabio Vignoli, Jettie Hoonhout

Context awareness

Context awareness is proposed to improve device usability by adapting the way a device behaves in response to implicit input acquired by the device or information from a distributed sensing environment. This concept is said to be a step forward from a traditional black-box paradigm that uses explicit user input [3]. The stimulus for context-aware research is catalyzed by advances in mobile electronics and connectivity as mobile devices accompany us on the move in a constantly changing context [1].

Efforts to make systems context aware generate some skepticism [2]. This skepticism relates in part to the limited intelligence that context-aware systems have demonstrated up until now. These systems have restricted means for recognizing context reliably and reasoning about it. As context-aware devices can then act on their own behalf or perform autonomously actions triggered by context changes, an additional concern is whether users will accept having to delegate part of the control to the system and, if so, for what tasks and situations this will be acceptable.

Context Aware Remote Control

Gerard Hollemans • Tatiana Lashina • Vincent Buil • Sander van de Wijdeven

Fabio Vignoli • Jettie Hoonhout

The aim of the project was to assess the user-perceived added value of context-aware features for home entertainment systems. It focused in particular on consumer electronics (CE) home entertainment systems, such as TVs and Home-Theatre-in-a-Box systems.

Concept

The remote control is the most mobile part of an home entertainment system. It is often faced with different contexts of use. For this reason we chose an Electronic Program Guide (EPG) on a remote control as the carrier application for our research. An EPG is easier to use when searching for preferred TV programs than its predecessor, the printed TV guide [4]. These days many TV sets and indeed some remote controls (e.g. Philips' iPronto) offer access to an EPG.

We extended the concept of this type of remote control with EPG by adding the following features: (1) a recommender function, which acts as a filter and presents only those programs that fit the preferences indicated in a user profile, (2) a reminder function, which enables the users to mark programs they want to be reminded about, and (3) a messaging function, which allows the user to send and receive suggestions for interesting programs from others, e.g. friends.

Because we have introduced a reminder and a messaging function, the Personal Remote Control (PRC) needs to take the initiative, informing the user when a program starts or a message arrives. As discussed, this can potentially lead to problems. Interviews with several representative TV consumers revealed a number of typical situations in which communication/alerting problems could easily occur. For each of these situations, a solution was devised using sensor-based context awareness, as described below.

a. *The remote control is in a (table) drawer or other confined space, which muffles the audio alerts of the TV program reminders.*
The remote control is generates a louder auditory alert. If the user does not react to the alert, the reminder is stored and repeated as soon as the user picks up the remote control.

b. *The user is away and cannot hear the audio alerts of the remote control that is lying on the table.* If nobody responds, the reminder is not repeated until the user is detected in the proximity of the device.

c. *The remote control generates audio alerts that are too loud while the user is holding it.* Quieter audio alerts are generated if the user picks up the device or if the device is already in the user's hand before the alert starts.

d. *The visual reminder window on the PRC screen opens full screen and overrides another application the user was using. An icon that indicates that there is a reminder or incoming message is used instead of a pop-up window if the user is using other device features.*

e. *Audio alerts for non-urgent program suggestions distract the user when watching an exciting TV show.* Incoming suggestions for programs that start after the program currently being watched are stored and presented as soon as the user starts zapping through the channels or switches off the TV.

Figure 1: *PRC demonstrator.*

The PRC demonstrator shown in Figure 1 is implemented in Personal Java on a mobile platform running Microsoft Pocket PC. The device communicates wirelessly with a desktop PC that controls a TV. To enable the context awareness of the PRC, six sensors are built into the casing of the device with the following functionalities:

• Two light sensors, one on the front and one on the back of the device.
• One touch sensor made of two metal strips on the sides of the device.
• Two passive infrared motion sensors that are sensitive to the narrow spectral band of infrared light emitted by the human body.
• One microphone.

The data from the sensors is converted into context information, triggering the behavior described.

Evaluation

The purpose of the user evaluation in HomeLab was to gain an understanding of the user-perceived benefits of context-aware features and the relevance of context awareness for specific applications. The relevance of the context-aware features of the PRC was compared with the relevance of the same features on a mobile phone. In view of the explorative nature of the study, a semi-structured interview was chosen.

Each of the participants (seven men and seven women who were representative of potential users) was exposed to three problem situations (a, b and c) once for the PRC and once for a mobile phone. For each problem the participant had to indicate how often the problem occurs and how serious it is on a 7-point scale. The possible solution was then presented using sensor-based context awareness. Following this, the participants were asked to indicate the attractiveness of this solution on a 7-point scale.

As shown in Figure 2, in the case of PRC the context-aware features were felt to be significantly more attractive (Wilcoxon signed ranked test, for all three p<.03) than analogous features in the context of a mobile phone. Respondents explained that they considered missing a reminder as a more serious problem because the reminder had been set by the user himself. In the case of a telephone call there is always the possibility of calling back later.

This study indicates that sensor-based context awareness can present attractive solutions, in this

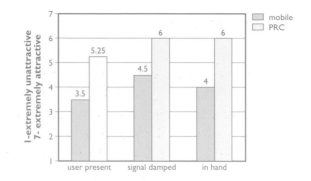

Figure 2: *Attractiveness of context-aware features for mobile phones and PRC.*

case for attracting the user's attention. Furthermore, the importance of an alert can be determined in part by the source, i.e. the user or someone else. This should be taken into account for future applications of context awareness to attract the user's attention.

References

1. Dey, A. K. (2000), *Providing Architectural Support for Building Context-Aware Applications,* Ph.D. thesis, College of Computing, Georgia Institute of Technology.

2. Erickson, Th. (2002), Some problems with the notion of context-aware computing, *Communications of the ACM* 45(2), 102-127.

3. Lieberman, H., and T. Selker (2000), Out of context: Computer systems that adapt to, and learn from, context, *IBM Systems Journal* 39(3&4), 617 - 632.

4. Swann, Ph. (2000), *TV dot Com: The Future of Interactive Television,* TV Books Inc. New York.

MediaBrowser
Gerard Hollemans • Vincent Buil • Sander van de Wijdeven • Jettie Hoonhout

MediaBrowser

Personal collections of entertainment media, such as photos, music, movies and home videos, are becoming digital. Because it is easier to collect more content when it is in digital form, collections tend to quickly increase in size. For example, digital photos cost virtually nothing and are easy to share. However, a large digital content collection may become difficult to access and manage. These days most of the digital content collections are stored on the computer. As the number of devices in the home with digital storage and connectivity rises, so digital content collections will start to be stored on these distributed media. There are a variety of CE appliances available on the market that enable consumers to enjoy content in an appropriate setting (the living room) by giving them access to the various storage devices in the home, particularly the PC [1,2]. Consumer devices are usually controlled from the living room using a remote control. In spite of its limitations, it is still the most attractive and cost-effective solution for this context.

Gerard Hollemans, Vincent Buil,
Sander van de Wijdeven, Jettie Hoonhout

The digital nature of the content makes it possible for photos, TV programs, DVDs, home videos and music to all be served from or via a single device in the living room. However, the consumer does not want to have to learn to use different interaction solutions to access different types of content. The aim of the MediaBrowser project was to conceptualize a single interaction solution that provides easy access to a growing digital content collection using a standard remote control and a TV screen.

Concept

The basic principle of the MediaBrowser, as the interaction solution that was devised is called, is that the user first selects content and then selects an action for that content, e.g. 'play', 'add to play list', etcetera. To select the content, the user nav-igates through the collection, which involves five stages, irrespective of the size of the collection. Going from stage to stage, the user can zoom in, arriving at the desired content item as described below.

- *The user selects the device on which the content is stored.* The user can omit this step if a single overview of all available content can be compiled from the different sources in the home network. However, even if an aggregated content overview is available, this step is still useful in some cases if the user knows where the content is (e.g. if he has just inserted some portable memory) and wants to go directly to that location.
- *The user selects the type of content he wants to use.* The type of content can be music, home video,

Browsing content in an easy and intuitive manner.

movies, photos, etc. What constitutes a separate type of content is determined by how the user uses content. A close approximation can be made by considering the metadata that defines the content. Home videos are largely defined by events (holiday), persons who appear in them (friends), location (France), and time (2003). Typical Hollywood movies are defined by their genre, actors, director, description, etcetera. Home videos and movies are therefore two different content types, even though both are 'video'.

- *The user selects the navigation method.* The user can select a different navigation method according to the activity he has in mind. If he just wants to reminisce, he may simply want to browse through the list of photos, but to show specific holiday pictures he may want to 'filter'. If the user filters content, he selects certain values for metadata fields, e.g. 'London' for location, or 'Jazz' for genre. The user can select more than one value for more than one metadata field. Based on these selections, the MediaBrowser will present content to the user that matches these criteria.

- *The user selects a content container from a list of containers.* All individual content items are stored in a container: music tracks in music albums, photos in photo albums, movie chapters in movies. Exactly which containers are listed depends, of course, on the criteria the user has selected.

- *The user selects one of the content items within the container.* All individual content items that are stored in a container (music tracks in music albums, photos in photo albums, movie chapters in movies) are listed for the user to select from.

MediaBrowser
Gerard Hollemans • Vincent Buil • Sander van de Wijdeven • Jettie Hoonhout

The MediaBrowser is operated using a standard remote control. On the screen the options of the current stage and the next stage are presented in two lists side by side on separate panels; see Figure 1. The user moves between stages using the left and right arrow keys. As the user moves through the stages, the panels move as well. For example, when the user moves to the next stage, the right-hand panel moves to the left, covering the left-hand panel and a new panel appears on the right. The options displayed in the left-hand panels can be selected or de-selected using the 'OK' button (which acts as a toggle). The bottom line of the screen contains several function labels accompanied by colored squares, which correspond to the color keys on the remote control. The functions presented can be activated using the color keys.

Evaluation

In the MediaBrowser the hierarchical tree structure, which is common for folders in PC operating systems, is not supported. Instead, a flat struc-

Figure 1: *The Easy Access MediaBrowser*

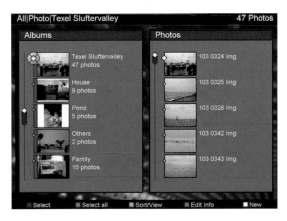

ture of containers (albums, movies) and items (songs, photos, chapters) is combined with a filtering mechanism. The conventional folder structure can become complex, inconsistent and hard to maintain. However, the advantage of a conventional folder structure is that users are familiar with it, whereas they are not familiar with the filtering mechanism. It was, therefore, decided to test the filtering mechanism against the conventional folder structure.

Two visually identical demonstrators were implemented, one with the filtering mechanism and one with the folder structure. Test participants were asked to bring their own photo collection and its folder structure was replicated in the demonstrator. Both demonstrators were used by all participants to perform a set of tasks tailored to the participant's collection.

Although it was manageable with the current size of their collection (from 900 to 1800 photos), participants realized that as collections increase at a rate of 1000 photos a year, the folder structure would soon become problematic and so they favored the filtering mechanism. They quickly learned to use filtering, usually taking only a single search task to master it, and liked the new ways of browsing the collection that this enabled, e.g. browsing by association. To make filtering work, it is required that the user links keywords to albums, rather than to individual photos. This effort considered acceptable by the participants.

Based on these user test results, we can conclude that consumers accepted the interaction solution, at least for browsing through photos. In subsequent formal and informal evaluations the concept as a whole was validated. Philips CE adopted the basic concept of the MediaBrowser for its products in the Connected Planet range. Although the filtering mechanism was initially not included, this planned extension is easy to realize from an interaction concept point of view as it was already part of the initial MediaBrowser concept. The final step required to get the full MediaBrowser onto the market is for the filtering mechanism to be adopted in CE products.

References
1. Microsoft Windows XP Media Center (online), (http://www.microsoft.com/windowsxp/mediacenter/default.mspx.
2. Philips Streamium (online), http://www.streamium.com/.

Touch Headphones

MP3 players enable people to enjoy listening to music when on the move. In order to give easy access to the playback controls many devices have a remote control in the wire between the player and the headphones. When on the move – walking, cycling or doing sports – the remote control can be reached to control the volume, switch tracks and start/stop playback. In our observation of others and ourselves we identified the following consumer insight; see also Figure 1:

Easy control of your music on the move.

Vincent Buil, Gerard Hollemans

If I'm listening to my MP3 player when I'm walking, cycling or doing other activities, it is always such a hassle to control the volume and other playback functions: the remote control gets tangled up in wires somewhere on or underneath my clothes, it is difficult to reach, and it's difficult to control and keep my eyes on the road at the same time. Wouldn't it be nice if there was an easy way to control my MP3 player when I am on the move, without all this hassle?

The aim of the Touch Headphones activity in the Easy Access project was to develop an interaction solution that (1) provides easy access to the main playback functions of an MP3 player when on the move, (2) avoids hassle with wires, clothing, etc., and (3) can be operated easily and conveniently without looking.

Concept

Hands-free headsets for mobile phones [1] and the emerging stereo Bluetooth headphones have controls for phone communication and music playback [2] incorporated onto the earpieces. This solves part of the problem because the user is no longer bothered by tangled wires and people's ears are usually easily accessible. However, there are a few more problems that will have to be solved if this solution is to become a success. These can be formulated as follows:

- The user cannot see his ears, so he has to find the right controls using proprioceptive and tactile senses only;
- There is little space on headphones for (multiple) controls, particularly in the case of in-ear headphones;

Figure 1: *An illustration of the use of an MP3 player*

- The inner ear is sensitive to pressure, which restricts the applicability of conventional button technologies for in-ear type headphones [3].

All of the problems listed above can be solved in one go by replacing the mechanical switches with capacitive touch sensors and several distinct touch sequences. Touch controls solve the issue of the operating force being passed through to the ear, while the use of touch sequences (i.e. tap, double tap, and hold) prevents the need for multiple mechanical controls for each earpiece.

Realization

The Touch Headphones have two touch sensors per earpiece; see Figure 2. The first sensor, placed near the speaker part, is used to detect whether the user is wearing the headphones. This is a known feature for headphones, as can be seen from [4]. The second sensor is placed on the outer part of the earpiece and functions as a button. The user operates this button by touching the earpiece with his finger.

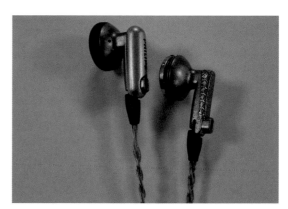

Figure 2: *Implementation of the touch headphones*

For each earpiece we have implemented three touch sequences that are well known from the standard mouse actions: tap, double tap, and hold (a prolonged touch on the earpiece). This provides access to a total of six functions, which we have mapped to the left and right earpiece according to frequency of use and the principle of 'right is more, and left is less' (based on the typical placement of volume and track controls on music players). This resulted in the function mapping shown in Table 1.

Table 1: *Mapping of touch sequences to playback functions*

Sequence	Left earpiece	Right earpiece
Single click	Pause	Play
Double click	Previous track	Next track
Hold	Volume down	Volume up

In addition to the explicit control commands, two implicit commands have been implemented. When the user takes off the headphones, this is detected by the sensors in the speaker part and playback is paused. In this way, the user does not miss any of the music and battery power is saved. Playback is resumed when the user puts the headphones back on.

The advantage of touch controls is that they require a very light operating force, which helps to avoid pressure on the ears when the earpieces are being operated. The drawback, however, is that touch controls can easily be activated inadvertently, for example when the user is holding the headphones in his hand or carrying them in his pocket. Traditionally, producers of portable devices provide a control lock switch, which disables the button controls when the device is being carried in a pocket. This control lock is often perceived as a barrier to quick access to the controls when the user starts to use the device and, furthermore, people often forget to put it on when they want to store the device. We have implemented an automatic control lock feature via intelligent interpretation of all four sensor signals over time. This feature disables the controls automatically when the user is not wearing one or both earpieces in the ears. It can discriminate robustly between when the user is holding the earpieces in his hand or has them in his pocket and when he is wearing them in his ears. The controls are only enabled again when the earpieces are inserted in the ears again. As a result, the user does not need to remember to switch the control lock on and off and yet any inadvertent playback from the MP3 player will be avoided.

Evaluation

Realization of the Touch Headphones has been carried out in an iterative process of evaluation with users. Since the start of this work in 2003, we have progressed via several intermediate steps.

Evaluation with users has resulted in various improvements to our prototypes, particularly in terms of reliability and usability. We have had to change the simple and cheap conductive touch technology to capacitive touch sensing due to the poor conductive qualities of earwax. We have adapted our pattern recognition for touch sequences, improved the automatic control lock feature and fine-tuned the general signal processing. Initial environment tests have been conducted to provide an indication of performance in various weather conditions.

We have conducted various usability evaluations, amongst others in emulated mobile use settings, where people were walking and operating the touch headphones at the same time. Furthermore, the touch headphones have been presented to and tried by large audiences at conferences, fairs and exhibitions, and were very well received. A field trial has been planned with full-size Bluetooth headphones that are currently under development.

References

1. Jabra BT200 wireless headset (online), http://www.jabra.com/JabraCMS/EM/EN/MainMenu/Products/WirelessHeadsets/JabraBT200/JabraBT200.

2. HP Stereo Bluetooth Headset (online), http://h10010.www1.hp.com/wwpc/nl/nl/ho/WF06c/A1-1693817-1694005-1694005-1694009-1694009-16023985.html.

3. Buil, V. and G. Hollemans (2005), Acceptable Operating Force for Buttons on In-Ear Type Headphones, *Proceedings of the IEEE 9th International Symposium on Wearable Computers (ISWC2005)*, pp. 186-189.

4. Dietz, P., and W. Yerazunis (2001) Real-Time Audio Buffering for Telephone Applications, *Proceedings of the 18th Annual ACM symposium on User Interface Software and Technology (UIST '01)*, November 2001, Orlando, Florida, pp. 193-194.

uWand – Universal Remote Control Wand for Pointing and Gestures

One of the most annoying problems in the home today is the complexity of the way we interact with technology. This is apparent, for example, from the fact that we are accumulating an increasing number of remote control units on our coffee tables. The advent of 'universal remote controls' promised to put an end to this, but only in return for greater complexity that is simply packaged in a single box. The remote control has now become a demanding system, requiring the user to switch between different modes, each corresponding to one of the controllable devices. And although there are now typically more than 50 buttons – sometimes crammed in at a density of seven per square inch – it is often not possible to avoid assigning multiple functions to a single button.

Pointing is an easy and natural way to control a wide range of applications.

Jan Kneissler

Figure 1: When aiming the uWand at a TV screen, a thumbnail mosaic menu opens and allows the user to make choices in a point & click fashion.

There is already great scope for improvement in the intuitiveness of the interaction with a single device. The classical example of VCR programming has now been transformed into the problem of scheduling recordings with current DVD/hard disc recorders: if you want to select one of tonight's programs just before you leave your home in the morning you will have to press the buttons 20 times or more! The purpose of the uWand project is to find a way to overcome these types of hurdles in our daily interaction with technology and to facilitate intuitive and universal ways of controlling devices.

User insights

The starting point is the elementary observation that human beings share a very basic style of communication in the form of gestures. Many hand gestures are easily and universally understood across all cultural contexts. A particularly salient and important example is pointing to objects: we

immediately fall back on this gesture if we do not know the word for something, e.g. when abroad, and small children are able to point to things they want even before they can speak.

It goes without saying, therefore, that a truly 'universal' remote control must make use of our large pool of intuitive gestures and also be able to recognize which device is the target of the current interaction. The result will be a single device, with just a few or perhaps no buttons at all, which can be used to point and control applications on displays according to point-and-click paradigm, as illustrated in Figure 1.

What's more, it can also be used to point at objects (e.g. your loudspeakers to change the volume), to

Figure 2: Demonstrator for clinical environment applications allowing direct interaction on multiple screens, volume control and 3D manipulation by intuitive gestures, drag and drop between screens and to a printer.

zap stations with a slight flick of the wrist, to turn on and off lights by 'shooting' at them, or even to drag and drop content between devices; see Figure 2. Such a universal pointing device will thus function as a virtual extension of your hand or index finger. It will allow you to operate appliances directly from a distance and will be a bit like a sorcerer's magic wand: an instrument that will enable you to exert power over the environment as if by will alone.

Technology

Naturally, one of our first tasks was to identify feasible technical solutions to enable direct pointing. There are already numerous approaches to object tracking in controlled environments which also allow determination of the direction in which a user is pointing. However, the required localization accuracy is quite high, even for moderate pointing accuracy, and, furthermore, the dependency on an expensive and often impractical permanent infrastructure excluded this approach from the start.

There are also relatively cheap technical solutions for hand-held relative pointing devices. A relative pointing device is, in effect, a wireless handheld mouse, i.e. relative movements of the hand are translated into x/y-coordinate changes of a mouse pointer displayed on a screen. The difference between this and the absolute pointing required by our concept is obvious: the system cannot know in which direction or at which device the user is pointing. Since the targeted point and the place at which the effect of the interaction is felt, i.e. the mouse pointer icon, do not coincide, a relative pointing device does not meet the direct manipulation requirement.

Figure 3: Accurate pointing control is made possible by a small directional component in integrated into the pointing device. The targeted objects are equipped with a reference marker (or two if 3D-mouse functionality is desired).

A crucial step in the process to create an absolute pointing device that is not dependent on an expensive localization infrastructure is therefore to find a sensor technology that allows absolute measurements made from the viewpoint of the user's hand, e.g. by a sensor or signal source which is located in the pointing device itself and whose intrinsic geometry is coupled to the physical axis of the pointing device, i.e. the assumed pointing direction; see Figure 3.

History

By investigating several technical options in parallel, we were able to present direct interaction by pointing in HomeLab in 2004. The content on an ultra-large display (the 'DreamScreen'; see Chapter 3.5) was selected by dragging it from a picture hanging on the wall onto the display. Visitors then followed the presenter into another room where – using the same device – the TV set was turned on by pointing towards it and music/TV/video content could be selected in a thumbnail mosaic view on the screen. To illustrate gesture-based control of continuous parameters, the luminosity of the Ambilight effects was changed by turning the pointing device around its axis like a volume knob.

The next step in pointing technology was then demonstrated in 2005, when interaction on multiple displays and drag-and-drop from the screen to physical objects (a waste-paper basket) was demonstrated. Pointing to loudspeakers was supported by visible feedback, and the volume could be adjusted.

Pointing control is certainly an excellent example for Sense and Simplicity, and was thus an integral part of the Simplicity event in September 2005 in Paris and other locations of the Next Simplicity campaign. The concept of an adaptive remote control (ARC) developed by Philips design envisions gestures as an essential part of future man-machine interaction using a wand that adapts automatically to the targeted device. At the annual convention of the Radiologist Society of North America (RSNA) in November 2005, a new medical user interface based on pointing technology was shown to medical experts. On the basis of an example of complete (but simulated) cardio-vascular intervention, we demonstrated the seamless interplay between pointing control and speech recognition that allows very efficient and easy interaction with all parts of the system. In the medical field the essential strength of pointing lies in the fact that it enables direct control on multiple screens and systems, making it unnecessary to have a number of different mice and remote controls.

The fact that our solutions for absolute pointing enabled intuitive interaction (zooming and rotation in addition to the usual 2D interaction) with 3D image data was particularly valued by doctors. In the questionnaire that was handed out at the Philips Research event the majority of visitors selected our demo – which was shown in combination with eye-tracking and touchless interaction for preparation of the case at the desktop – as 'the most innovative break through/idea/concept' presented on that evening. An additional user study at the end of 2005 in the Amsterdam medical center [1] indeed confirmed – by direct comparison – our assumption that users prefer direct pointing over relative hand-held mouse solutions.

Finally, in 2006 we were able to demonstrate a new technical approach to absolute pointing based on embedded hardware that allows very small form factors at a drastically reduced bill of materials. This opens up the road towards widespread implementation of direct pointing in many applications.

References
1. Coen Stefels (2006), UI *Wand and Gyromouse; Usability for Control of the Mobile Viewing Station in Sterile Environment*, Master Thesis, Delft University of Technology.

Emotion-sensing Chair

In the AmI vision we anticipate a world in which technology is integrated into the fabric of everyday life [1]. This presupposes the large-scale integration of electronic devices into our surroundings. The purpose of this is to make our surroundings smart and in this way to support us in our everyday life. The present-day availability of powerful, low-energy sensors with small dimensions enables us to embed sensor networks into furniture. In this study we investigate concepts for the design of a smart chair for the purpose of sensing biometrical information.

Martin Ouwerkerk, Frank Pasveer, Jim Oostveen

Concept

The aim of the *Emotion-sensing Chair* is to sense human physiological parameters, such as heart rate (ECG) or muscle strain (EMG) in a non-invasive manner. Small flat sensors on flex foil capture ECG and EMG signals by means of capacitive coupling. These sensors are placed behind the textile fabric of the upholstery of the chair. The flex foil capacitive sensors are therefore invisibly present in the back of the chair. As soon as a person sits down, sensing is activated and heart and muscle activity data can be extracted from the output. The high sensitivity of the sensors allows the measurement of the heart and muscle signals through both the textile of the chair and the clothing of the person.

Prototype

A prototype of the Emotion-sensing Chair was built using commercially available sensor equipment in a standard chair; see Figure 1. The chair contained sensors in the back and the bottom of the seat as well as in the armrests. A pad in the bottom was applied to ground the signals collected by the sensors. The sensor output was collected using standard computer equipment.

Applications

The idea is that this high sensitivity combined with smart noise reduction measures results in a high reliability in capturing the ECG and EMG signals. Moreover, additional digital signal processing can be used to obtain extra information. For instance, the onset of fatigue can be interpreted by analyzing muscle firing frequencies, or even emotional or mood changes can be derived from values such as the heart rate variability (HRV). The sensitivity of the HRV to emotional changes is obvious, but to ensure a correct and accurate interpretation requires careful study with users in a realistic context.

A promising application domain for the Emotion-sensing Chair is that of "Active Relaxation". By means of biofeedback, users can for instance be supported in achieving a more relaxed state. One project demonstrator uses the capability of the

Figure 1: Engineering the Emotion-sensing Chair.

chair to sense the heart rate of a person sitting in the chair and make the beating of the heart audible. Additionally, music is played with the same rhythm, as an alternative form of biofeedback. It is envisioned that slowly decreasing the tempo of the music can help people to relax both physically and mentally. With the project demonstrator in HomeLab, the effectiveness of explicit and implicit biofeedback, such as music, can be investigated.

Feasibility

Feasibility studies in a realistic environment, as provided by HomeLab, showed that apart from the electrical signals emanating from the person sitting in the chair a multitude of other signals are detected by the system. The most prominent is the 50 Hz signal caused by the mains power lines. These signals are actually impinged onto the human body of the person sitting in the sense chair from elsewhere in the room, causing the sensors to couple into them through capacitors. Notch filtering eliminates most of this noise problem.

A different problem that is much harder to tackle is interference from other people present in the same room. Motions of other persons causes charging effects in the person sitting in the chair, which in turn are picked up by the capacitive sensors. These strong signals are almost impossible to filter out, reducing the signal quality of the ECG and EMG signals severely. It also may happen that the induced charging effects due to peoples' motions turns the notch filters off sync, thus causing even more problems. Only when the static charge of moving persons and objects in the vicinity of the sense chair is reduced by counter-measures, such as ion showers, can this problem be solved. However, the latter can be regarded as unacceptable from a user point of view.

Lessons learned. The studies with the Emotion-sensing Chair showed that it was practicable to build a chair that could remotely sense biometrical information of an individual, such as his ECG and EMG. However, putting the chair into the real-life environment of HomeLab, where there are many interfering signals resulting from the presence of electronic equipment as well as other persons, buries the captured body signals in noise to a degree that they become immeasurable. This calls for the development of sophisticated noise reduction techniques. After this problem has been resolved, the question will remain how people will react to the feedback given by the chair and how they will use this information in their daily lives.

References
1. Aarts, E., R. Harwig, and M Schuurmans (2001), Ambient Intelligence, in: P. Denning (ed.). *The Invisible Future: The Seamless Integration Of Technology Into Everyday Life*, McGraw-Hill, New York.

Ambient Intelligent Lighting

Ambient Intelligent Lighting (AI-L) started in 2002 as a cooperation project between Philips Research and Philips Lighting. The project aimed to identify and demonstrate innovative applications of light in the home with a high added value from an end-user point of view. Many innovative product concepts, such as the Philips Senseo, build on 'soft' or 'emotional' user benefits rather than purely functional benefits. This indicates a shift from selling commodities to selling experiences; this is known as the experience economy [3]. Thus, the true added value is in the experience that technology can elicit, rather than in the technological functionality itself.

Elmo Diederiks, Jettie Hoonhout

User-centric innovation

The Ambient Intelligent Lighting project applied a user-centric innovation process. This process started with an ideation workshop based on contextual studies of how people live at home and on existing ideas for future lighting applications that were found in literature. This resulted in a large pool of ideas, ranging from light ambience recorders to adaptive light furniture. These ideas were then analyzed with input from trend studies, user studies and technology outlooks. The most promising ideas were worked out as short stories of envisioned real-life situations concerning people and their activities. These scenarios were used to obtain feedback on the ideas early in the product creation process, even before these ideas had actually been realized. Figure 1 shows an example of a scenario.

The scenarios were discussed with potential end users as well as technical and business experts. These evaluations already provided valuable insights, e.g. the fact that users are looking for new experiences, they want to relax at home, they always want to feel in control and new light solutions should be very easy to install. The sessions also gave rise to specific feedback on the different ideas.

The insights collected in the evaluation formed a basis for the selection of the best ideas. These were then implemented as experience demonstrators in HomeLab for further evaluation with users to help us determine the appeal of the concepts and to indicate further ways to improve the ideas. One of the winning concepts was *Living Light*.

Living Light

Living Light can be considered as the next step in the home cinema experience. It uses various light units to enhance the experience of watching film [1]. One could say that Living Light is aimed at people who normally just watch television, but once in a while want to take the time to watch a good movie in a cinema-like setting. They will switch off the

Ambient Intelligent Lighting
Elmo Diederiks • Jettie Hoonhout

Joey has invited his friends over to watch his latest DVD. When he fires up the Home Cinema system a dark purple glow amplifies the spooky atmosphere of the initial scenes. It is quite obvious that it is an SF thriller.

Suddenly they are startled when the light seems to fill the whole room. Luckily it was only lightning and not one of those alien body snatchers.

As the rumble of the thunder fades away, a green pulsating light coming from beneath the couch startles them: they can feel that the alien is near again. How scary!

Figure 1: *An example scenario.*

lights and get the popcorn out, but are not willing to redecorate their living room as a home theatre. Any additional features need to be integrated into their television or home-cinema set for them.

Living Light therefore uses light units that are built into the television and into the surround-sound speakers; see Figure 2. Furthermore, the lighting

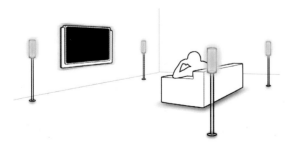

Figure 2: *The Living Light system.*

ambience and effects are directly linked to the on-screen content. The lighting ambience can safely be derived from the colors of the scene, since light and color are used in a scene to set the ambience as well. Special effects can also be easily derived from the video content, since explosions and lightning are almost always accompanied by fast and furious changes in light and color on the screen.

Evaluations

Evaluation with end users shows that the appeal of Living Light is quite high, especially in the case of film. The participants said that the addition of lighting effects made watching the movie fragments a very enjoyable experience. According to most participants it made them feel more involved. The light situated around the television set was particularly appealing: it seems to be the key factor in enhancing the content. Many participants also com-

mented that this light made the TV screen seem bigger. Finally, the participants indicated that the speakers should have a different function: a more general scene setting with only occasional special effects, in order not to be a source of distraction in the peripheral field of view [2].

The Living Light concept has resulted in the feature that later became known as Ambilight™ which was introduced in 2004 and can now be found in many of Philips' FlatTVs. Integrated into the back of the television, Ambilight provides a well-balanced amount of light that matches the scenes that are depicted on the screen. The viewer feels a part of the scene and the screen appears enlarged, giving rise to an authentic cinema atmosphere. Extensive market research has shown that, overall, more than 75% of respondents believe that Ambilight delivers a superior viewing experience and a recent Customer Satisfaction Survey revealed that around 90% of existing customers are satisfied with the Ambilight feature. Figure 3 gives an impression of an Ambilight TV.

It is not surprising that the Ambilight has been well received as a valuable innovation. The 37" 2005 LCD TV with Ambilight received an EISA award, was labeled "Best Buy'" by Home Cinema Magazine, declared "worth its price in gold" by T3 magazine, and embraced by Martin Scorsese as an experience enhancer for his films [4].

Light ambiences in the home

People also indicated that they would like to use this kind of light system without film to create a pleasant lighting ambience, for instance when they have friends over for drinks or for a nice family evening.

Figure 3: *An impression of an Ambilight TV.*

This was the starting point for further research in the area of *Light Ambiences in the Home*.

Light is considered to be a key factor for creating the right setting and ambience at home. In the evaluation of various ambience solutions it became clear that people like to have a good combination of functional and ambience light. They are interested in good light settings that are appropriate for the daily activities in their homes and would like to have presets to easily set the appropriate light ambience. These presets could thus very well be linked to common activities. On the other hand, light settings are very much a matter of personal taste and people would therefore like to have manual control in addition to the presets. It remained unclear, however, what level of control people would like to have and what aspects of the light they would want to be able to adjust.

Furthermore, people showed a clear difference in their need for functional light and ambience light with respect to color. Functional light is usually light that one 'sits in' and should therefore be predominantly white, perhaps with a hint of color. Ambience light, on the other hand, is usually light that one 'looks at' and can therefore be of much more saturated color, albeit with lower light intensities. All in all, these initial investigations in the area of lighting ambiences have provided some preliminary answers, but also indicated the need for a wide range of further studies.

References
1. Diederiks, E.M.A., and H.C.M. Hoonhout (2005), From picture quality to viewing experience. In: S. Wensveen, et al. (eds.), *Proceedings of the conference Designing Pleasurable Products and Interfaces (DPPI)*, October24-27, Eindhoven University of Technology, pp. 467-475.

2. Hoonhout, H.C.M., and P.C.J.G. Niessen (2005), *Living Light concept discussions: User assessment of LightSpeakers and Personalisation*, Philips Research, Eindhoven. Technical Note 2004/1140.

3. Pine, B.J. and J.H. Gillmore (1999), *The Experience Economy*, Harvard Business School Press, New York.

4. Press release August 17 2005, Philips Electronics India Limited, India (online), Philips Introduces Ambilight Technology, http://press.xtvworld.com/modules.php?name =News&file=article&sid=6245.

Living Light & Music

One of the cornerstones of the Ambient Intelligence vision is that consumers will increasingly be looking for more 'soft' or 'emotional' values in products and services. They will look for appealing and enjoyable experiences, over and above functional benefits. For example, consumers are looking for features in rendering devices that extend beyond the traditional, basic qualities, such as screen size, picture quality, and surround sound. Following this line, the Living Light concept was developed to further enhance the user experience of enjoying entertainment content, such as movies and music.

○ System Intelligence
○ User Evaluation

Ramon Clout, Patrick Niessen, Jettie Hoonhout,
Elmo Diederiks, Bram Kater

The mood of music

The Living Light concept has proven its value for film [2], and pilot studies in which users were presented with music combined with lighting effects have also shown that this could become an appealing proposition. However, for music it is important to realize that users commonly combine listening to music with other activities and that the lighting effects should not interfere with these activities. Dynamic effects in particular could easily be distracting and interfere in such circumstances. Static or very slowly changing lighting settings with colored light and with sufficient intensity might be more suitable. Given this general requirement, the next question is which lighting effects will nicely match with music of choice. To answer this question, a series of tests with users were conducted.

First studies confirmed that people would not appreciate disco-like effects in their living-room, but would prefer more subtle colors and lighting settings that reflect the 'mood of the music', or that would contribute to, or even enhance, the emo-tion expressed in the music. In follow-up studies with users, therefore, specific attention was paid to the relationship between music and the mood of a particular piece of music, and the color that would best reflect that mood or emotion. Initially, genre was considered as a potential basis for automatically creating appealing matches between songs and colored lighting settings. However, interviews with users revealed that genre is not likely to provide a reliable and consistent basis [1]. The respondents showed too much variability in their color preferences per genre. The reason for this appeared to be two-fold. First of all 'genre' is an ill-defined concept. People are likely to have different opinions about the content of a genre. These differences can also result in differences in the colors that are associated with a particular genre. Another reason is that genres consist of many different subgenres. Thus the variety of songs belonging to one genre could be too large to associate only one particular color with it. Based on this result a second experiment was conducted. For this second study, music features that were seen as important for the emo-

Living Light & Music
Ramon Clout • Patrick Niessen • Jettie Hoonhout • Elmo Diederiks • Bram Kater

tional characterization of a song were explored [1]. To start with, the possibilities of tempo and key were investigated. A literature study [1] indicated that both features were important for specifying a song's emotional character; more specifically, tempo and key are generally seen as important for specifying a song's degree of happiness and liveliness. And happiness and liveliness appeared to be labels often used by the participants in the first study to denote the emotional tone or characterization of a song.

Participants were asked to listen to 100 fragments of songs and indicate which color they thought went best with each fragment. Both tempo and key had a significant influence on people's color choices: slow tempo songs were associated with cold colors (purple, purple-blue, blue, blue-green, green), whereas up-tempo songs were associated with warm colors (yellow, yellow-orange, orange, orange-red and red). A clear distinction was also visible for key: songs written in a minor key were associated with cold colors, and songs written in a major key with warm colors. The strongest effects were found for the songs belonging to the up-tempo, major category and the slow tempo, minor category.

Color from music

Based on the results of these studies, an algorithm was implemented [3] that calculates a color for a song, given its tempo and key. The color is expressed in brightness, hue, and saturation. Hue refers to a particular color such as red or green. Saturation describes the purity of a color varying from intense colors (high saturation) to muted

or grey colors (low saturation). However, as the aforementioned studies showed no clear relation between the saturation and brightness of the color and these music features, only a suggestion for the hue is given. A pilot test conducted to measure the performance of the algorithm showed that, although the suggested hue often came close, the participant's preference was different [3].

Two other ways of relating music to light were explored, implemented, and tested. The first one was based on similarities on a physical level: both music and light can be represented as a combination of waves. Low-level wave properties of the audio signal were extracted to estimate the melody, volume and timbre of the music. These were then related to the hue, brightness and saturation of the light. As these properties change as the song progresses, the resulting light effects change in all three dimensions: brightness, hue, and saturation.

Figure 1: Living Light setup.

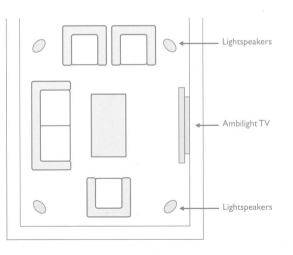

The second alternative was based on synaesthesia, a condition in which sensory input for one modality, such as hearing, is also projected onto a different modality, for example vision. The most common form of synaesthesia is audio input being projected onto the visual system, which resembled the conversion of music to light effects. The consistency between synaesthetes in pitch of the audio input and brightness of the perceived colors and the consistency in timbre and complexity were used in this second alternative. Hue, however, could not be specified in this way. The algorithms were customizable to increase or decrease the speed of lighting changes. This, combined with features from the music being measured over a longer period of time, resulted in light effects that were non-distractive as they changed slowly. In addition, output colors were represented in a perceptually linear color space. This allowed for smooth color transitions and contributed towards a subtly changing light atmosphere as opposed to the unwanted disco-like effects.

Evaluation with users

An experiment with users interested in listening to music was conducted in which people were asked to evaluate each of these three methods of generating light effects from audio features [3]. The experiment took place in a room in HomeLab with the Living Light setup depicted in Figure 1. In the room, four surrounding light speakers were positioned around the participant. A light speaker is a loudspeaker device with light units attached to it that are able to produce a wide range of different colors. The output of these light units could be varied using the three algorithms described above.

The participants were asked to customize the algorithms to create the most desirable light effects for a song of their choice. To do this they were presented with a user interface in which the following parameters could be varied: a preference hue, and the maximum change of brightness, hue and saturation over time. After that, the customized algorithm was applied to four pre-selected songs and the output result was evaluated by the participant. Participants were enthusiastic about the concept, especially as they saw it did not create the disco-like atmosphere they had expected. By customizing the algorithms participants were able to increase their appreciation of the output. The customized settings also performed well for the pre-selected songs, which could be attributable to the song-dependent input features.

Conclusion

The studies on the relation between light and music showed that combining music and light settings creates highly appealing experiences. Users appreciate a system that provides some initial suggestions for appropriate light settings to be combined with music; but they are also very keen on means to customize these settings, resulting in their own creative output.

References
1. Cruts, A., and H.C.M. Hoonhout (2003), *The color of music. Looking for a consistent association between music features and colors*, Technical Note TN2003/553, Philips Research, Eindhoven, The Netherlands.

2. Diederiks, E.M.A., and H.C.M. Hoonhout (2005), *From Picture Quality to Viewing Experience*, in: S. Wensveen (ed.), *Proceedings of Designing Pleasurable Products and Interfaces*, October 24-27, Eindhoven University of Technology, Eindhoven, The Netherlands, pp. 467-475.

3. Kater, B. (2005), *Music Based Light Effects*, M.Sc. thesis, Eindhoven University of Technology, Eindhoven, The Netherlands.

Gerard Harkin • Jettie Hoonhout

Light Atmospheres

Light Atmospheres

Back in 2003, Philips Lighting took the initiative to explore new markets where light could be used to create atmosphere. These new applications be based on meaningful light effects derived from insights about users. In addition, a major challenge was to develop appealing and easy-to-operate user interfaces that would enable people to interact easily with light in a variety of contexts [1]; see Figure 1. This challenge was selected for the Light Atmospheres project at CRE 2004. It was decided to contrast different user interface concepts and to show the demos in the main bedroom and the children's room of ExperienceLab.

New Applications
User Interaction

Figure 1: *The Relation between a person, a lighting system and light effect.*

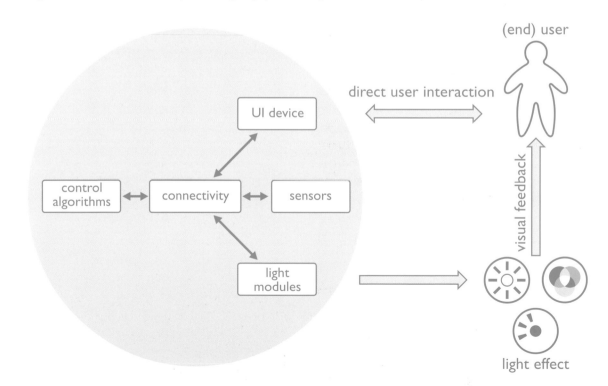

Gerard Harkin, Jettie Hoonhout

Light Atmospheres
Gerard Harkin • Jettie Hoonhout

Creating and Building Light Atmospheres

The approach adopted for the creation, construction and testing of demos for ambient lighting consisted of the following five steps:

1. *Determine and describe the intended experience in a design brief*

   Writing the design brief involved understanding the users of the demos and their different activities in the different rooms (e.g. main bedroom: waking up, romance), as well as their desired experience and expectations. The design brief also captured the spatial aspects, patterns of use and the leading light qualities.

2. *Identify the elements over which you have control*

   The following elements could be influenced:
   - Spatial articulation (room layouts in 3 dimensions)
   - Light scenes built with effects in space
   - User interface devices
   - Patterns of use/experience when demos are shown to users

3. *Determine how to create the intended experience*

   Spatial articulation: options for the floor plan, furniture, etc., were determined in an idea-generating session.

   Light scenes: a brainstorm session was held to define the light conditions for the different atmosphere impressions. Light scenes were described in terms of the following aspects: general lighting, accent and architectural lighting.

   User interface: a conventional touch-pad concept offering advanced functionality and two new playful concepts with modest functionality.

   Pattern of use: the room demos at CRE 2004 could host up to 10 persons and the tour was approximately 15 minutes. The demo in the main bedroom took people through a defined script (e.g. going to bed, waking up), while in the children's room people could play with the user interface concepts.

4. *Develop the concept into a working solution*

   Dozens of light sources were needed to create the atmosphere impressions in the main bedroom. Light sources were integrated into the bedframe, the ceiling and the furniture; see Figure 2. Consequently, there were many parameters to be controlled and this highlighted the future challenge for user interface devices. The light qualities of brightness, color, dynamics and direction were used. For the main bedroom, light scenes were pre-programmed per activity and users were able to select, modify and store light scenes via the portable touch screen.

   Three luminaires with color and brightness capabilities were used in the children's room. Here the activities were about play & fun and the user interface concepts enabled users to select pre-defined light scenes. One concept comprised colored marbles (with wireless RFID tags inside) and a bowl with an antenna; see Figure 3. When a marble was placed in the bowl, the light effects would change to the color of the marble. It was also possible to mix the colors of the light effects by combining different colored marbles in the bowl. The second concept for the children's room was a hand-sized cube; see Figure 4. The side facing up determines a pre-defined light effect via built-in wireless sensors that communicate with the lighting system.

5. *Evaluating the concepts: results*

   Tests with users were conducted in the children's bedroom of the Homelab. The purpose of the tests was to explore the user's response to colored lighting and to collect some initial information on their requirements in terms of the application of colored lighting in the home

Figure 2: *The main bedroom.*

Figure 3: *The marbles concept.*

Figure 4: *The cube concept.*

domain, as well as to obtain feedback on the user interfaces. The test was performed with 15 participants (8 women, 7 men) aged between 25 and 55. A detailed description of the test approach is given in [2]. The key results of the tests are presented below.

Colored lighting settings for the home

The concept of colored lighting for the home was generally well liked. The participants indicated that it offers interesting ways of creating appealing and appropriate atmospheres. However, for reading (and similar types of tasks) participants tended to prefer a whiter light, which was warm but quite bright. Generally speaking, there was not one color setting available in the test that all of the participants liked or disliked. The participants found some of the settings to be just right, too saturated, too bright, too dim, to be awful or to have a nice hue, or to be right for one type of task or situation, and completely wrong for other tasks. The participants thus differed in their preferences with regard to the various settings: a setting that was liked very much by one participant could be disliked by the next participant. This highlights the importance of personalizing the choice of settings.

In conclusion, colored lighting was felt to be appropriate for relaxing, chatting with friends and family, watching TV, listening to music and for parties. Colored lighting was considered to be less appropriate for tasks such as reading and cooking.

Marbles and Cube concept

The marbles and the cube concepts were generally well liked by the participants and these concepts were not only felt to be of interest to children. Both user interfaces were considered more appealing and attractive than conventional remote controls. Some participants stated that they already had too many remote controls lying around the house, and felt that these devices would make a nice change. Of course, many participants suggested changes to the design, e.g. replace the wooden bowl of marbles with a bowl made of another material, and of a different size or shape. However, the general opinion was that a conventional remote control is not something that one would be proud to have lying on the coffee table, whereas the marbles and the cube were seen as nice objects that would look good on a coffee table. In response to the question about what they saw as the benefits and drawbacks of the marbles, the key comments were: they are playful, fun to experiment with; however, it was not clear how one could dim the light – something that was felt to be an important function. Also, the whole device was expected to take up a relatively large amount of space on the table. In answer to the same question, but now with respect to the cube, the participants made the following comments: the cube is very easy to use, it provides immediate feedback on the options available, and it does not take up much space. Although the device does not allow colors to be mixed, the number of presets (5 in the case of the cube) provided was felt to be adequate, as long as the user could adapt these to suit his personal taste.

The two user interfaces did not yet have a dimming function incorporated. However, all participants wanted to have this function. Furthermore, several participants expressed concern about how to switch off the system. They were not satisfied with removing all the marbles from the bowl or turning the black face of the cube up to switch off the lights. That would be fine for switching the lights off temporarily, but there should also be a more secure way to switch off the system.

Conclusion

The response to colored light was generally positive in this test. Of course, the participants did only spend one hour in the test room and they were involved in a test situation rather than going about their own daily routines. Longer-term exposure to colored light settings and integration with daily activities are important issues that need to be investigated. In addition, the potential differences between user appreciation of fluorescent lamps

Light Atmospheres
Gerard Harkin • Jettie Hoonhout

and colored light generated by LEDs, for example, need to be investigated. Furthermore, with regard to the user interface part, there are many issues that require further research. There is one question that immediately comes to mind in connection with the two interfaces that were evaluated in this preliminary test: what would be the best way to enable users to create their own presets? Finally, all participants stated that it is very important to them that a new lighting system is easy to install. And when asked what aspects of the installation of new systems they would like to change, the participants invariably answered that they would like to get rid of wires as much as possible.

Acknowledgements
We greatly appreciate the very valuable contribution made to the project by T. Bergman, T. van den Broek, R. Cortenraad, E. Diederiks, J. van Kemenade, and M. de Kruiff.

References
1. Harkin, G., D. Seebode, and L. Scholten (2005), *Create and Build Atmosphere*, Philips Lighting internal publication, Eindhoven.
2. Cortenraad, H.M.R., A.H. Bergman, and H.C.M. Hoonhout (2005), *Tangible User Interfaces for Color Lighting Systems*, Philips Research Technical Note, TN 2005/44.

Exploring Light and Fragrance Combinations

Ambience Creation
User Evaluation

Light is an important 'atmosphere creator', but what about fragrance?

In today's world people want their homes to be a place that provides more than just shelter. "Their homes are their castles" and people spend much effort and money on making it their own special place. Although most of the time we are not consciously aware of it, two factors have a large impact on how we assess a place: lighting and odor. We feel at home because it smells good – 'like home'. And different lighting conditions could make us feel for example comfortable and relaxed or tense and uneasy. But even though lighting and scents are considered to be important atmosphere creators, little appears to be known about how these factors in combination affect an individual's experience of an environment. And even less data is available about the combined effect of *colored* lighting and fragrances. A literature review [1, 3] pointed out that neither ambient scent nor

(colored) light appears to have much effect on people's *mood*. But a couple of studies have demonstrated that fragrances and lighting, each on its own, can affect the environmental assessment of, say, shops.

Environmental *assessment* comprises in this case affective reactions (how does one appreciate or feel about the different environments), and descriptive reactions (does the space appear cleaner, larger, stifling, more spacious, etc.). Changing the appearance and the appreciation of a room by using lighting and scent could be an interesting option, not just for shops —other more or less public places could also benefit from this. Examples are hotel rooms, lobbies, waiting rooms, and of course people's homes. However, as we have said, the question is still open of how to apply these two elements together in order to create certain desired effects. We therefore conducted a series of studies in which we explored how combinations of scents and lighting settings could help to establish a more positive experience in a hotel room or bedroom context.

Elly Pelgrim, Jettie Hoonhout, Tatiana Lashina

Exploring Light and Fragrance Combinations

Elly Pelgrim • Jettie Hoonhout • Tatiana Lashina

Figure 1: *Refreshing lighting ambience.*

Figure 2: *Relaxing lighting ambience.*

Developing fragrance-light combinations

Two settings were chosen as themes; a refreshing (morning) setting and a relaxing (evening) setting. These settings were considered to be appropriate for a hotel room or bedroom environment. These themes were the starting point for designing 4 fragrances and 5 colored lighting settings [2]. The scents were created by a professional scent designer on the basis of an extensive design brief on both themes. For the design of the light settings, several light designers were consulted, again using the design brief.

The scents and lighting settings were separately evaluated in a pre-test in order to check their suitability. The participants (10 men, 10 women) were asked to judge the intensity, the pleasurability and the stimulating / relaxing association of the scents and the lighting settings. Based on the results of the pre-test, two scents (one refreshing and one relaxing) and two colored lighting ambiences (one refreshing and one relaxing were selected as stimuli for the main test; see Figures 1 and 2). The results showed that the selected scent stimuli only differed in terms of relaxing and stimulating associations, but were perceived as equally pleasant and intense, which was essential to avoid bias in the results of the main experiment.

Putting the fragrance-light combinations to the test

Conducting studies with ambient scents is rather complex: a number of problems have to be dealt with, such as scent neutralization and maintaining a constant scent concentration [1]. In order to control the scent dispersion issues as well as possible we used a specially designed scent dispersion device (see [2] for more details), and a ventilation device to remove the scents.

Apart from two congruent conditions (refreshing and relaxing), two incongruent conditions were tested in which a relaxing scent was combined with a refreshing lighting setting and vice versa. For the refreshing condition a citrus scent and yellow colored lighting were selected, while for the relaxing condition a musky scent (consisting of a mix of, among other things, lavender and cinnamon) and violet colored lighting were selected. Together with neutral conditions for both scent and colored light (i.e. no scent dispersed into the room and 'neutral' whitish lighting), this resulted in nine different conditions.

For the main test 90 participants (46 men, 44 women) were invited to come to HomeLab to participate in a test about appearances of hotel rooms. The participants were told that in this study the master bedroom in HomeLab represented a hotel room. Participants were assigned to one scent condition and successively experienced all three lighting conditions (refreshing, relaxing, neutral – in balanced order) within that scent condition. Having the participants experience all three scent conditions (refreshing, relaxing, neutral) would involve a time-consuming process of ventilating the room to remove the scents after each condition. So, in formal terms, lighting was measured by means of a within-subjects design, while scent was measured by means of a between-subjects design. To determine the participants' affective responses (e.g. pleasure, arousal, excitement and relaxation) and descriptive responses (e.g. spaciousness, innovativeness, luxurious appearance, tidiness, inviting impression, feeling at home and feeling comfortable), 7-point scales were used. At the start of each condition participants were asked to perform a short task to ensure that they could get accustomed to the environment before they started filling in the questionnaires. After each condition the participants were asked to leave the room for a short while so that the next lighting setting could be selected. The tests were concluded with an interview in which participants were asked about their preferences and associations.

Results

The results indeed showed that a combination of a scent with colored lighting produced more positive evaluations than a neutral or partly neutral condition, i.e., no scent with either a refreshing or a relaxing lighting setting, or a neutral lighting setting with one of the scents. It is important to note that some scent-lighting combinations received more positive responses than others. In particular, the yellow lighting-musky scent combination scored high on most scales – even though this was one of the incongruent combinations. Based on results reported in the literature, we had expected that incongruent combinations might score lower than congruent combinations. It is clear that the issue of congruency between lighting and scents needs further investigation.

Consistent with results reported in the literature, this study demonstrated that lighting positively affects the assessment of an environment. But in this case we demonstrated this for colored lighting: the colored lighting settings elicited more positive evaluations of the room than the neutral, white lighting. Interestingly, the room with the yellow lighting was experienced as being more pleasurable than the room with the violet lighting.

It is also remarkable that more significant effects were found for colored lighting than for scent – the colored lighting settings generally received more positive marks on the scales than the scent conditions. Even so, the room was evaluated more positively in both scented conditions than in the unscented condition. There were no differences between the two scents.

The interview results also contained some interesting outcomes. The majority of the participants (61%) reported that they would choose a hotel room with scents and colored lighting over a room including only one attribute or none. However, it appeared that people were more cautious in applying scents and colored lighting in their own bedroom, although 45% of the participants still reported that they would try it out when a system incorporating both factors became available.

The study described here only focused on the short-term effects of colored lighting and scent on the assessment of an environment. It would be interesting to investigate people's responses after prolonged exposure to combinations of lighting and scents. Berlyne [4] argues that when stimuli are new, the novelty of a stimulus is its dominant property. As a person becomes more familiar with the stimulus, other stimulus properties such as arousal potential and (perceived) complexity become more important. In his research into novelty and complexity Berlyne also found that increased familiarity with complex stimuli produces more positive responses, although increased familiarity with simple stimuli can result in boredom. This has of course implications for the design of lighting-scent combinations.

Conclusion

This study demonstrated that colored lighting and ambient scent can be used to alter people's impressions of locations such as bedrooms and hotel rooms, and make them appear as appealing places.

Exploring Light and Fragrance Combinations

Elly Pelgrim • Jettie Hoonhout • Tatiana Lashina

Acknowledgements

We would like to thank Benedicte van Houtert (Philips Lighting, now at ATOS-ORIGIN), Jan Engel (CQM and Philips Research), Antoine de Riedmatten, Christian Margot, Lyse Tranzeat, Wessel Jan Kos, and Yann le Gauffey (all Firmenich, Geneva), Wijnand Ijsselsteijn, and Yvonne de Kort (both Technical University Eindhoven) for their much-valued contribution to this project.

References

1. Pelgrim, P.H., H.C.M. Hoonhout, T.A. Lashina (2005), *Scent and its effect: a literature study on the effects of scent on mood and perception*, Technical Note TN2005/1000, Philips Research, Eindhoven, The Netherlands.

2. Pelgrim, P.H., H.C.M. Hoonhout, T.A. Lashina (2005), *Creating atmospheres: exploring the effects of fragrance and coloured lighting on environmental perception*, Technical Note TN 2005/1001, Philips Research, Eindhoven, The Netherlands.

3. Pelgrim, P.H., H.C.M. Hoonhout, T.A. Lashina, J. Engel, W.A. Ijsselsteijn, and Y.A.W. de Kort (2006), Creating atmospheres: the effects of ambient scent and coloured lighting on environmental assessment, *Proceedings of the Fifth Conference on Design and Emotion*, September 27-29 2006, Gothenburg, Sweden.

4. Berlyne, D. (1970), Novelty, complexity, and hedonic value, *Perception and Psychophysics* 8, 279-286.

New Applications
User Interaction

Human Factors in Matrix LED Illumination

Although most people usually do not give it much thought, our lives, basically our whole society would be very different without artificial light. Light allows us to make more of the day (or night, if you like), to perform tasks, which would otherwise be very difficult if not impossible to do. And generally the invention of artificial light ensures us a more comfortable and pleasant life. Of course, electrical lighting added even more comfort (and increased safety) to the concept of artificial light.

Developments in consumer and professional lighting have resulted in a shift from a focus on functional lighting, although still very important, to a desire to create a nice atmosphere [2]. Of course, creating an appealing atmosphere is not just about light, but it does play a very important role. New developments in technology – in lighting and in other domains (e.g. networking and sensor technology), combined with a growing interest in more personalized, and more imaginative lighting schemes (mood setting, creating atmospheres), now make it possible to actually play with diverse lighting settings.

A matrix of LEDs

Many situations in homes, shops and offices require good lighting but at the same time the creation of a nice atmosphere. And in order to realize such a nice atmosphere, it would be great if one could play with light colors, light patterns, and intensities – in short, if one could have a range of options to adapt the light settings and thus create an immersive experience. This is exactly what Matrix Illumination proposes: a pixelated illuminating device,

Jettie Hoonhout

which can be made in a range of sizes, capable of offering a wide variety of lighting settings to meet functional task lighting requirements, and atmosphere lighting desires; see Figure 1. The Matrix Illumination shown in Figure 1 is constructed with Light Emitting Diodes (LEDs) that are placed in a matrix array. The LEDs are grouped in pixels, each pixel consisting of a red, a green, a blue, and a white LED. The LEDs are combined with optics that collimates the light and driving electronics to make a flexible and adaptive pixilated illumination device. The device can be mounted above a table, or above a floor, with the light reflecting on the surface.

The illumination device can show temporal changing patters or statically lighting patters, e.g. to light out objects. For example, one can create the appearance of clouds drifting slowly over the table (see Figure 1.), or one can make coloured balls bounce from left to right over the surface, simulate a sunrise, or water drops falling on the table. And it can be equipped with e.g. a sensing and vision system to make it responsive to user input.

Figure 1: Indoor Matrix Illumination, with **left:** functional lighting for tasks such as reading, and at the **right:** a dynamic atmosphere pattern. The device shown here consists of 1280 LEDs, grouped in 320 pixels of 4 LEDs (red, green, blue and white), and arranged in 16 rows x 20 columns.

Evaluation with users

Since little is known about the effects of dynamic, colored lighting as produced by technologies such as LED based matrix illumination [1,2], we conducted a series of tests in HomeLab. In these tests, we exposed end-users to the Matrix Illumination addressing the following questions.

- How is the experience that can be created with the IMI (Indoor Matrix Illumination - the name used for the Matrix Illumination demonstrator) evaluated by consumers, i.e., quality, type of atmosphere, and task fit?
- How is the color rendering evaluated? The different (colored) lighting settings might alter the appearance of common objects, or of human skin.
- General feedback on this type of lighting application, and suggestions for possible applications.
- Given different tasks and activities, e.g., reading, writing, computer use, chatting, how are different (dynamic) settings appreciated?
- Are there effects of prolonged exposure to colored and dynamic settings on visual and mental fatigue measures?

These questions were addressed in two separate tests. In the first test, the first three questions were tackled; the remaining questions were addressed in the second test. In the first test, 28 participants (14 women and 14 men, aged between 22-60 years) were presented with 12 different settings (varying dynamics, colors, and patterns), and they were asked to evaluate these settings on a number of scales. In addition, they were asked to complete a number of other tasks; each test ended with a closing interview. In the second test, 42 participants (16 women, 26 men, aged between 21-60 yrs) were presented with one of three different dynamic settings. They were asked to engage in the following activities: reading, writing, laptop use, and reading again. The duration of each test was approximately 1.5 hours. The participants were asked to complete a range of tests, to determine visual fatigue and mental effort. Again, each test was concluded with a closing interview.

Evaluation results

Participants clearly had different opinions on the various settings: a setting liked by some, could be strongly disliked by others. But generally, cool-blue settings, and settings with large contrast differences over time (light bursts) were not appreciated much by most participants. Appreciation of settings was also dependant on the situation or context in which a setting would be applied. The color rendering was commonly judged to be poor, but this was seen as acceptable for certain settings. For example, many participants said that good color rendering would be less important in bars, or at parties: as long as people's skin would not look sickly, poor skin color rendering was not seen as problematic. Dynamic lighting settings were generally seen as inappropriate for tasks such as reading. The data showed that reading in these conditions did require more effort on the part of the participants, but no major visual fatigue issues were found. But again, fast dynamics in the settings, and large contrast differences were not liked.

Overall, the IMI was seen as a flexible, appealing application. Possible application domains that were mentioned by the participants ranged from offices, hospitals, bars, lounge bars, saunas, therapy settings, and restaurants to discotheques. It was by most seen as less suitable for the home. As arguments for this the following issues were mentioned: the device was considered to be too large for homes, one expected it to be too expensive, and one was concerned about the energy consumption. Many participants indicated that the IMI should preferably be built into the ceiling, to make it appear less as a very large object.

Lessons learned

The Indoor Matrix Illumination is seen as a flexible application, innovative, with interesting possibilities. People clearly see potential in colored lighting, and in flexible lighting devices. Of course, the appreciation is also dependant on the application domain, on the situation and on the tasks that have to be carried out. People seem to have a more reserved opinion about dynamic lighting effects – these are seen as suitable for a much more restricted number of applications and situations. The pacing of the dynamics, and the contrast differences in the effects are going to be important factors in this.

Given the large personal differences in the appreciation of settings, and dynamic patterns, it is clear that any device should provide a range of options, to allow people to choose their personal preference.

Acknowledgements
The IMI was developed by an enthusiastic team: Peter Duine, Roel van Woudenberg, Remco Breen, Lars Waumans, Jean-Paul Jacobs, Elena Vicario. Many other people at Lighting and Research provided their input and support.

References
1. Boyce, P.R. (2003), *Human Factors in Lighting*. London: Taylor and Francis.
2. Harkin, G., D. Seebode, and L. Scholten (2005), *Create and Build Atmosphere*, Philips Lighting, Eindhoven, Internal publication.
3. Hoonhout, J., J. van Kuijk, L. Bruninx-Poesen (2002), *Ambient Intelligent Lighting. Literature Survey*, Philips Research, Eindhoven, Technical Note 2002/180.

Photonic Textiles

One of the great challenges in the realization of the AmI vision is the development of technologies that enable the integration of electronics into textiles [1]. The integration of electronic lighting devices into textiles would be especially groundbreaking. At first glance, objects such as clothing, towels, upholstery, and drapes would seem unlikely places on which to place intelligent and interactive systems. Yet these low-tech objects figure prominently in our lives. By integrating flexible arrays of multi-colored light-emitting diodes (LEDs) into fabrics—and doing so without compromising the softness of the cloth—Philips Research has brought these inert objects to life.

A new technology

To meet the challenge of creating light-emitting cloth objects that retain their softness, we have developed an interconnected and drapable substrate made entirely of cloth. This is achieved by weaving diffuser optics and miniaturized driver electronics into textiles. On the highly flexible substrates we have placed passive matrices of compact RGB LED packages. Similarly, we have been able to create flexible and drapable substrates from plastics and films.

Figure 1 shows an example of a pixelated luminaire with a relatively large distance between the RGB pixels embedded in a cushion. Other examples of similar applications are backpacks and floor mats. Since the fabric material covering the miniature light sources naturally diffuses light, large pixels can be created from small LED light sources. The electronic components in the textile items thus remain small and unobtrusive, while the fabric retains its soft look and feel.

Martijn Krans

Interaction

Photonic textiles can also be made interactive by integrating other electronic devices into the textiles. We have achieved interactivity by incorporating sensors, such as orientation and pressure sensors, and communication devices, such as Bluetooth and GSM, into the fabric. In this way the textile object can be (wirelessly) connected to other electronic devices, allowing the exchange of information. Interactive light patterns can be generated for the purpose of sending messages or generating personalized ambiences.

Creating interaction between the textile devices and their surroundings makes possible a wealth of new electronic devices and applications in nomadic as well as static environments. It also opens the way for the development of novel services using light as a new interactive medium and it allows individual branding and self-expression for individuals, shop owners and enterprises. Below we present some of the first applications we have developed.

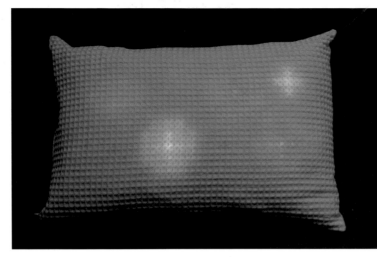

Figure 1: Lighting cushion.

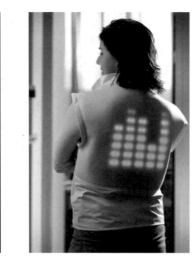

Figure 3: Body warmer made of electronic textiles.

Applications

Figure 2 shows a cushion and a cuddly toy that can both be used as a communication device. Scrolling text messages and full color animations sent from a mobile phone can be displayed on these soft textile items in, for example, the living room or the bedroom. This creates a soft and friendly atmosphere that can be made use of for the purpose of intimacy and comfort.

Figure 2: Lighting cushion and cuddly toy as communication device.

Figure 3 shows an example of a body warmer made of photonic textiles. The item can be worn as a normal jacket and is just as soft and comfortable. The addition of photonic textiles enables light signals to be displayed to the people in the vicinity for the purpose of security, identification or lifestyle expression.

Figure 4 shows a settee upholstered with photonic textiles. The back of the settee can display light patterns sent to the settee by an external source. The settee can detect if someone is sitting on it, thus allowing for interaction. The light patterns can be used to give the settee a specific color or brand flavor, depending on the position it occupies in a room.

Evaluation

We have received feedback on photonic textiles applications through a number of events.

User tests were conducted at HomeLab for the text-message cushion and cuddly toy. The body warmer and settee have collected feedback from attendees visiting fairs and shows where they have been displayed. People react very enthusiastically to the various applications. For most people this was their first encounter with light emitting textiles and therefore the show factor is quite high. For instance, they consider the cushion and the toys primarily as nice-to-have gadgets and thus do not have high functional expectations of the light properties. This is different for the body warmer and the settee. Both objects are regarded as items that can be used to show off and differentiate oneself from the general public to express oneself in a creative manner in order to display a certain lifestyle. For the settee we obtained similar reactions from shop owners, who see potential for using illuminated furniture to improve the shopping experience.

Conclusion

The results of these innovations are as various and promising as they are novel. Photonic textiles open up a wide range of applications in the fields of ambient lighting, communication, and personal health care. Photonic textiles are still a young business. Even at this early stage, however, Philips envisions partnerships with interior-decorating and apparel brands that see the potential of photonic textiles to revolutionize the very concept of fabric. Ultimate textile integration of electronic components requires the interconnecting substrate to be made only of fabrics. We are therefore developing a passive matrix substrate made entirely of woven textile. A woven structure made of non-conducting and conducting yarns has been created

Figure 4: *Settee upholstered with electronic textiles.*

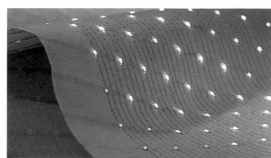

Figure 5: *Flexible LED array on woven textile substrate.*

on an automated loom, which is a first step in this direction. As an example, Figure 5 shows a piece of cloth in which RGB LEDs have been mounted directly on the textile substrate.

References
1. Reichl, H., C. Kalmayer, and T. Linz (2006), Electronic Textiles, in: E. Aarts and J. Encarnaçao (eds.), *True Visions: The Emergence of Ambient Intelligence,* Springer, Berlin, Germany, pp. 113-130.
2. Photonic Textiles (online), www.photonic-textiles.com.

Virtual Windows

Windows play an important role in people's lives. Windows in outer walls provide, for example, daylight in indoor spaces and allow us to stay connected to what is happening outside. It is well known that people generally dislike being in rooms without windows for longer periods of time. Nevertheless, such rooms are common, for example meeting rooms, offices, bathrooms and other spaces that are simply not adjacent to an outer wall. In other cases, a window to the outside may be present, but with a view that is very unattractive (for example a blind wall).

Daylight impression with the
virtual sunlight window.

Evert van Loenen, Willem Oosting, Ingrid Vogels,
Tatiana Lashina, Rick van Haasen, Corine Staats,
Onno van Tertholen, Aad Sempel

Virtual Windows
Evert van Loenen • Willem Oosting • Ingric Vogels • Corine Staats • Onno van Tertholen • Aad Sempel • Tatiana Lashina • Rick van Haasen

Until now artificial light or illumination has been mainly used as an enabler to see: making things visible to do your work, allowing you to read, making roads safer for nighttime traffic, etcetera. In addition, illumination within the home should provide a pleasant atmosphere and a feeling of friendliness. Novel lighting technologies have become available that are well suited for this purpose. Solid state LED technology makes possible small lamps that can easily be dimmed and can supply all colors. Furthermore, these lamps show excellent efficiency, reducing overall power consumption. Organic LED technology makes possible extremely thin lamps that emit light over large areas. In this way large-area lighting systems can be manufactured, such as a glowing floor, wall or ceiling. With new illumination systems being developed, a next step is to further enhance this atmosphere aspect to support people better.

Another drawback of today's lighting systems is the lack of flexibility. Even sunlight entering the house can only be controlled to a certain extent: closing the curtain simply reduces the light from outside but does not allow you full control of the atmosphere.

Concepts

To address the user needs as well as the limitations of today's lighting solutions, the concept of a Virtual Window has been developed. A virtual window is a system capable of creating a window experience in an otherwise windowless room. Note that the *Virtual Window* concept is complementary to the *Augmented Window* concept. The latter is an actual (transparent) window, capable of augment-ing or replacing the view, and therefore designed for spaces that do have windows. Both concepts are being studied in the DreamScreen project. An example of an Augmented Window is the Dream-Screen Intelligent Shop Window, described elsewhere in this book.

To better understand the requirements for a Virtual Window, a focus group study was performed to collect all the aspects that play a role in experiencing a window. Users indicated that the most important benefit of a window is the connection it provides to the outside world. Two key aspects of this connection are the view through the window, which mainly provides information on events happening outside, and the sunlight entering through the window, which provides light, but also a sense of time. Further important aspects are the heat or cold that is sensed when standing close to the window, the shadows cast by the sunlight behind objects in the room, reflections in the glass, and sounds that are transmitted through the window.

Prototypes

To explore which of these elements are most important for creating a window experience in a windowless room, two types of virtual window were designed: one that provides light with a surface area and brightness comparable to that of sunlight (by one of Philips Lighting's vision teams in cooperation with Philips Research), and one that uses a display to provide virtual views of the outside world. Both have been prototyped and implemented in the (windowless) kitchen of HomeLab [2]; see Figure 1.

The prototype *Virtual Sunlight Window* should enhance the feeling of being in a room while not being fully separated from the outside world. Several aspects support this: the amount of light should be large to mimic daytime. Furthermore the light must come from the side, as from a window, should have some directionality, as from a sunbeam, and may vary over time in intensity and/or color. To this end a prototype artificial window has been built in a window-look frame; a number of red, green and blue fluorescent tubes provide the light needed. As these tubes can be controlled individually, both the brightness and the color of the light can be adjusted over a wide range. The tubes are mounted behind a diffuser plate to prevent people looking directly into the lamps and to allow a smooth light patterning over the area, depending on the individual tube control setting. With the upper lamps emitting blue light and the lower lamps emitting yellow/greenish light, a simple "beach feeling" results. When more red tubes are switched on a "sunset" feeling is created. Within the window frame a lamp is added to produce a beam of light entering the room; the directed light and associated shadow mimic the sun. This lamp and its direction can move within the window frame from left to right to introduce a rough feeling of time. All lamps are programmable and controllable over time to produce a slowly changing atmosphere in the room. The controller contains a number of programmable presets like sunny day or sunset, but it might also be coupled to the daylight rhythm directly or be fully remotely controlled from your favorite holiday destination. Such a system might even be coupled to your TV as an additional Ambi-Light. For the *Virtual View Window*, a large (50") HD flat display is used. A simple image or video presentation would be a poor rep-

Figure 1: The two virtual windows in HomeLab.

resentation of a window view, since it lacks, among other things, brightness, depth, and it is invariant with respect to a user's head position. To create a more realistic window view experience, user studies were performed on the application of occlusion and motion parallax principles to generate a depth impression in 2D images. This will be described in more detail below. The results have been incorporated in the prototype window: the virtual view adapts to changes in a viewer's head position, as a real window view would. The two solutions rep-

resent the two key characteristics of a complete window view. To enable comparative user studies, they are mounted behind identical, real window frames, fitted with glass and sun shades. Feasibility and user studies are being set up to find an optimal solution for the creation of virtual window experiences.

User studies of the Virtual Sunlight Window

Initial experiments with people in windowless rooms with normal illumination where such an

artificial window has been added have resulted in a positive perception. The room is less dull and the light has a soothing effect, while in some cases the test person was not even aware of the fact that the window was artificial. This was particularly the case when the window was not directly visible, but could only be seen through Venetian blinds or curtains. Applications in hospitals are also envisaged, not only for patients but also for personnel, who are often faced with totally windowless rooms, such as small kitchens or cellars. Hotels and exhibition areas were indicated as other applications for such windows. As the window frame is transportable, it can be placed anywhere for optimal fit with existing furniture in the room, without the need for large holes in the wall or ceiling.

Additional functionality might be included by adding blue light for better stimulation of melatonin production to improve sleep/awake cycles for elderly people, as used in one of the applications presented in Chapter 3.41.

Depth perception cues for Virtual View Windows

When a virtual view is created using a 2D display or projection, it is immediately obvious that the view is not realistic because of the lack of depth in the image. A perception study was performed to investigate the efficacy of three monocular depth cues in arousing a window-like 'see-through experience' using projected photorealistic scenes [1]. The cues being investigated were: (1) motion parallax, simulated by transforming the relation between the window frame and the outside view, based on head movements, without transform-

Virtual Windows
Evert van Loenen • Willem Oosting • Ingrid Vogels • Tatiana Lashina • Rick van Haasen
Corine Staats • Onno van Tertholen • Aad Sempel

ing the relation between objects contained within the view; (2) occlusion, implemented by adding a cross-shaped window frame; and (3) blur applied at the boundaries of the window frame.

Participants were seated behind a table and looked at a projected photorealistic image while making slow lateral head movements, which were measured with a magnetic head tracker. When motion parallax was presented, the part of the image that was displayed depended on the participant's head movement and corresponded to the view that would be visible if the scenery was located behind a window. Hence, the visible part of the image shifted to the left when participants moved to the right. In a control experiment the optimal ratio between head movement and movement of the image was determined. For each of the six conditions (with or without motion parallax, with or without occlusion, and with or without blur), participants were instructed to evaluate the 'see-through experience' on a scale from weak to strong.

All three manipulations had a significant effect on the 'see-through experience'. Interestingly, the greatest effect was produced by motion parallax, even though the implementation was strongly simplified. Since the implementation is computationally inexpensive, in contrast to image-based rendering techniques, it creates the opportunity to develop a virtual window with any photorealistic static or moving scene. The experiment also revealed an interaction effect between motion parallax and occlusion, especially for the test image, where the occluding frame partially obstructed the view of objects of interest. Motion parallax alone

gives the illusion that a stable foreground is available through which an independent background can be viewed. Apparently, additional framing provides more evidence for the stability of the window frame in relation to the outside view.

In addition, an explorative user study was conducted to reveal the most important requirements of a virtual window. Users were given the opportunity to experience the Virtual View Window with still picture content, including automatic adaptation to head position. To most participants, this simple form of virtual window was not adequate for use as a view generation option. The presence of motion parallax had no influence on their level of appreciation, since many other requirements were not yet met. A focus group discussion revealed the most important functions of windows in daily life (providing light, explicit information gathering, ventilation, protection, atmosphere creation, communication, escaping from the average and orientation) and how successful this version of the Virtual View Window was in fulfilling these functions. The results are taken into account in further user studies being conducted to compare the Virtual Sunlight Window and the Virtual View Window concepts, and in the design of a Virtual Window that combines the most important aspects of both.

Conclusions

Feedback from potential users is quite positive for both types of virtual window, but people seem to have different preferences. Some consider the virtual sunlight window to be attractive, impressive and sometimes even relaxing. Others are

intrigued by the virtual view window. Somehow the simple video recording of a random street is sufficiently interesting. Perhaps it is just the right level of dynamics to create a sense of 'outside' in the background, or maybe it is simply nice to look at if one wants to unwind and clear one's mind.

The mixed feedback implies that further research needs to be conducted to get deeper insight into why people prefer either the virtual sunlight window or the virtual view window. This will also provide directions for future technology research on such topics as depth perception for virtual windows.

References

1. IJsselsteijn, W., W. Oosting, I. Vogels, Y. de Kort, and E. van Loenen (2006), Looking At or Looking In: Exploring Monocular Cues to Create a See-Through Experience with a Virtual Window, accepted for publication at the *PRESENCE 2006 Conference*, Cleveland, August 24-26.

2. Loenen, E. van, W. Oosting, I. Vogels, T. Lashina, R. van Haasen, C. Staats, O. van Tertholen, and A. Sempel (2006), DreamScreen: Virtual Windows, in: T. Lashina, J. Hoonhout, and E. Diederiks (eds.), *New Business through User Centric Innovation: A key role for Philips' ExperienceLab*, Philips Research Europe and Creada, Eindhoven, The Netherlands.

The Interactive Mirror

The Interactive Mirror project explores the scope of novel interactive applications and interaction solutions for mirror displays in the home context. It is based on the visionary scenarios that were created on the basis of the context-of-use analysis as well as socio-cultural and technology trends. The applications identified and the context of use set challenging requirements for innovative interaction with the mirror display and stimulated new patentable solutions. These interaction solutions were evaluated in HomeLab with end users in a controlled experiment that demonstrated a firm preference for 'touchless pointing' as the method of interaction with the mirror display.

New Applications

User Interaction

Concept rationale

The scope for interactive applications was explored with a focus on the end-user benefits, both functional and hedonic [1]. This exploration process included conducting ethnographic studies, end-user and expert interviews and ideation workshops.

Mirrors are generally used as functional and decorative elements in the home interior. Although there is quite some diversity with respect to where mirrors are installed in the house, in all cases the mirror is an integral part of the bathroom space. A recognized trend recently observed is that the bathroom is no longer a solely functional space for the purpose of personal hygiene. It is gradually becoming a center of care and comfort. One sign of this tendency is the increased number of private Jacuzzis and multi-spray showers with waterfalls. The amount of space allocated to the bathroom has also increased. The bathroom has gained a sophisticated interior, reflecting significant spend-

Tatiana Lashina, Joost Horsten

ing on the decorative materials and sanitary furniture. These tendencies are a reflection of the role taken on by the bathroom in our modern lifestyles, fuelled by our aspirations for body-and-mind balance and personal wellbeing, for example. Until recently, the bathroom was a little-explored context for innovative electronic technologies that offer new and appealing applications. These trends and observations led us to choose the bathroom as the context in which to explore new interactive possibilities for the mirror display.

An extensive context-of-use analysis conducted partly in people's homes delivered an overview of bathroom activities and the relevant needs. This information increased our understanding of important context variables relating to different consumer groups, activities, time of day, etcetera. The insights obtained were then verified with end users, high-end bathroom manufacturers, the beauty industry and technology experts. In this process the following directions were identified for further exploration: multitasking in the hectic morning rush, the ideal of environment integration and enchanting beauty care.

Multitasking in the hectic morning rush

You jump out of your warm bed when you are still half asleep, rush through your washing-shower-ing-shaving-styling routine, down your breakfast in no time at all and chase your children to hurry up and get ready for school in order to get everything done in time. A normal morning can easily become a nightmare.

How about a bathroom that reacts to your presence in the morning and triggers a gradual light transition simulating the sunrise that will gently trigger your natural awakening. As you approach the Interactive Mirror enabled with person identification it greets you personally and displays information services that are relevant to you. Later, you can check today's weather forecast whilst you brush your teeth to help you decide which outfit to wear. Alternatively, you can have a look at the traffic situation and, if necessary, think of a detour to avoid the traffic jams on your route to work.

The ideal of environment integration

Nowadays, to monitor health-related parameters like weight, blood pressure and body fat, we use dedicated devices for measuring the specific parameter. In order to interpret these measurements we often need to obtain additional knowledge or to seek advice from an expert.

A better approach to health monitoring is demonstrated in the HomeLab bathroom with the Weight

Figure 1: The *Weight Coach user interface on the Interactive Mirror.*

Coach application; see Figure 1. There are sensors embedded in the floor and ceiling that provide measurements, e.g. weight and height. The data is then analyzed automatically using recognized physiological models, interpreted and then presented on the mirror display in a form that is accessible to non-experts.

Enchanting beauty care

The Style Coach concept shown in Figure 2 is part of the beauty care track and is an example of a

service on the Interactive Mirror that satisfies the aspirations of a young fashion-conscious woman. It displays personalized information on the mirror, such as inspirational hair styles and make-up options that could be helpful when experimenting with one's own style. Consumers and beauty professionals considered the availability of relevant beauty-care information on the mirror to be a strong benefit of the Style Coach, since this application enables you to experiment with your looks straight away.

In addition, the Interactive Mirror can turn into a magnifying mirror in an instant and enlarge your virtual reflection to ensure you can see everything clearly. To facilitate hairstyling, it can even display the back view of the person standing in front of the mirror.

Interaction concept

After defining the applications, the next challenge was to come up with an interaction solution that would be intuitive and at the same time suitable for the mirror display. In our exploration of different possibilities, the scope was limited to technologies that could be integrated into the mirror itself to avoid using a separate input device. This choice was determined by considerations relating to user convenience and future commercial exploitation. When existing interaction solutions were considered, it was concluded that if any conventional direct-touch technology were used unsightly fingerprints on the mirror surface would make it less attractive. The bathroom context further reinforces this issue because users often get their hands wet or dirty here. The consideration of this context-of-use constraints triggered us to explore the follow-

The Interactive Mirror
Tatiana Lashina • Joost Horsten

Figure 2: *The Style Coach user interface on the Interactive Mirror*

ing two interaction solutions: 'interaction with the mirror frame' and 'touchless pointing'.

- *Interaction with the mirror frame.* Although fingerprints on the mirror are not desirable, touching the mirror frame is less of an issue, since it can be textured in such a way so that any fingerprints are invisible. In the mirror-frame interaction concept the frame is made touch sensitive, e.g. by means of a capacitive touch strip that detects the linear finger position along the frame, and the user interface visual feedback is provided on the mirror display close to the edges of the mirror. Using this style of interaction users can perform selection, activation and dragging tasks.

- *Touchless pointing.* In touchless pointing the finger is detected when it is close to the mirror. As the user points at the user interface hot spots for selection and activation, visual feedback signals to the user that the finger has been detected a

few seconds before actual physical contact with the mirror surface takes place. This is done, for example, by displaying a graphic image of a pressed-in button. This interaction style also enables the user to use a scrolling gesture to navigate a carousel menu, for instance.

Evaluation

A comparative experiment was conducted in the HomeLab to evaluate the two interaction solutions for the display mirror. Conventional touch-screen interaction was used as one of the experimental conditions to provide a reference point. The experiment evaluated the time taken to become acquainted with the method, performance, ease-of-use, usefulness and affect [2]. In the last phase of the experiment participants ranked all of these methods in their order of preference. There was a remarkable outcome here because although a conventional touch screen was experienced as the most easy-to-use method, 'touchless pointing' was clearly preferred for use with the mirror display, followed by the 'interaction with the mirror frame'. During the experiment it was observed that the majority of the participants spontaneously made a negative comment about the likelihood of leaving fingerprints on the mirror surface. When asked directly to rationalize their preferred interaction method, the majority of people mentioned the fingerprint issue and others indicated that they had an uncomfortable feeling when touching the mirror surface with their finger.

References

1. Hassenzahl, M. (2005), The quality of interactive products: hedonic needs, emotions and experience, chapter, in: Claude Ghaoui, *The Encyclopedia of Human Computer Interaction*, Idea Group Publishing, New York.
2. Keinonen, T. (1997), Expected usability and product preference, *Proceedings of Designing Interactive Systems DIS'97 International Conference*, Amsterdam, pp. 197-204.

The Fitness Coach

Objects frequently encountered at yard sales, or gathering dust in the attic are home fitness equipment. Apparently, many people try to improve their health by initiating regular exercising at home, yet they find it difficult to stay motivated and continue once absence of noticeable progress or boredom has eroded their initial enthusiasm. Factors causing this include lack of time, motivation, fun and confidence whether the exercise is done properly. Thus, a need exists for home fitness equipment that is more gratifying to stimulate the athlete to continue exercising. Consequently, we felt that using a virtual landscape through which athletes could maneuver would be more enticing and boost motivation. Additionally, we felt that providing athletes information about how well they were doing against their goals would raise their confidence, perceived control, competency and motivation, particularly when a virtual coach provided this information. Factors that we therefore aimed to evaluate in various experiments.

A virtual environment and coach can be motivating in fitnessing.

Marko de Jager, Joyce Westerink,
Michiel Roersma, Ronald Bonants, Jorg Vermeulen,
Jan van Herk, Yvonne de Kort, Wijnand IJsselsteijn

The Fitness Coach
Marko de Jager • Joyce Westerink • Michiel Roersma • Ronald Bonants • Jorg Vermeulen
Jan van Herk • Yvonne de Kort • Wijnand IJsselsteijn

Figure 1: *Composite photograph of the experimental set-up, with the stationary bicycle in front of the projected virtual landscape.*

Evaluating concepts

To test the feasibility and effectiveness of these ideas, we created a virtual cycling room in HomeLab. We focused on evaluating 1) the effect of a virtual landscape, 2) the impact of providing feedback on exercise intensity, and, specifically, 3) the influence of the characteristics of the virtual coach (gender and coaching style) on the athlete's motivation and the coach-athlete relationship. Two experiments were done: first, we investigated the main effects of the virtual coach and the virtual landscape [1,2]; second, we zoomed in on the effects of the virtual coach characteristics [3].

The basic experimental set-up was similar in both experiments; see Figure 1. A stationary exercise bike stood in front of a large screen (size: 160 cm wide, 110 cm high) on which we projected the virtual landscape and, if present, the virtual coach (in the upper right corner), while the participant was cycling. To direct the participant to a moderately intensive exercise, the coach provided feedback on exercise intensity based on heart rate measured

with a chest belt. None of the participants exercised frequently.

In the first experiment, we compared a detailed with an abstract virtual landscape and the presence with the absence of a virtual coach. The fairly detailed landscape was an interactive, computer-generated visualization of a person cycling through a landscape; see Figure 2. Interaction with this environment took place via the steer (for direction) and biking velocity. The abstract landscape was a bird's eye view of a racetrack, with a dot indicating the position of the biker; see Figure 3. Interaction with the environment was limited, since participants did not have to steer to stay on track, nor could they influence the velocity of the dot on the track (although most participants were not aware of this). The virtual coach was an avatar-like female that appeared briefly every minute to give feedback, based on measured heart-rate; see Figure 4. She would say that the heart rate was either 'too high', 'too low' or 'ok', and add an explicit instruction, e.g., 'cycle faster', to direct participants towards moderate exercise intensity. We measured intrinsic motivation [4] and average speed.

In the second experiment, we compared gender (male/female) and coaching style (autocratic/democratic) of the virtual coach, while participants cycled through the detailed virtual landscape. Now, the virtual coach was a photograph of a male or female coach projected on a separate screen to the right of the bike. The coach gave instructions by voice, again, to direct the participants towards a moderately intensive exercise. Yet now the instructions were phrased in either a democratic style,

Figure 2: *Impression of the detailed virtual landscape.*

Figure 3: *Impression of the abstract virtual landscape.*

Figure 4: *Impression of the virtual coach animation.*

e.g., 'Come on, you can do better, your pace is still rather slow for reaching your target' or an autocratic style, e.g., 'Your speed is too low, you must cycle faster'. We measured intrinsic motivation [4], extrinsic motivation [5], and the coach-athlete relationship [6].

Results and lessons learned
The first study showed that a more realistic virtual landscape heightens the fun the athlete is having, and thus improves motivation: participants reported more interest and enjoyment, more perceived competence and control, and – perhaps even more importantly – they cycled faster! Additionally, we found some effects of the virtual coach, but not quite what we expected: neither training intensity nor intrinsic motivation was higher with the coach. Her presence, however, lowered perceived pressure and tension – which is good – and perceived control. This last finding was somewhat striking since we expected the sense of 'being in control' to increase with feedback.

Perhaps receiving strict directions ('cycle faster') counteracted this effect. This was confirmed in the second experiment, which showed that coaching style influenced the athlete: with a democratic virtual coach, athletes feel a higher perceived control and a better relationship. We also found that, generally, male and female athletes reacted differently to the virtual coach: 1) male athletes find male coaches more useful, while female athletes find female coaches more useful, 2) male athletes feel more pressed to perform with either a democratic male coach or an autocratic female coach, while the reverse is true for female athletes, and 3) all athletes feel a better relationship with a democratic coach.

Conclusions
Both a virtual coach and a virtual landscape enhance the athlete's motivation in home fitnessing. The mechanisms, however, differ: the virtual environment strengthens intrinsic motivation, while virtual coaching mainly enhances extrinsic motivation. As in real life, personality and gender of the (virtual) coach have an effect, with athletes favoring a coach of the same gender and with a democratic style. It struck us that we could measure these effects already after a short exposure. Our future research will investigate the effects of virtual coaching characteristics in the long run, when we continue to disentangle these effects to make virtual cycling better than the real thing.

Acknowledgements
The authors kindly thank the AIM-team of Philips Digital Systems Lab, Eindhoven, for their Virtual Coach animations. The detailed virtual landscape was generated by TACX T1900 'i-magic' VR trainer software (Wassenaar, NL).

References
1. IJsselstein, W., Y. de Kort, R. Bonants, J. Westerink, J., and M. de Jager (2004), Virtual Cycling: Effects of Immersion and a Virtual Coach on Motivation and Presence in a Home Fitness Application, *Proceedings Virtual Reality Design and Evaluation Workshop*, January 22-23, University of Nottingham, UK.
2. IJsselsteijn, W., Y. de Kort, J. Westerink, M. de Jager, and R. Bonants (2004). Fun and sports: enhancing the home fitness experience, in: M. Rauterberg (ed.), *Proceedings of the Third International Conference on Educational Computing (ICEC 2004)*, September 1-3, Eindhoven, The Netherlands, Lecture Notes in Computer Science, Volume 3166, Springer Verlag, Berlin, pp. 46-56.
3. Westerink, J., M. de Jager, Y. de Kort, W. IJsselsteijn, R. Bonants, J. Vermeulen, J. van Herk, and M. Roersma, (2006), Raising Motivation in Home Fitnessing: Effects of a Virtual Landscape and a Virtual Coach with Various Coaching Styles, abstract, *The ISSP 11th World Congress of Sport Psychology*, Sydney, Australia, August 15-19, pp.
4. Intrinsic Motivation Inventory (online retrieved on 01-10-2003), http://www.psych.rochester.edu/SDT/measures/word/IMIfull.doc.
5. Self-regulation Questionnaire (online retrieved on 01-10-2003), http://www.psych.rochester.edu/SDT/measures/word/srqfull.doc.
6. Jowett, S., and N. Toumanis, (2004), The Coach - Athlete Relationship Questionnaire (CART - Q): Development and initial validation, *Scandinavian Journal of Medicine and Science in Sports*, 14, 245-257.

The iCat User-Interface Robot
Albert van Breemen • Bernt Meerbeek • Jettie Hoonhout • Peter Bingley
Boris de Ruyter • Privender Saini • Panos Markopoulos

The iCat User-Interface Robot

Interaction Technology
New Applications
New Market
User Interaction
User Evaluation

iCat, a user-interface robot with
social intelligence.

Albert van Breemen, Bernt Meerbeek,
Jettie Hoonhout, Peter Bingley, Boris de Ruyter,
Privender Saini, Panos Markopoulos.

Robots capable of expressing emotions are generally considered to be a new and promising paradigm in interfacing between the user and all kinds of systems. These novel interactive devices can be used in homes or offices to control the environment or to perform tasks such as managing incoming information streams and emails as a true personal assistant, or simply as a companion to household members. Most of these robots apply advanced interaction technologies such as vision and speech processing, which have reached an impressive level of sophistication over the years. But for robots to interact with users in a natural and appropriate way more is needed than speech and vision capabilities. It is generally believed that emotional expressions and appropriate personality characteristics are key elements of such natural interfaces. To investigate this hypotheses the iCat project was started, with the purpose of developing an open interactive robot platform with emotional feedback.

Early developments

The iCat project started with the development of a robot called Lino [4]; see Figure 1. Lino is a domestic companion that is able to navigate through HomeLab and interact with users in a socially acceptable manner. For this purpose it has been given an anthropomorphic head capable of showing facial expressions. Lino was Philips Research's first attempt to build a domestic companion that acts as a mediator between the physical and the digital world. The strengths of such a domestic companion has already been observed in demonstrations. When Lino shows a happy face users also react with a smile. This type of social interaction between a domestic companion and a user supports the interaction with all kinds of devices, and makes them easier and more enjoyable to use.

Figure 1: Lino.

The iCat concept

In order to further investigate social interaction aspects between users and a domestic companion with facial expressions a new research platform was needed that could be used as easily by roboticists as by psychologists. For this purpose the iCat [1], or interactive Cat, was developed, resulting in a first working prototype in early 2004; see Figure 2.

Figure 2: iCat, here as a game buddy for children.

iCat is a 38-cm-tall robotic character that is not mobile, so that research with the iCat can specifically focus on the robot-human interaction aspects. The robot's head is equipped with 13 standard radio control servos that control different parts of the face, such as the eyebrows, eyes, eyelids, mouth and head position. With this setup many different facial expressions can be generated that are needed to create an expressive, socially intelligent character; see Figure 3.

A camera fitted in its head is used for different computer vision capabilities, such as recognizing objects and faces. Each foot contains a microphone to record sounds, perform speech recognition and determine the direction of the sound source. A speaker is installed to play sounds (WAV and MIDI files) and speech. iCat is also connected to a home network to control domestic devices, e.g. lamps, a DVD recorder, TV, radio, and to obtain information from the Internet. Finally, touch sensors and multi-color LEDs are installed in the feet and ears to sense whether the user is touching the robot and to communicate further information encoded by colored light. For instance, iCat communicates to the user its mode of operation, such as sleeping, awake, busy, and listening, by means of different colors of the LEDs in its ears.

Psychology meets technology

Research with Lino has already shown that it is not the internally coded artificial intelligence that makes a domestic companion a success, but the way users perceive the level of intelligence. The new iCat prototype made it possible for work on technologies for increasing this so-called 'perceived intelligence' to be started and studies were initiated for the purpose of understanding in greater depth the social interaction between humans and robots. The core of these technologies is applying techniques from the field of animation to robots, which has led to the creation of domestic companion applications in which the personality of the companion is used as a way of improving the level of perceived intelligence.

Research indicates that these personalities raise expectations with the users regarding the behavior of these devices. The idea is that if the robot has some awareness of the most salient characteristics and traits of the other party this certainly helps in determining the most appropriate response and interaction style. So, to support interaction with iCat and enhance the notion of iCat being a robot person rather than a computer, iCat is provided with a personality. One of the key questions addressed in our research is what the ideal personality (or

The iCat User-Interface Robot

Albert van Breemen • Bernt Meerbeek • Jettie Hoonhout • Peter Bingley

Boris de Ruyter • Privender Saini • Pancs Markopoulos

personalities – since different applications and different users might require different personalities) would be for iCat.

Research community

When the first iCat prototype was made, many requests were received from both internal Philips Research groups and universities to have a copy of the iCat made available for their research. The iCat technology was therefore made available to other research groups and universities. The software was re-written into the Open Platform for Personal Robots (OPPR) software and manuals were created. To support an iCat Research Community a website [3] was launched with a discussion forum to initiate discussions and knowledge exchange among researchers. The first iCat Users Workshop was also organized in March 2006. In November 2005 the first iCat Research platforms were shipped to customers. This led to a high level of media attention and the iCat was labeled one of the 'Coolest Inventions of 2005' by Time Magazine. Currently, many universities are using the iCat for various research agendas, including care of the elderly, child care, truck driver companion, game buddy, diabetic coach, and many others. By making iCat available to universities, access is gained to knowledge that could not be generated by Philips Research alone.

Evaluations with users

Research with iCat at HomeLab has focused on the evaluation of application concepts for iCat, for example as a game buddy for children or as a robotic TV assistant that helps users find a TV programme that matches their interests. Questions that were addressed in these studies included: What personality do users prefer? What level of control do they prefer? The results of the user study with the iCat as a game buddy indicated that children liked playing games with the iCat much more than playing the same games on the computer. The participants were also able to recognize the differences in personalities between differently programmed versions of iCat. Overall, the more extravert and sociable iCat was preferred over a more "neutral" personality.

The results of the user study with iCat as a TV assistant [5] confirmed that young and middle-aged adults were also able to recognize the differences in personalities between different iCats.

Figure 3 iCat expressions.

Four prototypes were developed by combining two personalities and two levels of user control. In the high control condition, a speech-based command-and-control interaction style was used, while the interaction style in the low control condition consisted of speech-based system-initiative natural language dialogue.

Overall, the preferred combination was an extravert and friendly personality with low user control. One of the most interesting results found was that the personality of the robot influenced how much people feel in control. This finding is very relevant in the context of intelligent systems that work relatively autonomously to take over more and more tedious tasks from humans. It suggests that the robot's personality can be used as a means to increase the users' feeling of being in control.

This underlines that if even the smallest hint of human behavior is present, people tend to apply

Figure 2: *iCat, the friendly TV assistant.*

all human-human interaction rules and scripts to their interaction with computers and other devices [6]. To investigate this a separate study on the effects of social intelligence for robotic characters was conducted.

Social intelligence

There has recently been significant interest in social intelligence in the field of computational and robotic characters, but the benefits that such intelligence might provide have not been demonstrated or at least not been clearly identified [7]. One might therefore wonder what the effects of social intelligence in a robotic home dialogue system, such as iCat, actually are.

To this end, research was conducted to explore the apparent shortcoming of social intelligence in a user-interface robot. It comprised a Wizard of Oz experiment with iCat as a user interface for a DVD recorder and for an auction site. Two conditions were created: a socially intelligent condition and a socially neutral condition.

The robot was equipped with synthesized speech accompanied by lip synchronization. In the first condition iCat blinked its eyes throughout the session and displayed facial expressions and head movements. In this condition iCat would demonstrate socially intelligent behavior such as being empathetic. In the second condition iCat did not display any facial expressions and did not blink its eyes. It talked and used lip synchronization. It responded verbally only to explicit questions from the participant.

The results reported suggest that the implementation of socially intelligent behavior in a home dia-

logue system could elicit positive attitudes towards the technology embedded in the home environment. The study showed that a few socially intelligent behaviors in a robot are enough to remove a lot of the discomfort brought about when moving interactive systems into the background. While most research into social robotic characters has concentrated on the interaction with the robot, this study focused on the role of the user-interface robot itself. The robotic interface here served as a tool for effecting changes in the environment and accomplishing tasks. iCat acted as a user interface for the applications and thus interaction with iCat was not the participants' priority.

Despite its background function, iCat and the behaviors it displayed had a significant effect on the level of satisfaction with the embedded systems, acceptance of the technology, and sociability towards the system. This study opens an avenue for future research into the interaction between humans and Ambient Intelligence technology. The concept of social intelligence is important not just for direct interaction with robotic or even screen characters, but has relevance in systems that do not necessarily have a social function.

Outlook

Predictions indicate that domestic robots will be a huge market by 2015 [2]. While the current market has robots such as robotic toys and vacuum cleaners, new product categories will emerge. For instance, in the area of products for senior citizens an enormous market for robots will be created due to the rising cost of health care, manpower shortages and the aging population. When the func-

The iCat User-Interface Robot

Albert van Breemen • Bernt Meerbeek • Jettie Hoonhout • Peter Bingley

Boris de Ruyter • Privender Saini • Panos Markopoulos

tional basis of these robots has been mastered, a need for more socially behaving robot products will arise. The technology developed in the iCat project will make this social behavior possible.

Acknowledgements
We would like to thank Dennis Taapken, Peter Jacobs, Janneke Verhaegh, Jacques Terken and Ko Crucq for their valuable contributions to the iCat project.

References

1. van Breemen, A.J.N. (2006), Animation Engine for Believable Interactive User-Interface Robots, *IEEE/RSJ International Conference on Intelligent Robots and Systems (IROS2004)*, Sendai, 2004.

2. European Robotics Platform (EUROP) Strategic Research Agenda (online), May 2006, http://www.roboticsplatform.com/.

3. iCat Research Community Website (online), http://www.hitech-projects.com/icat.

4. Kröse, B.J.A., J.M. Porta, K. Crucq, A.J.N. van Breemen, M. Nuttin, and E. Demeester (2003), Lino, the user-interface robot, in: *Proceedings of the First European Symposium on Ambience Intelligence (EUSAI)*, Eindhoven, The Netherlands, November 2003.

5. Meerbeek, B., J. Hoonhout, P. Bingley, J. Terken. (2006), Investigating the relationship between the personality of a robotic TV assistant and the level of user control, In the *Proceedings of IEEE RO-MAN 06, The 15th International Symposium on Robot and Human Interactive Communication*.

6. Reeves, B., Nass, C. (1996), *The Media Equation: How people treat computers, television and new media like real people and places*. CSLI Publications and Cambridge University Press, Cambridge.

7. de Ruyter, B., P. Saini, P. Markopoulos, and A. van Breemen (2005), Assessing the effects of building social intelligence in a robotic interface for the home, *Interacting with computers*, 17, Elsevier, pp. 522 - 541.

Dimi, The Smart Companion

Philips Home Dialogue Systems is creating the technology for a product that simplifies the way in which consumers access the digital world. Having abandoned the idea that consumers must adapt to technology, Philips Home Dialogue Systems is developing a human-like interface which uses a physical embodiment that interacts with the consumer in a natural way through speech, vision and body language. The resulting Smart Companion is a new type of consumer product, the value proposition for which is based on three pillars.

The Smart Companion, called *Dimi*, is an extendable application platform that provides easy and intuitive ways to experience digital media, to send or receive messages, to access daily information or to control the home. It interacts with the user in a natural way by understanding spoken requests, giving replies, recognizing faces and by using body language with head movements, such as nodding and shaking, and colored light. It turns its head to follow the user as he moves around the room. Finally, the Smart Companion invokes an emotional bond with the user and exhibits a 'personality', thus truly becoming a companion that joins the user's experiences and assists him with daily activities; see Figure 1.

Intuitive Interaction
The purpose of the Smart Companion is to create a product that communicates just as humans do. To that end, the Smart Companion not only speaks, listens and looks at you attentively, it also nods and shakes its head. The result is that the Smart Companion enables us to use the technology by which we are surrounded in an easier, more natural and more intuitive way.

Functional Capabilities
The Smart Companion forms a bridge between the user and the technology in the home. Because the Smart Companion is such an effective intermediary, the user is able to focus on the experience rather than on the complex processes that make the experience happen. For example, if you wish to watch a movie, you need only say the name of the movie. Dimi will find the movie, turn on the television and start playing it. Dimi can even dim the lights and raise the temperature in the room. The number of ways in which the Smart Companion can be put to work is limited only by the human imagination.

By adding applications to the human-interaction platform, developers can shape Smart Companions to carry out countless tasks – from searching the Internet and providing language training to serving patients and the elderly in their homes.

Harry Angenent

Emotional Strength

The Smart Companion is not just a head: it has a heart. Being more or less anthropomorphic, Dimi is like an electronic member of the household, recognizing you when you walk into the room and learning your likes and dislikes. Our tests have shown that users of the Smart Companion begin to feel as if they are dealing with a friend [1]. As trust and ease grow, so interaction with Dimi – and therefore with the technology in the home through Dimi – becomes enjoyable and fun.

Figure 1: *Interacting with Dimi should be as easy as communicating with your friend.*

Evaluation

Obviously, iterative optimization of the three values mentioned and thorough user testing in a home environment are essential to unlock the full potential of the consumer proposition. Thorough testing of the product functionality by target users is already routinely standard in consumer electronics. Unlike most usual products, the Smart Companion requires far greater elaboration in terms of Intuitive Interaction and Emotional Strength in the

testing cycles. The Smart Companion technology is still not able to match human capabilities for understanding certain interaction contexts, and the compromises that have to be made in order to provide reliable and robust user interaction have yet to be optimized to make them as intuitive as possible [2]. Providing they are well designed, the motions of the head, the light patterns and the 'look and feel' of the embodiment are some of the main elements that contribute to the emotional bonding between the Smart Companion and the user. Because the Smart Companion is such a new device, a lot has still to be learned about what consumers like or dislike about the personality of a product. Ultimately, after extensive user testing, we will be able to master these sociological elements in the Smart Companion's values so we design a product that will be successful in the consumer market.

HomeLab has turned out to be very valuable in this optimization process. It provides the right ambience for test users to work with Dimi in a natural environment and the HomeLab's observation facilities have provided us with valuable feedback on the use. We have used HomeLab to demonstrate the Smart Companion to various audiences on a number of occasions. These results have helped considerably to optimize the Smart Companion and to bring the technology used in it up to the current level, at which it is ready to be implemented in the first consumer products.

Conclusion

Having started only four years ago with the idea that people need a physical character as an interaction point with which to communicate, we are now on the verge of introducing a new way of using and experiencing the technology surrounding us. Philips Home Dialogue Systems is currently working with a number of parties to implement this technology in the first consumer products. These will be launched onto the market in due course. We envision that Smart Companions will become a commodity in the home but, unlike television sets or DVD players, each product will be different in the way it looks and behaves. Each consumer can choose their preferred version of the Smart Companion yet all versions will benefit from a standardized platform which offers a wealth of applications.

References
1. Saini, P., et al (2005), The Effects of Social Intelligence in Home Dialogue Systems. *Proceedings of Interact 2005*, pp 510-521.
2. Os, E.A. den, L. Boves, S. Rossignol, L. ten Bosch, and L. Vuurpijl (2005), Conversational agent or direct manipulation in human-system interaction. *Speech Communication*, 47, pp. 194-207.

PartyDJ
Vincent Buil • Gerard Hollemans • Dennis Luijer • Aadjan van der Helm

PartyDJ

People listen to music together for many different purposes: to share the joy of a performance, to dance at a party, to get in the mood at a bar, or for example to explore each others favorites at a gathering with friends. People have different tastes in music though, which can make it hard to find music that is really liked by everyone. In a mixed group of people, the music selection often suffers from the 'Beatles effect': the selection is accepted by many – because it contains popular songs, but is liked by few – because of overexposure to these songs [1,2].

Intuitive Interaction Solutions
Ambience Creation
User Evaluation

Social settings

For younger people, it is not uncommon to bring their own music to the party. In this way, in theory, everyone could make sure that his music is played at the party, next to music of others. In practice however, often a few people take over the stereo and play their own favorites, frequently switching songs while the previous one wasn't even finished yet, resulting in the interrupted music experience illustrated in the left drawing of Figure 1.

The aim of the PartyDJ project, executed together with StudioLab at the Delft University of Technology, was to develop a solution to this problem. PartyDJ aims to offer a simple way to allow users to bring their own music to the table, while distributing each user's air-time fairly and generate a smooth music experience, as depicted in the right drawing of Figure 1.

Vincent Buil, Gerard Hollemans,
Dennis Luijer, Aadjan van der Helm

Figure 1: An undesired versus desired shared music listening experience.

PartyDJ
Vincent Buil • Gerard Hollemans • Dennis Luijer • Aadjan van der Helm

Concept

The PartyDJ system is a flat and squarish device that can be placed on top of your stereo, with multiple USB ports placed on a circle made up of LEDs; see Figure 2. Users can place their own USB stick or MP3 player in one of the ports to include their music in the shared music experience, generated on basis of the other USB devices present in the device. When the current song ends, the system will randomly select one of the inserted USB devices. This action is shown to the user by a circling light on top of the surface, like the ball on a roulette wheel. Alternatively, a user may press the centre dial to move to a new song. From the USB device at which the light ends an MP3 file is selected and gently cross-faded with the currently playing song.

Figure 2: *Artist impression of the PartyDJ device.*

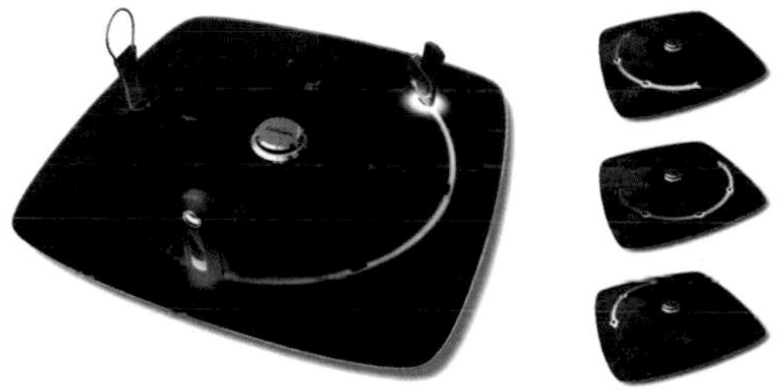

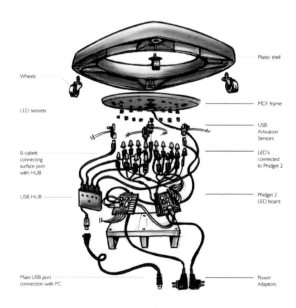

Depending on his desire, the owner of the product can decide to accept any type of music to be played via the PartyDJ device, or he can constrain the system to play music of a certain genre only. In this way he can maintain a certain atmosphere and avoid extreme transitions from for example heavy metal to Schlager music. The knob in the middle, which normally functions as a volume control, is then used to tune to a certain genre, much like tuning to the radio station of your preference.

Realization

A working version of the PartyDJ device has been prototyped with help of so-called PHIDGETS (hardware components) and MAX/MPS/Jitter [3,4]. Four USB ports and 16 LEDs were mounted on a piece of hardboard that, in turn, was mounted in an acrylic frame; see Figure 3.

The whole setup is connected to a PC that runs the music control software to read the ports and control the LEDs, and playback the selected MP3 songs. The system is designed to be placed on top of and to be connected with a standalone stereo system with speakers.

Figure 3: *Exploded view of the PartyDJ prototype.*

Wheels

LED sockets

B-cables connecting surface port with HUB

USB HUB

Main USB port connection with PC

Plastic shell

MDF frame

USB Activation Sensors

LED's connected to Phidget 2

Phidget 2 LED board

Power Adaptors

Evaluation

Random music selection has been marketed very successfully by Apple, with the iPod Shuffle that is marketed with slogans like "Enjoy uncertainty", "Life is random", and "Choose to lose control". The iPod Shuffle is loved for it, and for its simplicity [5]. In this context, we hoped that PartyDJ will be well received, as it drives on similar properties. Note that the principle behind PartyDJ – random selection between users' music collections – was already conceived in 1999.

So far the PartyDJ prototype has been exposed to users during iterative development in an office space with students, and during a Christmas party in HomeLab, as shown in Figure 4. The idea of PartyDJ was well received, although it suffered from a few technical limitations. For example, users could not yet plug in their own MP3 sticks, while also smooth cross fading between the songs was not yet implemented. Currently, the prototype is developed further in preparation of further evaluation with users.

With respect to the provided solution, many questions are still open: what level of control do users want over the selection process, and how much should the system do to control song transitions? For example, the LikeMusic algorithm [6] could be used to select a next song similar in sound to the currently playing song, but not necessarily of the same genre. Also other algorithms are available within Philips Research which could improve the overall multi-user listening experience. These questions are to be answered in future iterations and evaluations of the PartyDJ concept.

Figure 4: *Still shots of the PartyDJ prototype at the HomeLab Christmas party.*

References

1. North, H.C. and D.J. Hargreaves (1997), Experimental aesthetics and everyday music listening. In: North, H.C. and D.J. Hargreaves (Eds.), *The Social Psychology of Music*, Oxford University Press Inc., New York, pp. 84-92.

2. Peretz, I., Gaudreau, D., & Bonnel, A.-M. (1998), Exposure effects on music preference and recognition. *Memory and Cognition*, 26(5), pp. 884-902.

3. PHIDGET (online), http://www.phidgets.com.

4. MAX/MSP 4.5 Jittter 1.5.2, and Cycling 74 (online), http://www.cycling74.com.

5. Hill, D. (online), The rise and rise of shuffle, http://www.cityofsound.com/blog/2005/01/the_rise_and_ri.html

6. Picciotto, N. (online), Solutions to A Millennium of Inventions, http://www.derf.net/inventions/solutions.html.

Multimedia Applications and Content Services

Advances in digital networking, processing and storage technologies are contributing to an enormous and steadily increasing availability of multimedia content. Despite massive investment in digital multimedia technologies, the average user is still less able to interact with and manage large multimedia collections than to handle other types of documents, such as text. This is mainly due to the temporal and multi-modal nature of multimedia and the large size of the associated medium.

System intelligence
New Applications

Mauro Barbieri, Hans Weda

The *MACS* (Multimedia Applications and Content Services) project aims to create next-generation multimedia applications and services that will allow users to effortlessly summarize and combine multiple types of media to give them enhanced experiences and convenient content management.

User insights

In spite of the abundance of content, consumers do not have any more free time to enjoy it. Users are faced with the emerging problems of filtering and selecting what to consume from the dozens of options available. On the other hand, content providers are struggling to capture and maintain the customers' attention to promote their digital entertainment products. Our survival and excellence inside this world of media overload is guaranteed only if we are able to *abstract* and *summarize* the meaningful information from a sea of data.

Improving efficiency can be considered one of the main drivers for technological progress. *Automatic summarization* aims to create efficient representations of multimedia to facilitate browsing, retrieval and, more generically, management of content. Automatically generated summaries can support users when they are navigating large archives and can help them to take decisions more efficiently about selecting, consuming, sharing or deleting content [1].

Summarization

Content analysis techniques comprise algorithms from image processing, pattern recognition and artificial intelligence that aim to create automatically annotations of multimedia content. Such annotations vary from low-level signal-related properties, such as color and texture, to higher-level information, such as the presence and location of faces. By integrating low-level features with textual metadata, such as speech transcripts, movie scripts and manual annotations, algorithms can be developed that achieve a higher-level understanding of the multimedia content. Based on them, we develop automatic summarization algorithms that represent the core components of innovative services and applications. Presentation of results and user interaction with the system are

More of this

Mauro Barbieri • Hans Weda

Multimedia Applications and Content Services

of key importance. In the MACS project we follow a user-centered design to define and validate new concepts for content-based services and applications. HomeLab is a very useful facility for evaluating new concepts and test prototypes.

Traditional content analysis aims to achieve automatic understanding of multimedia content by extracting various features from the visual (color, texture, shape, motion) and audio (energy, frequency spectrum, etc.) domains. Using low-level features, content analysis algorithms try to imitate the human brain by recognizing concepts such as faces, objects, silence, music, etc. However, it is not possible to achieve a complete understanding of multimedia semantics using traditional content analysis. The current algorithms can, in fact, recognize only a small set of semantic concepts with limited precision. Automatic summarization and other applications based on video understanding are therefore limited by what artificial intelligence can achieve.

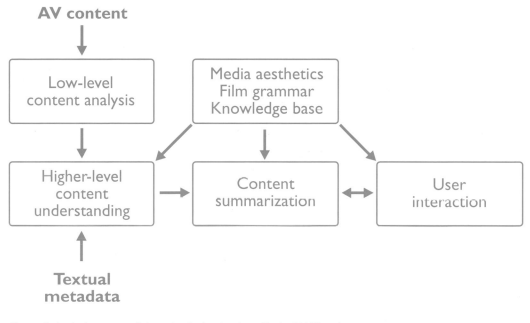

Figure 1: *Logical structure of the technologies developed in the MACS project.*

A novel approach

In the MACS project we want to show that the application of knowledge of media production rules and aesthetics, such as *film grammars,* can greatly enhance automatic multimedia understanding and summarization. Figure 1 shows an overview and the logical structure of the technologies that are being researched and developed in the MACS project. Our hypothesis is based on the assumption that, in professionally created video, filming techniques and editing operations play a fundamental role in shaping the message conveyed. Professional video production uses cer-

tain common conventions often referred to as *film grammar* [2,3]. For example, to convey the message that two persons are involved in a dialogue, it is common practice to use close-up shots of the two persons alternated with medium shots showing the two persons together in the same location. Other conventions relate, for example, to the use of camera angles or the selection of certain sounds and music to manipulate the audience's mood. In line with the objectives of HomeLab, research into these and other mechanisms that influence the user-media interaction enables the design of better applications [4].

Applications

Based on the logical components depicted in Figure 1, the MACS project is developing new applications and services around automatic summarization.

For commercial content, we have developed *movie-in-a-minute* [5]: a summarization method that generates a short video preview composed of automatically selected portions of a video recording. It is designed to help users choose what to watch by conveying key aspects of a program and its story in an efficient and entertaining manner.

This summarization application has been evaluated with end users. The aim of this evaluation was to compare different methods of generating movie-in-a-minute of a digital film. The participants were asked to compare two different movie-in-a-minute of the same film and to indicate their preference. Since movie-in-a-minute is an application that is typically used in a home environment, the test was conducted in HomeLab; see Figure 2. This gave participants the feeling of a home atmosphere and their behavior was more natural.

The concept is being extended to sports programs (*sport-in-a-minute*). The goal is to automatically create a summary of the highlights of a sports event. For this application, the research challenge is to find clever user-interaction solutions that can compensate for the current limitations of content-understanding algorithms. Usability aspects therefore play a crucial role in the project and HomeLab thus represents a key facility for this type of research.

With the rapid proliferation of digital video camcorders and digital still cameras with video recording capabilities, more and more consumers are becoming involved in video production and editing. It is no longer just amateur video enthusiasts who are recording their experiences and documenting their lives, virtually everybody is doing so – even people with no prior experience of video production and editing. They create a huge amount of personal content which is, unfortunately, stored and never touched again. The main reason for this is that unedited raw material is too long and boring or lacks visual appeal. Users rarely find the time or have the skills to use lean-forward video editing tools on PCs, which are tedious, difficult and too time-consuming. Nevertheless, there are many home video users who would like to make their video appear like a professional production before they share it with family and friends. It is for this type of self-created content that we are developing a new application called *edit while watching*; see Figure 3. It allows the user to create and change an automatically created summary of a home video in an easy, intuitive and lean-back way.

In addition, we are investigating efficient representations of content collections such as photo albums. Users accumulate huge collections of content items and summaries of single items are not sufficient to enable them to organize them more effectively. The next step is the so-called *meta-summarization*, which consists of the combination of multiple sources and the translation from one medium to another to provide useful information about the collection quickly and efficiently and in a personalized way. For example, text retrieved from an Internet website can be translated into synthetic voice that can then be mixed with a slide show of related images retrieved from an Internet service in an automatic way.

Conclusion

The key to automatic summarization is still to abstract multimedia narrative content while at the same time preserving the logical plot and narrative line. This would allow, for example, the creation of *readers' digest summaries* or abridged versions of

Figure 2: *HomeLab experimental set-up for user evaluation of movie-in-a-minute.*

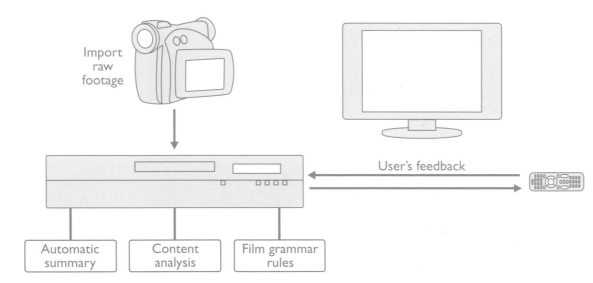

Mauro Barbieri • Hans Weda

Multimedia Applications and Content Services

Figure 3: *overview of usage of the edit while watching system.*

References

1. Barbieri, M., L. Agnihotri, and N. Dimitrova (2003), Video Summarization: Methods and Landscape, *Proceedings of SPIE International Conference on Internet Multimedia Management Systems IV (ITCom 2003)*, September 7-11, Orlando, USA, pp. 1-13.

2. Mascelli, J.V. (1965), *The Five C's of Cinematography – Motion Pictures Filming Techniques*, Silman-James Press, Los Angeles, USA.

3. Phillips, W.H. (1999), *Film – An Introduction*, Bedford St. Martin's, USA.

4. Reeves, B. and C. Nass (1996), *The Media Equation*, Cambridge University Press, New York.

5. Barbieri, M., H. Weda, and N. Dimitrova (2006), Browsing video recordings using Movie-in-a-minute, *Proceedings of the IEEE International Conference on Consumer Electronics (ICCE 2006)*, January 7-11, Las Vegas, USA, pp. 301-302.

a narrative multimedia content item that can be consumed more efficiently than the original without any significant loss of information. To achieve this objective, in the MACS project we are investigating how to exploit effectively multiple sources of textual information associated with the multimedia content (e.g. manually entered annotations, movie transcripts, movie scripts) and how to fuse them with the metadata that is extracted automatically from the AV signals.

Another key aspect that is vital for the success of novel content-based services and applications is *personalization*. Multimedia summarization-based applications and services need to be tailored to the specific needs and preferences of each individual user. Services and applications should be customizable in content, functionality, interaction and presentations styles. In its future work, the MACS project will investigate the above-mentioned different aspects of personalization and the impact of these as perceived by end users.

Personal Content Management Made Easy

With the proliferation of digital capturing devices, users will need intuitive and integral solutions to deal with the ever-growing amount of digital personal content they create. Creating photos and videos has always been a very important means for modern consumers to capture their experiences, share them with family and friends and express their creativity. On the one hand, in the past the physical nature of photos on paper allowed users to deal with these photos intuitively due to a high degree of familiarity with paper as a medium. On the other hand, digitalization offers a host of new possibilities for dealing with photos and videos, such as easy and fast capturing, automatically annotating content items with relevant metadata and browsing through hundreds or even thousands of content items.

Freddy Snijder

A solution combining the best of both worlds is required that deals with the loss of intuitiveness of handling personal content in the digital domain. Such a solution should not simply focus on making one aspect of personal content management easy, such as showing photos to others. It must be an integral solution, allowing users to deal intuitively with the personal content at every step in its life cycle: from creating photos and videos, to uploading, annotating, organizing and archiving this content, to browsing, showing and sharing it; see Figure 1.

Media-Bubbles: a new device class

A Media-Bubble is a new class of devices that aim to provide the user with such a solution. Every Media-Bubble implements a basic set of personal content management functions, allowing the user to deal intuitively with his or her entire personal content life cycle. Any device could become Media-Bubble-compliant by implementing these functions. In a Media-Bubble-compliant world users can intuitively perform the same type of personal content management tasks on any device, which is able to interoperate with other devices to help accomplish the user's task.

The Media-Bubble personal content management functions leverage the technological trends towards seamlessly interconnected and context-aware mobile devices. In the near future consumer electronics devices will have more processing power and will integrate more functions such as wireless networking and methods of detecting device context [1,2].

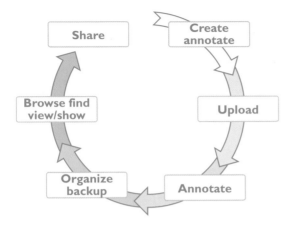

Figure 1: *An overview of important steps in the personal content life cycle. At the beginning of the cycle the user creates personal content; while this is being done annotations can also be added. Annotations are very important for helping the user organize and find content. A user must be able to upload created content to his/her home network; at home more annotations can be added. To enable users to locate content more easily they need to be able to organize content between multiple devices in the network. To protect their experiences, users need to be able to back up their personal content. Users want it to be easy to find content, view it and show and share it with family and friends.*

These trends will enable devices to display more intelligence, intelligently interact with other devices and better anticipate the user's demands based on context information. The Media-Bubble functions are based on the following three pillars enabled by these trends:

Pro-active autonomous behavior
More processing power makes it possible to give devices more intelligence. This, combined with the ability of devices to sense context, for instance the environment and internal state, can make devices trigger reactions autonomously, starting up processes that aid the user.

Device collaboration
More processing power, together with the ability to communicate in a network, makes it possible for devices to interact with each other intelligently. This in turn enables them to collaborate, solving problems for the user; collaboration among devices is a form of multi-agent collaboration, see for instance [4].

Task initiation through physical interaction
Physically changing the context of a device can be an intuitive way for users to initiate a task. For instance keeping a device close to another device could trigger the devices to interact. This could allow the user to show content on one device although it is stored on the other.
The next sections further explain the Media-Bubble functions and describe how these three pillars are used.

Semi-automatic annotation

Metadata describing the context and content of photos and videos are crucial to enable powerful handling of personal content. Users require this information to easily find content of interest, to have content automatically organized or even to create automatically generated edits and collages of content collections.
The problem is that users do not usually want to go to the considerable effort of annotating their personal photos and videos with relevant metadata. Moreover, many users most likely do not even know what kind of annotations they should make. A solution is thus required to reduce the user's annotation efforts. The user should only be asked for feedback when the system is unable to infer required metadata autonomously. In addition, the feedback asked for should be formulated as a very specific question, for instance "who is this person?" or "where was this picture taken?". Feedback from the user should of course be used efficiently: a system should learn and infer new results from the feedback, limiting or even progressively reducing the number of new questions put to the user in the future. Annotation of personal content is an active field of research, see for instance [3,6,7].

A solution addressing these requirements is currently being developed whereby Media-Bubbles try to annotate new content in collaboration with other Media-Bubbles in the network. The collaboration element allows the Media-Bubbles to make use of the heterogeneous knowledge and capabilities available in the network, which should increase the automatic annotation quality. Knowledge and capabilities are in this case, for instance, the faces that are known by a device and the quality with which it can recognize those faces respectively. If the collaboration does not give rise to results with a sufficiently high degree of confidence, annotation questions for the user will be generated and sent to an "annotation center".
This allows users to answer simple annotation questions in lean-back mode; see Figure 2 for

Joe sees that a (stationary) Media-Bubble is blinking.

He sees that there are new annotation questions:

Media-Bubbles in the network try to help annotate newly uploaded pictures.

Joe starts the annotation centre and answers the annotation questions in lean-back mode.

Figure 2: A Media-Bubble usage scenario.

an artist's impression of how the user could experience this solution.

The current focus is on creating annotations about who appears in the content, when the content was created, where it was created, and why it was created. The latter annotation type can also be called the occasion or event of the photo or video: for instance "Dan's birthday party" or "Summer holiday trip".

The solution under development is clearly based on pro-active autonomous behavior and device collaboration, as is the self-organization function described in the next section.

Self-organization of content

Currently it is very cumbersome for users to get the right content on the right device. For instance, if a user wants to take his latest family pictures somewhere, he would need to manually find, select and transfer the content to her mobile device. In addition, many users would probably still prefer to use the local storage of their mobile devices, since broadband access to content outside the home is not free of charge.

The self-organization function [8] addresses this issue. It allows Media-Bubbles to work together in such a way that the right content is always available on the right device in the right format, automatically. Based on a self-organization profile set by the user, Media-Bubbles know what kind of content they need to gather. Whenever content items arrive on a Media-Bubble, the networked Media-Bubbles start to negotiate how to organize the content on the network. This negotiation is based on the self-organization profiles and, for instance, on device constraints such as available storage capacity.

Since the self-organization can result in Media-Bubbles having a very specific content collection, the user could 'physically' browse for those collections by looking at the visual collection summaries on the different devices. By these means Media-Bubbles could be used as electronic photo albums that are automatically filled with the right content!

'Physical' user interfacing

Users can perceive the digital world as being very abstract: digital photos and videos are not tangible and thus cannot be handled in a tangible fashion. It is however possible to create "physical" metaphors [5] to perform personal content management tasks.

Applications of such "physical" metaphors are currently being developed for Media-Bubble functions. An example of an intuitive 'physical' user interface is to start uploading or sharing content with a second Media-Bubble, simply by keeping the two Media-Bubbles near each other. The same idea can be used to enable the user to initiate a content slideshow on a TV display; see Figure 3 for an artist's impression of how the user could experience this solution.

There are multiple requirements for making physical metaphors truly intuitive. The devices

Suzy is visiting her parents; she wants to show them the pictures of her last holidays with Joe.

She takes out a Media-Bubble device containing the pictures.

She keeps the device close to the Media-Bubble TV.

She uses the Media-Bubble as a remote control unit, showing the pictures to her parents in lean-back mode.

Figure 3: *A Media-Bubble usage scenario.*

involved should make use of the available context to resolve what the user's actual intention is; besides the physical metaphor action the required additional user interaction should be kept to a minimum. Further, the physical metaphor action should be indifferent to variations in how the user performs it.

Towards truly easy personal content management

Combining the described functions into a single Media-Bubble device will provide the user with unprecedented power to deal intuitively with personal content throughout its life cycle. However, this power can only be achieved if the user experience is used as a basis for designing and implementing the functions. Users could have more than one Media-Bubble at home, all displaying pro-active autonomous behavior, all collaborating in the network, for different reasons. This complex dynamic behavior calls for good interaction solutions for single users to oversee

and control these devices. HomeLab provides an ideal experimental home environment in which these interaction solutions can be tested with real users. This will allow us to develop the Media-Bubble concept further towards making personal content management truly easy!

References

1. Aarts, E., and S. Marzano (2003), *The New Everyday: Views on Ambient Intelligence*, 010 Publishers, Rotterdam ,The Netherlands.

2. Dey, A.K. (2001), Understanding and Using Context, *Personal and Ubiquitous Computing Journal*, 5(1), pp. 4-7.

3. Davis, M., M. Smith, J. Canny, N. Good, S. King, and R. Janakiraman (2005), Towards Context-Aware Face Recognition, in: *Proceedings of 13th Annual ACM International Conference on Multimedia (MM 2005)*, Singapore, ACM Press, pp. 483-486.

4. Ferber, J. (1999), *Multi-Agent Systems: An Introduction to Distributed Artificial Intelligence*, Addison-Wesley Professional.

5. Hoven, E. van den (2004), *Graspable Cues for Everyday Recollecting*, Ph.D.-thesis, Department of Industrial Design, Eindhoven University of Technology, The Netherlands.

6. Wenyin, L., S. Dumais, Y. Sun, H. Zhang, M. Czerwinski, and B. Field (2001), Semi-Automatic Image Annotation, in M. Hirose (ed.), *Human-Computer Interaction Interact '01*, IOS Press, pp.326-333.

7. Wu, P. (2004), A Semi-automatic Approach to Detect Highlights for Home Video Annotation, IEEE *International Conference on Acoustics, Speech, and Signal Processing (ICASSP)*, Montreal, Canada, May 2004.

8. aceMedia (online), European IST project, http://www.acemedia.org/aceMedia/index.html.

System intelligence
smart sensors

PowerPad

In recent years there has been a marked rise in the use of mobile electronic devices. However, although a lot of attention has been devoted to the communication between these devices, their electric power supply has long been neglected from the point of view of ease of use. When the battery is empty, a 'wireless device' still needs to be connected via a cable in order to be recharged. To prevent the need for any cables at all, we are now proposing a solution that allows wireless charging of mobile electronic devices. This consists of a tablet or pad the size of a mouse pad and allows arbitrary placement of the mobile device. With the PowerPad the idea is that you just 'put it on the pad and let it charge'.

Concept

The solution we propose is based on an inductive power transfer similar to that used in a electronic toothbrush or shaver, except that the device can be positioned arbitrarily and the PowerPad is universally suitable for various devices; see Figure 1.

Figure 1: *Just put your electronic gadgets on the pad and let them charge.*

Eberhard Waffenschmidt

The pad can recognize the different devices that are put on it and is able to adjust the charging conditions accordingly. This gives rise to a number of user benefits, as follows:

- *Convenience*. The most important feature of this innovation is the simple and intuitive use of this invisible technology. The charging action is initiated simply by placing the device on the pad.
- *Universal use*. One universal charging pad can be used for different kinds of devices, different voltages and power levels.
- *Ubiquity*. Such a charging pad could be found in many locations. Much like a telephone socket, it could be provided as a service in many public or private places.
- *Functionality*. The housing of the mobile devices can be sealed tightly in an easy and reliable way. Such waterproof devices offer a range of new applications, e.g. integrated into washable clothes or used in rough and dirty environments.

Although the application shown in HomeLab focuses on consumer devices, further applications of this technology are possible in different areas of Philips' business. The PowerPad can therefore be considered as a technology platform for other wireless power applications.

Technical realization

The PowerPad consists of an array of transmitter coils that can generate an alternating magnetic field vertical to the PowerPad surface. The mobile devices contain a receiver coil in which a voltage is induced to power the device and to charge a battery. The transmitter coils are spiral inductors made from cheap printed circuit board (PCB) tracks. We applied transmitter coils based on the original design by Hui [1]. In our design they are laid out in an interleaved pattern, as shown in Figure 2. This makes it possible to achieve a sufficiently homogeneous induced voltage (gray line) if several transmitter coils (red, green, blue) are switched on. In order to reduce the magnetic field emission and the idle losses, the original concept is improved, the transmitter coils can be switched locally and only the part where a receiver is located is switched on. Each transmitter coil contains such a sensor, forming a basic cell. By repeating a number of basic cells, the pad can be scaled arbitrarily to any size. This represents an advantage over proposals for a similar application put forward by the competitor company Splashpower [2].

Possible concerns

During the further development of the charging pad a number of issues arose that will have to be solved before we have a valid proposition. They can be formulated as follows:

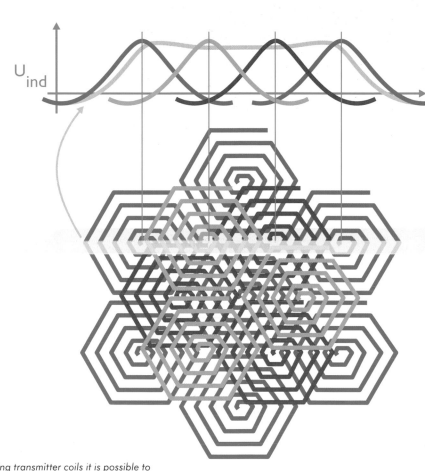

Figure 2: By overlapping transmitter coils it is possible to achieve quite a homogeneous induced voltage (gray line) if several transmitter coils (red, green, blue) are switched on.

- *Efficiency.* With only one array coil powered, efficiency in excess of 80% will be possible. Any further losses in the unused parts of the Power-Pad will reduce the efficiency. We have measured an efficiency of 30% when transmitting 1.5 W on a non-optimized first prototype, when the entire PowerPad was powered. This has to be compared with a typical efficiency of 50% to 60% for 50 Hz transformers in low-power applications and 70% to 90% for switch-mode power chargers. A switched coil solution for the charging pad has a similar efficiency.

- *Magnetic field emissions*. If we select a design with many turns in the coils a low magnetic field is possible. Measurements on a first prototype showed that for operation with only a single array coil powered, the magnetic field emissions were 5 times lower than the limit defined by the German workplace standard BGV B11 close to the top of the coil. Thus, the impact on human beings is comparable with that of other electronic equipment.
- *Cost*. The main additional cost is incurred for the coil array of the PowerPad and the array of sensors. However, if the PowerPad is used for several mobile devices, this cost can be shared.

Challenges

In order to take the idea further into the product creation phase, the following issues need to be addressed:

- *Power limit*. From a technical point of view, we have not yet worked out where the limit of power transmission is without exceeding the limits set by specific standards or losses. This is going to be important for reducing charging times.
- *Cost reduction*. One way of optimizing the cost of the charging pad could be a high level of modularization with standardized, identical and thus low-cost sub-cells. As well as possibly reducing cost, this would offer the largest scalability. A contrasting solution would be to combine functions as much as possible into centralized control units. It is not yet clear which solution will give rise to the lowest overall cost.
- *Standardization*. To achieve acceptance by the users, it is not only Philips portable devices that

need to be equipped for 'Wireless Power'. A large extend of standardization is required.
- *Market introduction*. In our view, the main challenge is the introduction of the concept onto the market. In order to ensure a significant benefit for the user, more than just one mobile product will have to be equipped with a Wireless Power receiver. Large-scale coordination is therefore going to be essential.

The first step, however, will be to use and prove the concept in niche markets to gain experience with the technology.

Conclusion

PowerPad is a powerful concept in more than one respect. It serves a basic need for people who use mobile devices because it reduces the need to connect up devices for recharging. The proposed solution is efficient and self-explanatory in its use, and therefore meets the Philips brand promise of Sense and Simplicity.

References

1. R. Hui, and W. Ho (2004), A new generation of universal contactless battery charging platform for portable consumer electronic equipment, *Proceedings of the 35th IEEE Power Electronics Specialists Conference, June 20-25*, Aachen, Germany, pp. 638-644.

2. Splashpower (online), http://www.splashpower.com.

Sensors and Ambient Intelligence: SAINT
Willem Fontijn • James Chen • Mylan Chen

Sensors and Ambient Intelligence: SAINT

Storage and processing are essential ingredients for achieving intelligent behavior in devices. When connected to networks, these devices can achieve even higher levels of perceived intelligent behavior by communicating with each other [1,2]. SAINT was started in 2003 to investigate the implications of large networks of such connected devices without any centralized server or authority.

Network Technology

System Architecture

Smart Sensors

Intelligent System Behavior

Intuitive Interaction Solutions

Sensor networks

The first step was to look at the technical implementation issues, which applications would be possible and how such a system would demonstrate intelligent behavior towards the user. It quickly emerged that the acquisition, storage and processing of, in particular, context information was central to this and it was decided to focus on the management of sensor data in distributed and decentralized wireless sensor networks with the aim of extracting context information from the environment and providing meaningful descriptions of human activities.

SAINT studies the system architecture for context-aware applications based on sensor networks, as well as the easy deployment of the sensor network infrastructure and of context-aware applications using that infrastructure. SAINT aims to develop a generic platform for context-aware applications [3] to be used in, for instance, healthcare applications. In ShopLab the carrier application is a lighting control application in a professional environment.

Usability and feasibility aspects

The detection, recording and analysis of context information, such as user presence, location and activities, as well as environmental conditions, enables the system to detect patterns in user behavior and use them to predict user wishes and preempt user actions. This method of controlling the system by observing the user is called implicit user-system interaction as opposed to explicit user interaction where the user consciously and deliberately controls the system with explicit actions, e.g. the manipulation of objects as in the case of StoryToy; see Chapter 3.10.

Some level of learning by the system is involved but to enable the deployment of applications that are functional from the start, some explicit knowledge about the user, or typical users in general, is also required. The combination of explicit knowledge, auto-configuration of system/data management and sensed context makes the system particularly powerful.

Context awareness is one of the most important elements in the realization of the Philips vision of Ambient Intelligence. However, there is also a

Willem Fontijn, James Chen, Mylan Chen

shorter-term, more concrete issue that is specifically addressed by the SAINT system in ShopLab. It deals with how Philips Lighting is to support the increasingly complex operation of its lighting systems without increasing the complexity of the user interface. A self-configurable and decentralized sensor network to detect context information provides a natural way for the system to interact with people, adapting to the context of the user by creating an atmosphere suitable to that context and thus providing a desirable user experience.

Shop lighting

Shop lighting is seen as a promising field of application for LED technology. Shop owners have been interviewed to assess how LED lighting can benefit them. One scenario that emerged features a rest corner for a high-end fashion shop. Shop owners commented that the fact that the husband is hanging around, actually wanting to leave, rushes the woman. To improve sales, this feeling of rush has to be taken away, and therefore a more advanced relaxing corner seems to be an interesting idea. Shoppers will be likely to spend more time shopping if their companions have an enjoyable and comfortable experience such as the rest corner provides. Other information that is of interest to shop owners may also be collected, such as how many people are in the shop at any time, what routes buyers and non-buyers take, where they spend their time, etcetera. Shop owners have indicated that such information is very useful, e.g. to optimize the layout of their stores.

The SAINT system in ShopLab demonstrates an adaptive rest area for shopping companions or

Sensors and Ambient Intelligence: SAINT

Willem Fontijn • James Chen • Mylan Chen

Figure 1: *Rest area in ShopLab.*

tired customers as shown in Figure 1. It changes the lighting atmosphere and conditions according to their activities. The system can estimate whether a person in the shop is interested in shopping or not by using several cues, such as movement tracking. A shopper usually goes directly to the stacks, while a bored shopping companion just hangs around the main path. If a bored or tired person is detected, the system will attract him to the rest corner using the lighting system.

In the rest corner the customer finds a bookstand and several seats. Different functional lighting is provided automatically without explicit control, based on the state and activities of the customer. For example, when the customer opens a magazine the lighting atmosphere changes to match the magazine's theme. If the customer happens to sit down when the magazine is open a spotlight will target the seat and magazine. A soothing lighting script relaxes the customer when he is sitting in one of the seats without reading.

To implement this, a wireless sensor network is deployed throughout ShopLab with an elevated

density of nodes in the rest corner. As depicted in Figure 2, the sensor nodes are located mainly inside objects and embedded in the ceiling. Each sensor node connects to one or more sensors. Sensors used include PIR (Passive Infra-Red), 3D accelerometer and binary switch sensors. The activity recognition system analyzes the sensor data and outputs the detected context information to the lighting management system. The context information provided includes customer location, their interaction with objects, and the states of objects.

Lessons Learned

The SAINT infrastructure has only recently been deployed in ShopLab. As a result no conclusions can be drawn yet from user studies there. However, a previous demonstration set-up that focused on habit watching in an office environment enables us to draw some preliminary conclusions regarding certain implications of implicit user-system interaction.

To be able to detect human activities with an accuracy high enough to anticipate user wishes while remaining unobtrusive requires a relatively dense sensor network. In addition, to be able to react in a timely manner requires a relatively high sample rate for the sensors. In combination, this leads to a substantial amount of sensor data to be processed. Sending all this data over wireless connections would put undue strain on the available bandwidth. As a result it is necessary to process the data close to the source, preferably on the sensor node acquiring it. Given that constraint, it is entirely feasible to use a sensor network to preempt user actions based on habit monitoring.

References

1. Fontijn, W.F.J., and P.A. Boncz (2004), AmbientDB: P2P Data Management Middleware for Ambient Intelligence, *Proceedings of IEEE International Conference on Pervasive Computing and Communications (PerCom) Workshops*, March 14-17, Orlando, USA, pp. 203-207.

2. Fontijn, W.F.J., J.A.D. Nesvadba, and A.G. (2006), Integrating Media Management towards Ambient Intelligence, 3rd International Workshop on Adaptive Multimedia Retrieval, Glasgow, UK, July 28-29 2005, *Lecture Notes in Computer Science,* 3877, Springer, Berlin, Germany, pp. 104-109.

3. Chen, J.N.J., W.F.J. Fontijn, Q. Zhang, and M. Chen (2005), A Framework for Ambient applications, *Proceedings of the International Conference on Sensor Networks (SENET 2005),* August 14-17 ,Montreal, Canada, pp. 348-354.

Figure 2: *Overview of the main sensors distributed throughout ShopLab.*

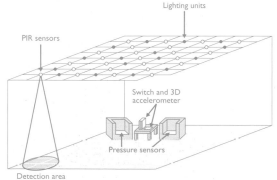

Flexible Light Management Systems

Network Technology
System Architecture

Developments like solid-state lighting and the experience economy are changing the focus of the lighting business from functional lighting with stand-alone lamps towards lifestyle lighting in systems with many connected light sources. This is clearly apparent in the retail domain. A pleasant atmosphere in a shop, strongly influenced by the lighting, increases the time that people spend in the shop and the chances that people will return. Furthermore, market research into retail lighting shows that many shops, particularly high-end fashion shops, change their interior regularly, as often as once a month, to continually reinforce the attractiveness of the shop. These changes, which involve selecting different accessories, re-painting walls and re-adjusting the lamp control parameters, are at present costly and time-consuming. Finally, a shop chain typically wants to express a consistent brand image to the market in all its individual shops. The lighting in and around the shop can strongly support the brand image of the chain.

Distributed lighting concept

Designing or changing the lighting for a shop with current solutions means that the lighting designer has to determine the intensity, color, direction, etcetera, for every light unit in the shop. Given the fact that shops can contain hundreds of light units, this is a very time-consuming and costly process, which severely limits the use of lighting as a marketing or branding tool. Ho'wever, an easy way to design light and an automatic process for rendering the light in a shop would significantly reduce this effort and increase the flexibility and value of light. The aim of the LightMan project is to provide the technology that enables attractive light atmospheres with such a networked lighting system, which can be created in an easy and flexible way. Important user requirements are:

Mark Verberkt

- Easy creation of light atmospheres for large lighting installations.
- Support for a wide range of lighting technologies (LED, Halogen, HID, TL, ...).
- No significant increase in system installation and commissioning.
- Support for frequent relocation of wares in the shop.
- Support for shop chains.

The LightMan technology consists of an atmosphere description language, a rendering algorithm and an infrastructure of networked lamps, as depicted in Figure 1. The XML-based atmosphere description language enables a lighting designer to describe the desired light for a shop or even a complete shop chain, regardless of the layout

Figure 2: *Examples of atmospheres realised in ShopLab.*

and lighting infrastructure of a specific shop. The language enables a lighting designer to describe the type of light that should be created at a certain abstract location at a certain point in time. Incorporation of sensor information, e.g., occupancy, permits adaptive atmospheres. The rendering algorithm translates the abstract light description into specific control values for the light sources in a given shop, using information on the available light elements, sensor values and time constraints. Runtime control is realized in a networked light management system featuring robust communication supporting wireless and wired connectivity using a distributed light operating system with easy set-up and maintenance.

First impressions

The first prototype, installed in ShopLab, shows automatic rendering of an abstract light description in a complex lighting system, consisting of more than 60 light units with more than one hun-

dred control parameters featuring a mix of wall washing, spot lighting and ambient lighting, using various network technologies. A few examples of rendered atmospheres in ShopLab are depicted in Figure 2. Changing the shop's interior, e.g., by moving furniture or modifying the functional layout or lamp availability, demonstrates the system's flexibility. User tests with lighting designers will be carried out in the newly built ShopLab to validate the power of LightMan's abstract description language and rendering algorithms.

Acknowledgements
The author would like to thank the LightMan Team: Salvador Boleko, Wolfgang Budde, Dirk Engelen, Bozena Erdmann, Robert van Herk, Pieter Koenen, Armand Lelkens, Arjen vd. Linden, Felix Ogg, Ron Pijpers, Oliver Schreyer, Volkmar Schulz, Leon van Stuivenberg, Matthias Wendt.

Figure 1: *The LightMan system stack.*
Although this solution is currently targeted at shops and chain stores, it can also be applied in the hotel and consumer domains.

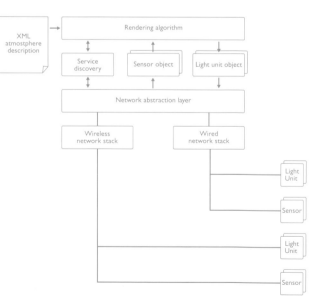

Intuitive Interaction for Lighting Atmospheres

Richard van de Sluis

Elmo Diederiks

The aim of the IILA (Intuitive Interaction for Lighting Atmospheres) project is to come up with a new user interaction style for creating and controlling lighting atmospheres. The retail domain is taken as the starting point since there is a strong need for easy ways to change the atmosphere in shops. Product collections in shops are being refreshed at an increasing frequency, especially in fashion. Shopping has also become one of the most important leisure activities in the Western world. It is important to realize that people do not only go shopping because they need to buy certain goods. In many cases it is the shopping activity itself that fulfils people's need to experience nice atmospheres and to discover novel trends and attractive products [1]. The creation of pleasant atmospheres in shops is important because this can help to keep people in the shop for longer and increases the chance that they will come back. And if people do revisit a shop several weeks later, they prefer to see something new. Shops therefore want to create a fresh feel by continuously updating both the product collections and the atmosphere in the shop.

Atmosphere requirements

At present the atmosphere in a shop is changed by regularly changing the accessories, posters and by repainting certain colored walls or elements. New technologies will provide more flexible ways to change the overall atmosphere. Advances in solid-state lighting technology in particular will create new ways for changing the atmosphere in a shop at the push of a button. These new lighting elements can be integrated seamlessly into the interior. They also enable the creation of colored lighting, dynamics and interactive atmospheres.

It should be possible for someone, such as the shop manager, to change the atmosphere in an easy and enjoyable way. For instance, when new clothing products arrive in the new season's fashion colors, the manager may want to change the color of the luminaires or, if the shop ambience needs to be geared to a specific event or theme, like 'Christmas', 'Summer' or 'Sale', it may be desirable to adjust the distribution of light intensity in the shop or to define a dynamic lighting atmosphere.

One problem with color control is that people have difficulty navigating a colored space because they are unfamiliar with it. When people have to choose or describe a color they often refer to colors in their environment. This is the reason why we are investigating various user interaction solutions that make use of a color sensor. In this way, people can simply pick a color that they like from their environ-

Richard van de Sluis, Elmo Diederiks

Richard van de Sluis • Elmo Diederiks

Intuitive Interaction for Lighting Atmospheres

ment and have it scanned so it can set the color of the luminaire. This color control method also opens up a new and playful type of interaction that is expected to encourage people to explore the possibilities of the new color lighting systems. People can scan colors from any object, such as their clothes, furniture, art work or magazines, and try these colors out to see if they look nice as colored light.

Concepts

Based on the user insights we have derived from the atmosphere requirements discussed above, we generated a large pool of concepts. Evaluation of these concepts with shoppers, shop owners and other stakeholders resulted in the selection of four color-control concepts and three interactive lighting concepts. These have been worked out in more detail and implemented as experience demonstrators in ShopLab.

The color-control concepts that are topic of further research are:

- *The ColorScanner:* a slit into which a piece of paper of the desired color can be inserted.
- *The ColorSensor:* a sensor that allows a user to hold an object of the desired color in front of a sensor.
- *The ColorWheel:* a touch wheel that enables simple navigation around a color circle.
- *The LightWand:* scanning and pointing device that enables the user to 'paint with light'.

The first three concepts can be used to set the color of a single luminaire, or a group of luminaires that all need to have the same color, whereas the *Light-Wand*, is suitable for controlling a large number of different colored lights. It allows a user to pick a color by either pointing to another luminaire or touching a colored surface in the vicinity, as illustrated in Figure 1, and to 'paint' with this color by pointing the LightWand at the target luminaire.

In-depth user studies need to be carried out to establish the pros and cons of these color control concepts and to identify possible improvements. For instance, is there a need for an 'undo' function, or for color fine-tuning after a particular color has been copied using the LightWand?

Figure 1: *The LightWand can be used to sample the color of garments and then 'paint' to set the color of lighting elements in the shop.*

The interactive shop lighting concepts that are being explored in the project are: the interactive clothing rack, the smart display cube and the adaptive spotlights. The interactive clothing rack uses a dynamic spotlight to highlight the clothes

a person is looking at when 'browsing' through a clothing rack. Many high-end fashion shops create a dimmed lighting atmosphere because this makes the shop look exclusive. As a result, the products in the shop need to be illuminated separately so that shoppers can see the colors of the garments correctly. The interactivity makes it possible to respond in a subtle manner as people are looking at and touching the clothing in the rack; see Figure 2. This response can make shoppers feel they have been noticed and that they are appreciated. It enables the shop environment to respond to the customer's behavior without a shop assistant immediately having to engage in a conversation with them.

Figure 2: *The Interactive Clothing Rack creates a dynamic spotlight on the garments people are looking at.*

The smart display cube is a display cube like those commonly used in shops to display fashion accessories with the addition of integrated color lighting and a camera. The camera image is processed and geared to match prominent colors in the item on display and the light color of the inside of the

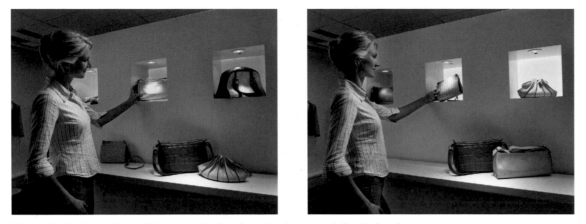

Figure 3: The Smart Display Cube automatically adapts its color to match the displayed goods.

cube. For instance, the interior of the cube is lit in a color that contrasts the color that is most prominent in the object. The color of the display cube can therefore be changed easily and this means it is no longer necessary to paint the cubes when the goods in the display are exchanged; see Figure 3. The adaptive spotlights are spots that can be used to illuminate certain products in the shop. As soon as a shopper comes close the spotlight changes beam width; see Figure 4. In this way the attention of shoppers can be drawn to the product in a subtle manner. Similar to the interactive clothing rack, it creates the notion of an attentive shop environment that is able to respond to the presence and behavior of shoppers.

Early observations
Advanced lighting systems are already being used to create atmosphere in high-end fashion shops. However, in many of these shops it is still not easy to change the atmosphere and in most cases only

a lighting technician is able to change the color of a color panel. The concepts described here aim to make these atmosphere lighting systems easy to control and to introduce the first step towards interactive atmospheres. This is expected to help shops to create a differentiating shop atmosphere and to turn shopping into a more exciting experience.

Figure 4: An impression of the adaptive spotlights with a wide beam on the left and a narrow beam on the right.

Preliminary feedback from visitors in ShopLab indicates that people very much appreciate the various color-control concepts. They feel that the ease with which a color can be set using for instance the ColorSensor is impressive. They also indicate that they would prefer the ColorWheel if they would need to set a very specific color. Finally, people indicated that the interactive features of the adaptive spotlights and the display cubes are subtle yet attractive ways to guide people's attention. More extensive user studies will be done in ShopLab with various end-users, such as shoppers, shop managers and retail experts. The results of these studies will be used to validate and improve the proposed innovative interaction solutions and inspire future directions for research on enhancing the shopping experience.

Acknowledgements
The authors would like to thank the IILA team: Tom Bergman, Peter van de Biggelaar, René Cortenraad, Jettie Hoonhout, Joost Witsenburg and Mehmet Yalvac.

References
1. Michel Van Tongeren (2004), *Retail Branding: From Stopping Power To Shopping Power*, Gingko Press, ISBN9063690436

Active Beam Manipulation

New Applications

Lighting is an essential ambience element in our lives. People like to be able to adapt lighting conditions to the activities they are engaged in. For example, a spotlight used for task lighting, e.g. for reading, in a living-room needs to be switched to a more diffuse and warm lighting if friends come over for a visit. Similarly, spotlights suspended above the dining table should provide warm light during dinner, but a larger area needs to be illuminated when the table is not in use. At the moment, there are no easy-to-use solutions for switching lighting conditions between various states to suit different requirements. As a result, this still needs to be done manually by changing the direction of spotlights by hand or by dimming various light sources separately.

Concept

Since the introduction of solid-state lighting (Light Emitting Diodes, or LEDs), it is now very easy to switch between saturated colors and to obtain any desired color temperature from a light source. In addition to these possibilities with LEDs, the Active Beam Manipulation project offers simple thin switchable flat optical elements to enable us to control the shape, direction and collimation of a light beam. These elements do not have moving parts and can simply be placed in front of a luminaire so that the small form factor of LEDs is retained. Application of a voltage from a variable source changes the characteristics of such an optical element, which in turn adjusts the beam. The technology for producing these optical elements is simple and suitable for mass production, so that the elements can be introduced onto the market quickly. Figure 1 shows five white LED spots illuminating a wall. In the inactivated state the spots have narrow collimation. Using DMX [2] or direct control one

can produce precise settings and change the beam angle continuously. It is also possible to introduce dynamic changes at various speeds.

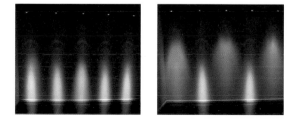

Figure 1: *Photos of LED spots illuminating a wall: A) None of the optical elements in the activated state B) Some of the elements in the activated state.*

In the same way we have produced elements that can change the collimation of the beam accompanied by a color temperature change integrated into the same element. Figure 2 shows the effect. The spot with a high color temperature is easily switched to a wide beam showing lower color temperature for comfort.

Rifat Hikmet, Ties van Bommel

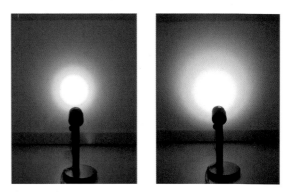

Figure 2: *Photos of LED spots illuminating a wall: A) Optical element in the off state B) The optical element in the on state.*

Applications

In the area of general lighting we are looking into various segments, such as homes, shops, restaurants, etc. As at the moment the beam control function is in its infancy in these segments, we are investigating application areas for this new increased functionality in order to find out about the benefits for the user. It is also our aim to find out how the user perceives such functionality and what kind of user interface is needed for ease of use.

In a home environment the shape of the beam and/or its direction can be switched between various states depending on the user's mood or activity. For example, a spot lamp in a living-room used for task lighting, such as reading, can be switched to a flood light with warmer color temperature when visitors arrive. In the same way lamps hanging above a dining table can be spot lights during meals that can be switched to illuminate a larger area when the table is not in use.

Active Beam Manipulation
Rifat Hikmet • Ties van Bommel

In a shop environment the beam control functionality can be used for various purposes. It can be used to attract the attention of a customer by focusing the beam on an object. It can be used in a cabinet containing jewellery, where changing beam shape or collimation can induce glittering effects as a result of changing reflection angles. It can also be used in the relaxation area of the shop, where gradual changes in the beam can provide relaxing effects. In the same way simply illuminating a large area can be turned into a spot effect illuminating the seat occupied by a person.

The beam control function is in its infancy at the moment. It is therefore important to investigate possible new applications for this technology. With the demonstrators in the HomeLab and ShopLab [1] we have conducted preliminary investigations into how consumers, lighting designers and shop owners would like to use this technology and what kind of user interfaces for light beam control would be preferred. Early results indicate that all those who have seen the demos are very interested in the elements and the possibilities they offer, especially with respect to the demonstrator in ShopLab

This is underlined by additional concept investigations with a number of small Italian retailers. They stated that the beam angle variation is more interesting than color temperature variation, and that the shop window seems to be the most logical application. These is only preliminary feedback, which requires more in depth investigation and validation, for instance with high-end retail chains.

References
1. Rifat Hikmet and Ties van Bommel (2006), LEDs in Lighting Applications: Active Beam Manipulation, in: Lashina, T., J. Hoonhout, and E. Diederiks (eds.) (2006), *New Business Through User Centric Innovation: A Key role for Philips' ExperienceLab*, Philips Research Europe and Creada, Eindhoven, The Netherlands.
2. The USITT DMX 512 standard (online), http://www.usitt.org/standards/DMX512.html

Evert van Loenen • Tatiana Lashina • Mark van Doorn • Kero van Gelder
Vic Teeven • Werner de Bruin • Rick van Haasen

Interactive Shop Windows

Interactive Shop Windows

The Dreamscreen project aims to create attractive experiences by augmenting or replacing the view through otherwise transparent windows. Our goal is to find out as early as possible what value propositions can be created based on end-user insights, to provide requirements for the technologies that are needed, and eventually to create complete prototype systems including appropriate interaction solutions.

Evert van Loenen, Tatiana Lashina,
Mark van Doorn, Kero van Gelder, Vic Teeven,
Werner de Bruin, Rick van Haasen

In the first phase of the project, we made an inventory of a broad range of DreamScreen applications in the professional, public, automotive and home domains. These applications were ranked based on their user benefits, technical challenge and strategic fit with the Philips businesses. From this initial ranking, smart shop and display windows emerged as one of the most attractive applications. The concept of an *Intelligent Shop Window* was developed and selected as the main application because shop and display windows can be used for a wide variety of different purposes, allowing experimentation with different concepts and technologies. Furthermore, retail is an important segment for the professional CE and Lighting businesses of Philips. Last but not least, we believed it was technically feasible with the current state of the art in technology to realize an intelligent shop window. To design and implement an attractive shop window experience, we followed the user-centric research approach: Shoppers were observed, and shop owners and shoppers were interviewed to learn how they use shop windows today, and why. Additional domain knowledge was collected through interviews with retail consultants.

Over the past decades, shopping has increasingly become a leisure activity. The largest indoor shopping mall in the world, West Edmonton Mall in Edmonton, Canada, features over 800 stores and services, 27 movie theatres, 110 eating establishments, an indoor theme park and much more. [1] It is a destination in itself. Mark Gottdiener's *"The Theming of America"* [2] provides an investigation into why the built environment we inhabit is increasingly cluttered with shopping malls, theme parks, fast food franchises and hybrids of these three. Shop owners are increasingly aware of this reality, but for most shop owners the options for augmenting shop and display windows with interactive media are very limited, as they are costly to install and maintain. From interviews with shop owners and retail experts we have learned that shop windows are important marketing tools, with three important functions:

- To express the type and style of the shop.
- To create the appropriate atmosphere and attract people.
- To inform people about the products available and their features.

- For shop owners the ability to customize or program the shop window is important because products on display change quite regularly. For shoppers it is of great importance that the shop windows are extremely easy to use and experience, because it cannot be expected that they should spend time on learning how to use them. With these functions and user insights in mind we designed a use-case scenario for the Intelligent Shop Window to enhance all of these functions, and to provide some entirely new experiences for shoppers and shop owners. This use-case scenario has been implemented in ShopLab and is being evaluated with end users, shop owners and retail consultants. Both the use-case scenario with its underlying interaction concepts and the prototype in ShopLab are discussed in the remainder of this chapter.

Scenarios

Emily and Olivia have an afternoon off from work and decide to go shopping for fun. When they approach the high-end fashion store near the central plaza of the shopping mall, they see moving images of the latest women's collection on the shop window. Attracted by the sight of pictures that seem to be hanging in mid air, Emily moves closer to the shop. The shop window tries to capture her attention by playing music and showing pictures near her. Emily follows the music and turns towards the shop window. Soon her attention is drawn to the pair of shoes on display. After a few moments she sees information about the shoes appear on the shop window in front of her (see Figure 1 for a sketch of the nearby interaction mode). The shoes in the store are also highlighted. "Come over

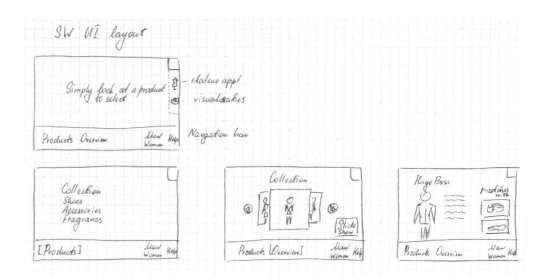

Figure 1: *Sketch of nearby interaction mode*

At the end of the week, Harry, the shop owner, decides to change the appearance of the shop window. The summer sale is approaching and the store needs to be updated. Harry stands in front of the shop window and, as he is recognized, a special user interface appears where Harry can change the settings of the different lamps in the shop window while he is looking at the results. Harry picks the summer preset but modifies the color of the spots in the ceiling. Satisfied, Harry closes the application.

here", she says to Olivia. As Olivia approaches the shop window, she is not greeted with music and imagery because Emily is still interacting with the shop window. Olivia walks up to the shop window section next to Emily and points to a dress in the shop window. Immediately, a product catalog appears on the shop window and Olivia starts to browse through the collection and sees more items she would like to buy. Olivia and Emily decide to go inside.

Interaction concepts

In the above scenarios several interaction concepts can be identified. In this section and the next section on the end-user programming we discuss these concepts in detail and describe how they have been implemented.

First, the intelligent shop window augments the view of the products on display in the shop window. To achieve this, the shop window is equipped with a holographic foil that enables a multimedia projector to project images and videos onto the glass at a specific angle, creating the augmented view. For the holographic foil we have chosen DNP technology [3].

Interactive Shop Windows

Evert van Loenen • Tatiana Lashina • Mark van Doorn

Vic Teeven • Werner de Bruin • Rick van Haasen • Kero van Gelder

Second, the interaction style depends on the distance betwee the user and the shop window. The idea behind this is that potential shoppers must be attracted, but not scared off. Therefore, we divided the area in front of the shop window into several zones, similar to the ambient displays of Vogel and Balakrishnan [4]. Furthest away is the attraction zone, meant to express the style and type of the shop and to create interest. Closer to the shop window is the attention zone, meant to grasp people's attention. Directly in front of the shop window are several interaction zones where people can call up information about the products on display. By moving into the interaction zone, the shopper indicates that he desires explicit interaction. To determine the position and orientation of shoppers we use a pressure-sensitive floor.

The next concept is that of private shopping experiences. Directional audio and video provide each shopper with personal and private interaction. This form of narrowcasting gives the shop owner the possibility to target individual customers in front of the shop window. For the directional audio we use Panphonics [5] speakers and an audio beaming technology developed in-house. The video is made more private by using only that part of the screen that is directly in front of the shopper.

Another characteristic is that the explicit interaction with the shop window is very natural. Simply by looking at products in the shop window or touching the screen, users can call up extra information. No learning is involved, which makes the show window very easy to use and easy to experience. For the touch screen we use a solution provided by

Figure 2: *A shop owner programming the look and feel of his shop window.*

Ubiq'Window [6]. The gaze tracker in our current setup is technology from SmartEye [7].

The last interaction concept related to the shopping scenario we want to mention here is that of immediate feedback with multiple modalities. If people interact with the shop window they will not only receive feedback through the screen, but also via light and audio cues. In this way the selected object is also augmented in ways that are helpful to people with disabilities.

End-user programming

The shopper is not the only user of the intelligent shop window. As we mentioned earlier, the shop owner wants to have the flexibility to change the appearance of the shop window depending on the collection on display or the time of the year, as illustrated in our scenario. A secondary goal of the Dreamscreen project is to make it easy for expert users to modify the desired behavior of the intel-

ligent environment as they see fit. For the shop owner in our scenario this means that he can conveniently change the appearance of the shop window. At present, the system only supports some customization of the look and feel of the intelligent shop window as mentioned in the scenario, but we intend to offer much richer forms of programming in which a shop owner can control every aspect of the experience; see Figure 2.

Whereas in the user-centric design philosophy the focus is on the end-user application, the focus in end-user programming is on the process that enables users to create and modify their applications. This difference in mindset has consequences on many levels. On a system architecture level, it means that the system must implement a programming model in which users can express their needs in an easy specific way that is relevant to their task. Examples can be seen in spreadsheets and CAD/CAM systems.

On the organizational level, end-user programming can help to bring producer and consumer into a constructive dialogue on the desired experience, thereby reducing the chance of miscommunication and products that do not match expectations. This opens up new opportunities to deliver even more tailored, personalized experiences.

Preliminary results

To be able to directly evaluate the feasibility, usability and actual end-user appreciation of different Intelligent Shop Window implementations, a fully functional test set-up has been developed and integrated in ShopLab: a controlled, yet realistic shop environment for the study of future shopping experiences. Here, different implementations, for example with explicit, implicit or combined interaction solutions, can be compared alongside one another.

At the moment of writing, feasibility and usability studies are being performed. First reactions of visitors to ShopLab have generally been very positive. Frequently made remarks have confirmed our assumption that the intelligent shop window would also be very useful for providing information after opening hours. The need for customization of the shop window was also expressed.

References

1. West Edmonton Mall (online), http://www.westedmontonmall.com/
2. Gottdiener, M. (2001), The Theming of America: American Dreams, Media Fantasies, and Themed Environment, Boulder: Westview Press.
3. DNP Holoscreen (online), http://www.dnp.dk
4. Vogel, D. and R. Balakrishnan (2004), Interactive public ambient displays: transitioning from implicit to explicit, public to personal, interaction with multiple users, *Proceedings of the 17th annual ACM symposium on User interface software and technology*, Santa Fe, USA, pp. 137-146.
5. Panphonics audio (online), http://www.panphonics.fi/
6. Ubiq'Window touch screen (online), http://www.ubiqwindow.jp/english.htm
7. Smart Eye gaze tracker (online), http://www.smarteye.se/smarteyepro.html

SmartBed

Andreas Brauers • Xavier Aubert • Alexander Douglas • Frank Johnen

SmartBed

The SmartBed is for taking care of people while they are asleep. It can help you stay fit, but it can also increase the quality of life for people with heart disease and increase their life expectancy. The SmartBed project aims to conceptualize and prototype a smart bed environment using sensing functionality that can enable monitoring of vital health-care and wellbeing functionalities.

Sensing in bed

A bed is the ideal place to monitor people's cardio-vascular and respiratory performance and – of course – their sleep [1,2]. It is a place that is used regularly and for a longer period of time. It enables long-term measurements to be taken without interfering with the user's daily routine. This is even possible without conscious user interaction. The user just goes to sleep as usual and the rest is taken care of automatically. To this end, we investigated sensors that perform the necessary measurements in a perfectly unobtrusive manner.

Figure 1: *Bed with sensors (here textile electrodes in the bed linen)*

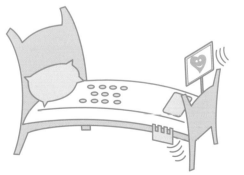

Andreas Brauers, Xavier Aubert,
Alexander Douglas, Frank Johnen

These sensors are integrated into the mattress, bedstead or textiles to allow transparent use rather than being attached to the body, as is typical in a hospital setting. As an example, textile electrodes that are part of the bed linen or the nightwear could be used to measure ECG signals during the night; see Figure 1. Breathing and activity can be monitored using mechanical sensors that are sensitive to small movements. It is even possible to monitor heart muscle activity in this way.

Sensor electronics and intermediate data storage are also integrated into the bedstead, while more elaborate data processing and feedback to the user is done using distinct user interaction device. A Bluetooth connection and dedicated protocols are used for data transmission. Depending on the application, the whole system maybe connected to a professional service, such as a disease management application; see Figure 2.

User requirements

User interviews with heart failure patients and cardiologists have shown that the unobtrusiveness of these measurements is of paramount importance

SmartBed
Andreas Brauers • Xavier Aubert • Alexander Douglas • Frank Johnen

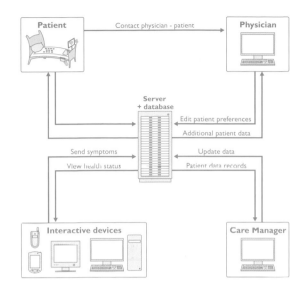

Figure 2: *SmartBed as part of a disease management system, e.g. for heart failure patients*

in order not to disturb the sleep of the person concerned but also – in the case of people who are ill – not to remind them of their illness. All of the cardiologists and patients interviewed said that the patients like using this technology and even feel safer when using it.

The use of these new sensors poses a challenge: using non-standard technology, how can we obtain information on standard vital bodily functions that will also be accepted by the medical community? The signals obtained from our sensors are non-standard and are also subject to noise. A very careful evaluation of signal quality and the development of suitable signal processing methods are the key to a successful realization of the concept

for applications that will work reliably in real life. The following two applications are currently our main point of focus:

- Disease management support for people with chronic heart failure by means of nightly monitoring.
- Monitoring of healthy persons to facilitate personal sleep management.

These applications are currently being evaluated as part of clinical and user studies in the MyHeart project and the sensors and algorithms developed in our project will be tested extensively as part of this.

Parameter monitoring

The parameters that need to be monitored to enable these two scenarios are: presence (in the bed), weight, activity, breathing rate and heart rate. Our studies could provide clear proof that it is feasible to obtain the desired information. For small signals, such as those from the pumping action of the heart, complex algorithms have been developed to extract the desired parameters for significant periods of time during sleep.

These parameters can be translated by specially designed information systems into information on the sleep quality or the status of the heart failure patients. In the case of sleep management, feedback to the user comes directly from the system. Here coaching strategies can be used to try to optimize the quality of sleep for the user. In the case of heart failure patients, feedback via medical services is recommended. The data obtained

in the bed can be used as a guide to medication to help optimize the treatment of the patient. This can enable the patient to stay out of hospital and to enjoy the best quality of life possible for someone who is suffering from a chronic condition such as theirs.

Even the simpler features, like presence detection in bed, can be used to great advantage. One example is the control of bedroom lighting, e.g. floor lighting that guides you when you get up in the night. Another example is presence surveillance in professional elderly care, where information on people leaving their beds can be transmitted to the night nurse so that accidents, such as falls, can be prevented.

References
1. Report of the National Commission on Sleep Disorders Research (1993), *Wake up America: A National Sleep Alert*, Executive Summary and Report.
2. Ishijama, M. (1997), Cardiopulmonary monitoring by textile electrodes without subject-awareness of being monitored. In: *Medical and Biological Engineering and Computing*, 35(6), pp. 685 - 690.

An Intelligent Home-monitoring System for Seniors

Intelligent System Behavior
New Applications
Ambience Creation

Ambient Assisted Living [1] constitutes a research field within Ambient Intelligence that is currently attracting much attention. The objective is to study smart sensor-based environments that can assist ordinary people in their daily life activities. Elderly people constitute a special target group within this domain since the size of the aging population is growing rapidly and therefore the cost of healthcare and well-being has reached a level that requires global action [2]. It is generally believed that smart environments may provide a solution to this problem because they can increase the period of time during which elderly people can continue to stay in their homes and maintain an independent lifestyle.

User insights

It is envisioned that in the future connected sensors will be integrated into peoples' clothing (body area networks), mobile devices and eventually their homes. These sensors can be used to collect data from which high-level information items can be detected such as context and action. As a next step this information can be used to support people in maintaining an active and independent lifestyle that includes social, wellbeing, health and entertainment elements. Over the years many user and concept studies have been carried out to obtain a thorough insight into the user needs of the elderly. Mikkonen et al., [3] have studied the merits of mobile communication services for the elderly and they concluded that elderly people have an open attitude towards wireless services and devices. This opens up the option of lifting digital support from mobile to ambient systems.

Boris de Ruyter

Concept

The 'Intelligent LifesStyle Assistant' (ILSA) system is an intelligent and adaptive home environment system that can support the elderly occupants of the home in maintaining an adequate quality of life as they grow older. Besides providing a feeling of safety and protection to the seniors, it provides a remote monitoring service that alerts care centers or relatives, as desired by the occupants. The ILSA project is targeted at developing interactive solutions for people who might need assistance, like elderly people, who have experienced a major event, such as losing their partner, or who are at risk, for instance of falling.

The technology realized in this project includes an intelligent monitoring system based on the integration of a range of distributed sensors. This system has a context-aware reasoning engine in order to translate sensor data into meaningful events. The

Figure 1: *CareLab interior with the living room (top), the bedroom (bottom left) and the bathroom (bottom right).*

- Enhancing the feeling of safety and wellbeing.
- Providing peace of mind for relatives of the seniors.
- Reducing the caregiver load and the risk of burnout.

The ILSA system will not only contribute to the wellbeing of seniors, but will also result in cost reductions at various levels in the healthcare supply chain in the following way.

- For the elderly by delaying or possibly eliminating the need to live in alternative but expensive care facilities.
- A reduced burden on the healthcare system by allowing care providers to spend time on other high-risk patients.
- Reducing the number of visits to hospitals by elderly people for check-ups as remote monitoring reduces the need for such visits.

The value of systems such as the ILSA system lies in their success in addressing manifest user needs.

CareLab

Developing application and services propositions that can deal with personal healthcare and wellbeing requires thorough feasibility and usability testing before they can be deployed in field settings. For that a laboratory infrastructure with close-to-real-life settings is needed. CareLab offers such a controlled, yet realistic testing environment for feasibility and usability tests of personal healthcare and wellbeing concepts before validating them in field settings. CareLab is a realistic probing environment with advanced sensing and reasoning

project furthermore comprises a flexible platform to interact with services chosen by the user. This system can offer a diversity of comfort services to seniors at home and alert care centers or relatives when needed.

User benefits

The primary goal of the ILSA project is to enable people to maintain an active, healthy and independent lifestyle. To that end, numerous benefits could be envisioned at the various levels of the healthcare supply chain. As the initial focus of the project is the elderly segment of the population, anticipated benefits for this segment and their relatives are:

- Helping the elderly in maintaining an independent lifestyle.

An Intelligent Home-monitoring System for Seniors
Boris de Ruyter

capabilities to study consumer health and wellness propositions in a home context. It is a regular elderly person's apartment consisting of three rooms: a living room, a bedroom and a bathroom; see Figure 1. It is equipped with the following sensors:

- 20 open/closed sensors for windows, doors, refrigerator, cupboards and drawers
- 3 waste-water sensors: 2 for the sink, 2 for the toilet
- 4 clean-water sensors: 2 for warm water, 2 for cold water
- 8 power sensors: for outlet in bathroom, bedroom, living room, and kitchen
- 4 humidity sensors: one per room
- 4 temperature sensors: one per room
- 5 brightness sensors: one per room, 2 in the living room
- 5 presence detectors: one per room, 2 in the living room
- 15 light control units (Dali units, Dim units)

Furthermore, CareLab is connected to the control and observation infrastructure of HomeLab.

Outlook

CareLab is still under development and the first extensive user studies are scheduled for the second half of 2006. The first experiments in CareLab indicate, however, that the sensor environment is working according to its specification and that the living environment reflects the real-life situation in an elderly person's apartment very well. So we are looking forward to the time when we can use the full potential of the facility.

References

1. Ambient Assisted Living (online), http://www.aal169.org/.

2. Zaengel, T., E. Thelen, and J. Thijs (2006), Perspectives in Personal Care, in: G. Spekowius and T. Wendler (eds.) *Advances in Healthcare Technology,* Springer, Berlin, Germany, pp. 439-462.

3. Mikkonen, M., S. Väyrynen. V. Ikonen, and M.O. Heikkilä (2002), User Concepts Studies as Tools in Developing Mobile Communication Services for the Elderly, *Personal and Ubiquitous Computing* 6, pp. 113-124.

Later Life Wellbeing and Lighting

Smart Sensors
User Research
User Evaluation
New Markets
Business Models

Ageing is accompanied by changes in visual performance. A large proportion of elderly people suffer from significant visual impairment under seemingly 'normal' lighting conditions. In order to compensate for their reduced eyesight, elderly people may require between three and five times higher lighting levels than young people; see Figure 1. What's more, they are also more sensitive to glare. Visual impairments reduce elderly people's ability to function independently and increase the risk of depression and injury from falls.

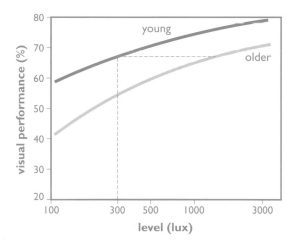

Figure 1: *The visual performance for a moderately difficult task for young and older people. The dashed line indicates that, in comparison to young people, older people need about 4 times higher lighting levels to achieve a visual performance of 65%. (Adapted from CIE source).*

Routines and rhythms

Lighting is not only required for visual activities, it also plays an important role in regulating our nat-ural body clock. Our biorhythm and sleep-wake cycle align to the 24 hour day cycle through the exposure to light. Biorhythm regulation is particularly important for the elderly as many elderly people suffer from sleep disturbances. Some examples include difficulties in going off to sleep and staying asleep, waking early in the morning and napping in the day. When these phenomena become more pronounced, this degrades the experienced quality of life for both the individual concerned and their family.

Exposure to high levels of sunlight or artificial light during the day promotes good sleep [1,2,3] and helps to reduce restlessness during the night [3]; see Figure 2. Blue light in particular is very effective in this respect [4]. However, with increasing age the transparency of the eye lens to blue light decreases dramatically, as shown in Figure 3, and more light is needed to achieve the same effect. As elderly people often spend a very limited amount of time outdoors, they rely a lot on windows and artificial lighting for body clock regulation.

Esther de Beer, André van der Putten,
Luc Schlangen, Ariadne Tenner, George Kok

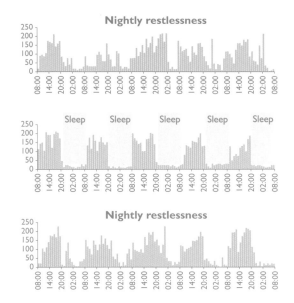

Figure 2: *Motional activity of a patient with Alzheimer disease during 5 consecutive days: 2 weeks before treatment (top), during 4 weeks of daytime bright light exposure (middle) and 4 weeks after (bottom) the last bright light treatment is given. During bright light exposure the nocturnal activity clearly decreases and the sleep quality improves. (Adapted from reference [3]).*

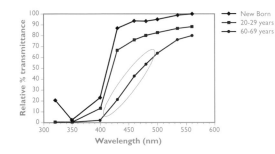

Figure 3: *The light transmission through the eye as a function of wavelength for three different age groups. (Adapted from reference [5]).*

If elderly persons have visual or sleep-related complaints, they tend to put this down to their age and are often reluctant to consult their doctor. Such age-related complications can, however, put a heavy burden on professional and non-professional caregivers and cause a strong increase in health-care costs. Elderly people are often prescribed a range of drugs for their health problems and many of these have side effects which tend to affect the elderly in particular. The hypnotics that are used to treat sleeping disorders often cause impaired day-time functioning, giving rise to falls and increased dependence on others. Light treatment is a non-pharmacological approach to improving the day/night rhythm and has virtually no adverse side effects.

Certain aspects of routine daily life and/or care at home may adversely affect vision and sleep in later life. These include a lack of exposure to sufficient levels of (natural) light, lack of physical activity, day-time naps and lack of night-time darkness in bedrooms. The efficiency of artificial light to control the biorhythm can be enhanced by careful selection of the spectral composition of the light source [4]. Philips Lighting works together closely with the care home industry to develop lighting solutions and recommendations that facilitate care for the elderly and improve the wellbeing and sleep quality they enjoy. Field tests are being carried out in the homes of elderly people and in care homes to evaluate what end users need and want, thereby improving the application concepts and specifications. New lighting concepts should fit seamlessly within the – usually quite rigid – daily routines of elderly people. Some examples are discussed below.

Bedroom

Most elderly people leave their bed more frequently at night. It is at times like this, when they are half awake and trying to find their way in the dark, that they are particularly likely to fall. This is why in CareLab special lighting is switched on automatically when a person leaves their bed. Corridors are lit effectively using colors and lighting levels that have been carefully selected to enable the individual to go back to sleep quickly.

Elderly people have a preference for more gradual transitions from rest to activity and vice versa. Dawn and dusk simulation in the bedroom is used as a tool to control ambience, mood and the rate at which someone wakes up or gets ready to fall asleep. The combination of dawn and dusk simulation improves sleep quality and sleep timing [6]. Dawn simulation helps people to wake up and reduces morning drowsiness [7].

Personalization is possible through feedback provided by intelligent sensors or by means of control settings like those found on an alarm clock. Similarly, dawn simulation can be linked to an alarm clock timer. Alternatively, sensors in the bed that monitor sleep quality could provide the necessary input for the lighting controls.

Living Room

To fulfill the user requirements of the elderly, living-room lighting must provide high lighting levels throughout the entire living area. Lighting levels can be set to match activities automatically, for instance always ensuring a well-lit workspace in the kitchen while someone is cooking.

Later Life Wellbeing and Lighting
Esther de Beer • André van der Putten • Luc Schlangen • Ariadne Tenner • George Kok

Different lighting requirements have to be met for activities such as reading, doing puzzles or needlework, for orientation during the hours of darkness and for creating a cosy atmosphere. The remote-controlled bright dining-room lamp is an all-in-one luminaire that supplies the right luminance and color temperature for each of these different purposes.

For the purpose of end-user testing, the luminaire is installed in the private living rooms of care-home residents. The preferred luminaire settings are monitored and the residents are interviewed on a regular basis. This helps to further specify user needs, to optimize the user interface and to assess the acceptance of this new product concept.

Philips Lighting works together with an Alzheimers clinic at a university hospital to investigate the effective use of light treatment for preventing or reducing sleep-wake rhythm disturbances and to record the consequences thereof for elderly people with dementia. A successful lighting solution should fit in seamlessly with the living environment and the daily routines of end users. In CareLab a light therapy luminaire is shown which has been designed to match the furnishings in an elderly person's room whilst at the same time providing the high lighting levels required for an effective light therapy device.

Lessons learned and outlook

Starting from the user perspective, expert knowledge in the area of medicine and chronobiology, lighting technology and user needs has been translated into concepts and specifications for new, attractive lighting systems. The combination of concept development and end-user testing represents a very powerful tool for evaluating people's needs and their levels of acceptance; it also provides specifications and supports claims for advanced lighting products.

References

1. Mishima, K., M. Okawa , T. Shimizu, and Y.Hishikawa (2001). Diminished melatonin secretion in the elderly caused by insufficient environmental illumination. *Journal of Clinical Endocrinol and Metabolism*, 86(1), pp. 129-134.

2. Wakamura T, and H. Tokura (2001), Influence of bright light during daytime on sleep parameters in hospitalized elderly patients. *Journal of Physiological Anthropology and Applied Human Science*, 20(6), pp. 345-351.

3. Van Someren E.J., A. Kessler, M. Mirmiran, and D.F. Swaab (1997), Indirect bright light improves circadian rest-activity rhythm disturbances in demented patients. *Biological Psychiatry*, 41(9), pp. 955-963.

4. Brainard G.C., J.P. Hanifin, J.M. Greeson, B. Byrne, G. Glickman, E. Gerner, et al. (2001), Action spectrum for melatonin regulation in humans: evidence for a novel circadian photoreceptor. *Journal of Neuroscience*; 21(16), pp. 6405-6412.

5. Brainard G.C. (1994), Ocular Mechanisms that regulate the human pineal gland. In: Möller, M., and P. Pévet, (eds). *Advances in pineal research*, 8, pp. 415-432.

6. Fontana G.P., K. Krauchi, C. Cajochen, E. Someren, I. Amrhein, M. Pache, et al. (2003), Dawn-dusk simulation light therapy of disturbed circadian rest-activity cycles in demented elderly. *Experimental Gerontology*, 38(1-2), pp. 207-216.

7. Avery D.H., M.E. Kouri, K. Monaghan, M.A. Bolte, C. Hellekson, and D. Eder (2002), Is dawn simulation effective in ameliorating the difficulty awakening in seasonal affective disorder associated with hypersomnia? *Journal of Affective Disorders*, 69(1-3), pp. 231-236.

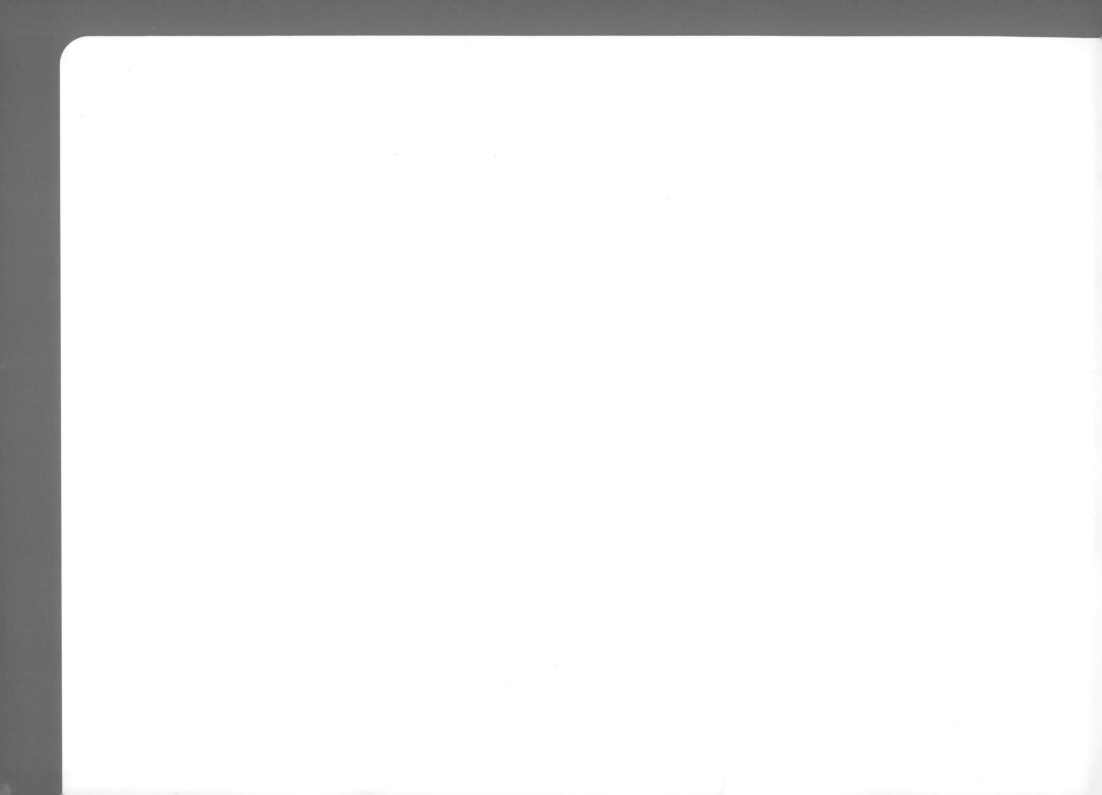